"Readers will be compelled by Daniel Shaw's differentiated a
trauma and non-recognition in the shaping of what has been c
intelligent and compassionate portrayal of clinical dilemmas involved in working with those who have suffered in abusive subjugating relationships is ideal for students and advanced practitioners. *Traumatic Narcissism* offers an original and captivating analysis of the relational configurations and painful emotions that lead to, and so often prevent emergence from, submission. While his thinking is informed by a broad theoretical knowledge, equally impressive is Shaw's exemplary dedication to exploring how we can use our own experience and personal honesty in order to transcend shame and confront the pitfalls of being an analyst while still maintaining our focus on recognizing the patient."

—**Jessica Benjamin**, *author of* Shadow of the Other

"Daniel Shaw has written a fascinating book that places his personal psychological journey in the well-researched context of his larger compelling theory of traumatic narcissism. Inspired by his own experience in a cult with a guru whom he eventually came to see as a traumatizing narcissist, and enlivened with numerous clinical case examples, this absorbing and far-ranging book traces the history of traumatic narcissism from ancient times to the vagaries of the current political scene."

—**Sheldon Bach**, *PhD, Adjunct Clinical Professor of Psychology, New York University Postdoctoral Program in Psychotherapy and Psychoanalysis*

"This book is a must-read for any of us who have worked with victims of traumatizing narcissists or been their victims ourselves. Whether drawing on his personal experience in the clinic and in cults, or analyzing literary productions and the inner worlds of their creators, Daniel Shaw brings vividly to life the relational world of those bent on subjugating others—and of those who have been subjugated by them. Not since Benjamin's *The Bonds of Love* has there been such a powerful analysis of the psychic life of domination and submission, complemented by a moving account of the effect of analytic love. Perhaps only someone like Shaw, who has known firsthand the psychic effects and needs fulfilled by living in a world of traumatizing narcissists, could have provided such a compassionate and helpful guide for clinicians engaged in the painful work of helping those who have been drawn into the traumatizing narcissist's relational system."

—**Lynne Layton**, *Harvard Medical School and Massachusetts Institute for Psychoanalysis*

"Daniel Shaw has written an astute, dramatic portrayal of the traumatizing narcissist's subjugation and destruction of another's subjectivity as it emerges in families, cult-like groups, and even in the psychoanalytic profession itself. He boldly offers 'analytic love' as the avenue of restoration of subjectivity. Professionals of all levels will be riveted as they expand their understanding of these phenomena."

—**James L. Fosshage**, *PhD, Clinical Professor of Psychology, New York University Postdoctoral Program in Psychotherapy and Psychoanalysis*

"Daniel Shaw's fine study of what he calls 'traumatic narcissism' explores the toxic forms of self-involvement in areas as diverse as the life of Eugene O'Neill, a number of his patients, and in his own experience with a guru. Shaw is at his best, however, exploring some of the dark corners of the cultic world of psychoanalysis itself. He holds a mirror up to those who claim the authority of self-understanding. Not all reflect well. Wisely, for all the anger and despair in this book, Shaw ends in hope that is cautious but authentic."

—**Charles B. Strozier**, *an historian at the City University of New York and a practicing psychoanalyst*

Traumatic Narcissism

In this volume, *Traumatic Narcissism: Relational Systems of Subjugation*, Daniel Shaw presents a way of understanding the traumatic impact of narcissism as it is engendered developmentally, and as it is enacted relationally. Focusing on the dynamics of narcissism in interpersonal relations, Shaw describes the relational system of what he terms the 'traumatizing narcissist' as a system of subjugation—the objectification of one person in a relationship as the means of enforcing the dominance of the subjectivity of the other.

Daniel Shaw illustrates the workings of this relational system of subjugation in a variety of contexts, theorizing traumatic narcissism as an intergenerationally transmitted relational/developmental trauma. He explores the clinician's experience of working with the adult children of traumatizing narcissists, the relationship of cult leaders and their followers, and examines how traumatic narcissism has lingered vestigially in some aspects of the psychoanalytic profession.

Bringing together theories of trauma and attachment, intersubjectivity and complementarity, and the rich clinical sensibility of the Relational Psychoanalysis tradition, Shaw demonstrates how narcissism can best be understood not merely as character, but as the result of the specific trauma of subjugation, in which one person is required to become the object for a significant other who demands hegemonic subjectivity. *Traumatic Narcissism* presents therapeutic clinical opportunities not only for psychoanalysts of different schools, but for all mental health professionals working with a wide variety of modalities. Although primarily intended for the professional psychoanalyst and psychotherapist, this is also a book that therapy patients and lay readers will find highly readable and illuminating.

Daniel Shaw, LCSW is a psychoanalytically oriented psychotherapist in private practice in New York City, and in Nyack, New York. He is a training analyst, teacher and supervisor of analytic candidates at the National Institute for the Psychotherapies in New York City.

Relational Perspectives Book Series

Lewis Aron & Adrienne Harris
Series Editors

The Relational Perspectives Book Series (RPBS) publishes books that grow out of or contribute to the relational tradition in contemporary psychoanalysis. The term *relational psychoanalysis* was first used by Greenberg and Mitchell (1983) to bridge the traditions of interpersonal relations, as developed within interpersonal psychoanalysis and object relations, as developed within contemporary British theory. But, under the seminal work of the late Stephen Mitchell, the term *relational psychoanalysis* grew and began to accrue to itself many other influences and developments. Various tributaries—interpersonal psychoanalysis, object relations theory, self psychology, empirical infancy research, and elements of contemporary Freudian and Kleinian thought—flow into this tradition, which understands relational configurations between self and others, both real and fantasied, as the primary subject of psychoanalytic investigation.

We refer to the relational tradition, rather than to a relational school, to highlight that we are identifying a trend, a tendency within contemporary psychoanalysis, not a more formally organized or coherent school or system of beliefs. Our use of the term *relational* signifies a dimension of theory and practice that has become salient across the wide spectrum of contemporary psychoanalysis. Now under the editorial supervision of Lewis Aron and Adrienne Harris, the Relational Perspectives Book Series originated in 1990 under the editorial eye of the late Stephen A. Mitchell. Mitchell was the most prolific and influential of the originators of the relational tradition. He was committed to dialogue among psychoanalysts and he abhorred the authoritarianism that dictated adherence to a rigid set of beliefs or technical restrictions. He championed open discussion, comparative and integrative approaches, and he promoted new voices across the generations.

Included in the Relational Perspectives Book Series are authors and works that come from within the relational tradition, extend and develop the tradition, as well as works that critique relational approaches or compare and contrast it with alternative points of view. The series includes our most distinguished senior psychoanalysts along with younger contributors who bring fresh vision.

Vol. 59
Clinical Implications of the Psychoanalyst's Life Experience: When the Personal Becomes Professional
Steven Kuchuck (ed.)

Vol. 58
Traumatic Narcissism: Relational Systems of Subjugation
Daniel Shaw

Vol. 57
The Play Within the Play: The Enacted Dimension of Psychoanalytic Process
Gil Katz

Vol. 56
Holding and Psychoanalysis: A Relational Perspective
Joyce Slochower

Vol. 55
A Psychotherapy for the People: Toward a Progressive Psychoanalysis
Lewis Aron & Karen Starr

Vol. 54
The Silent Past and the Invisible Present: Memory, Trauma, and Representation in Psychotherapy
Paul Renn

Vol. 53
Individualizing Gender and Sexuality: Theory and Practice
Nancy Chodorow

Vol. 52
Relational Psychoanalysis, Vol. V: Evolution of Process
Lewis Aron & Adrienne Harris (eds.)

Vol. 51
Relational Psychoanalysis, Vol. IV: Expansion of Theory
Lewis Aron & Adrienne Harris (eds.)

Vol. 50
With Culture in Mind: Psychoanalytic Stories
Muriel Dimen (ed.)

Vol. 49
Understanding and Treating Dissociative Identity Disorder: A Relational Approach
Elizabeth F. Howell

Vol. 48
Toward Mutual Recognition: Relational Psychoanalysis and the Christian Narrative
Marie T. Hoffman

Vol. 47
Uprooted Minds: Surviving the Politics of Terror in the Americas
Nancy Caro Hollander

Vol. 46
A Disturbance in the Field: Essays in Transference-Countertransference Engagement
Steven H. Cooper

Vol. 45
First Do No Harm: The Paradoxical Encounters of Psychoanalysis, Warmaking, and Resistance
Adrienne Harris & Steven Botticelli (eds.)

Vol. 44
Good Enough Endings:
Breaks, Interruptions, and Terminations from Contemporary Relational Perspectives
Jill Salberg (ed.)

Vol. 43
Invasive Objects: Minds under Siege
Paul Williams

Vol. 42
Sabert Basescu:
Selected Papers on Human Nature and Psychoanalysis
George Goldstein & Helen Golden (eds.)

Vol. 41
The Hero in the Mirror:
From Fear to Fortitude
Sue Grand

Vol. 40
The Analyst in the Inner City, Second Edition: Race, Class, and Culture through a Psychoanalytic Lens
Neil Altman

Vol. 39
Dare to be Human:
A Contemporary Psychoanalytic Journey
Michael Shoshani Rosenbaum

Vol. 38
Repair of the Soul: Metaphors of Transformation in Jewish Mysticism and Psychoanalysis
Karen E. Starr

Vol. 37
Adolescent Identities:
A Collection of Readings
Deborah Browning (ed.)

Vol. 36
Bodies in Treatment:
The Unspoken Dimension
Frances Sommer Anderson (ed.)

Vol. 35
Comparative-Integrative Psychoanalysis:
A Relational Perspective for the Discipline's Second Century
Brent Willock

Vol. 34
Relational Psychoanalysis, Vol. III:
New Voices
Melanie Suchet, Adrienne Harris, & Lewis Aron (eds.)

Vol. 33
Creating Bodies: Eating Disorders as Self-Destructive Survival
Katie Gentile

Vol. 32
Getting From Here to There:
Analytic Love, Analytic Process
Sheldon Bach

Vol. 31
Unconscious Fantasies and the Relational World
Danielle Knafo & Kenneth Feiner

Vol. 30
The Healer's Bent: Solitude and Dialogue in the Clinical Encounter
James T. McLaughlin

Vol. 29
Child Therapy in the Great Outdoors:
A Relational View
Sebastiano Santostefano

Vol. 28
Relational Psychoanalysis, Vol. II: Innovation and Expansion
Lewis Aron & Adrienne Harris (eds.)

Vol. 27
The Designed Self: Psychoanalysis and Contemporary Identities
Carlo Strenger

Vol. 26
Impossible Training: A Relational View of Psychoanalytic Education
Emanuel Berman

Vol. 25
Gender as Soft Assembly
Adrienne Harris

Vol. 24
Minding Spirituality
Randall Lehman Sorenson

Vol. 23
September 11: Trauma and Human Bonds
Susan W. Coates, Jane L. Rosenthal, & Daniel S. Schechter (eds.)

Vol. 22
Sexuality, Intimacy, Power
Muriel Dimen

Vol. 21
Looking for Ground: Countertransference and the Problem of Value in Psychoanalysis
Peter G.M. Carnochan

Vol. 20
Relationality: From Attachment to Intersubjectivity
Stephen A. Mitchell

Vol. 19
Who is the Dreamer, Who Dreams the Dream?
A Study of Psychic Presences
James S. Grotstein

Vol. 18
Objects of Hope: Exploring Possibility and Limit in Psychoanalysis
Steven H. Cooper

Vol. 17
The Reproduction of Evil:
A Clinical and Cultural Perspective
Sue Grand

Vol. 16
Psychoanalytic Participation:
Action, Interaction, and Integration
Kenneth A. Frank

Vol. 15
The Collapse of the Self and Its Therapeutic Restoration
Rochelle G.K. Kainer

Vol. 14
Relational Psychoanalysis:
The Emergence of a Tradition
Stephen A. Mitchell & Lewis Aron (eds.)

Vol. 13
Seduction, Surrender, and Transformation: Emotional Engagement in the Analytic Process
Karen Maroda

Vol. 12
Relational Perspectives on the Body
Lewis Aron & Frances Sommer Anderson (eds.)

Vol. 11
Building Bridges:
Negotiation of Paradox in Psychoanalysis
Stuart A. Pizer

Vol. 10
Fairbairn, Then and Now
Neil J. Skolnick & David E. Scharff (eds.)

Vol. 9
Influence and Autonomy in Psychoanalysis
Stephen A. Mitchell

Vol. 8
Unformulated Experience:
From Dissociation to Imagination in Psychoanalysis
Donnel B. Stern

Vol. 7
Soul on the Couch:
Spirituality, Religion, and Morality in Contemporary Psychoanalysis
Charles Spezzano & Gerald J. Gargiulo (eds.)

Vol. 6
The Therapist as a Person:
Life Crises, Life Choices, Life Experiences, and Their Effects on Treatment
Barbara Gerson (ed.)

Vol. 5
Holding and Psychoanalysis:
A Relational Perspective
Joyce A. Slochower

Vol. 4
A Meeting of Minds:
Mutuality in Psychoanalysis
Lewis Aron

Vol. 3
The Analyst in the Inner City:
Race, Class, and Culture through a Psychoanalytic Lens
Neil Altman

Vol. 2
Affect in Psychoanalysis:
A Clinical Synthesis
Charles Spezzano

Vol. 1
Conversing with Uncertainty:
Practicing Psychotherapy In A Hospital Setting
Rita Wiley McCleary

Traumatic Narcissism

Relational Systems of Subjugation

Daniel Shaw

NEW YORK AND LONDON

First published 2014
by Routledge
711 Third Avenue, New York, NY 10017

Simultaneously published in the UK
by Routledge
27 Church Road, Hove, East Sussex BN3 2FA

Routledge is an imprint of the Taylor & Francis Group, an informa business

Library of Congress Cataloging in Publication Data
Catalog record for this book has been applied for

ISBN: 978-0-415-51024-0 (hbk)
ISBN: 978-0-415-51025-7 (pbk)
ISBN: 978-1-315-88361-8 (ebk)

Typeset in Times
by Apex CoVantage, LLC

Contents

Preface

One day, more than a decade ago, I answered the phone at my office and a woman introduced herself to me. Victoria had read an essay I had written, published in the *Cultic Studies Review* and online, entitled "Traumatic Abuse in Cults" (Shaw, 2003b). She wanted me to know that she had studied narcissism for many years, though she was not a mental health professional. I learned that she is the daughter of a traumatizing narcissist mother, with an equally traumatizing narcissist stepfather, who had wealth and position and were extraordinarily neglectful and abusive to their children. Additionally, as a young woman she had been abused by and testified in court against a notorious guru—one of the very small number of victims of sexual abuses in religious groups other than the Catholic Church to speak out. She told me that I had explained something in my paper about narcissism that she had never really come across. She was referring to how I had used the example of a narcissist guru as someone who needed to believe that he was completely free, dependent on no one—the kind of narcissist who exploits and controls others, inflating himself by deflating those he surrounds himself with. I was arguing in this paper that he needs others desperately, but that he disavows dependency, which he views as weak and shameful. He needs to lure others into becoming dependent on him, which then allows him to persist in his delusion that only others are needy, not himself. As a result of his developmental trauma connected to dependency, he externalizes dependency, and with it, shame. Dependency and shame are repugnant weaknesses in his eyes, problems for his inferior followers, not for superior him. My new friend on the phone, Victoria, surprised me with her impressive grasp of the vast psychoanalytic literature, and I was very pleased to hear that she had found something new and meaningful in what I had written.

I had already received recognition for this particular paper—aside from its publication in a journal specifically geared to the ex-cult community, it was available on the internet and had been averaging 300 "hits" monthly for several years, had been translated into five languages, and had been used for a number of different college classes. However, what Victoria said led me to begin thinking about how I could present my ideas to my colleagues in the psychoanalytic community.

In "Traumatic Abuse in Cults" I defined a cult as a group that is led by a traumatizing narcissist, in which members are subjugated by the leader in various ways, mainly through the destruction of their subjectivity—their objectification. Only the leader's subjectivity is given validity in a cult; members are allowed validation only at the guru's whim, and only to the extent that they comply and submit as specified by the guru. My ideas about cults developed throughout my social work and psychoanalytic training, in the years following my own involvement with a religious group led by a guru for whom I had worked full-time for more than ten years. It was out of the literally hundreds of conversations I had with people who identified as former cult members in the first five years after I severed my ties with this guru that I began to develop the concept I present here—the relational system of the traumatizing narcissist.

I knew from the beginning of my effort to construct a psychoanalytic perspective on cults that this relational dynamic was not unique to cults—that in fact, it could be recognized in any relationship between significant others. My first analytic supervisor, the late Valerie Oltarsh, had suggested at the very beginning of my training that I read *Prisoners of Childhood* by Alice Miller (1981)—the classic book about narcissist parents and how their children are traumatized. Much of what I read there confirmed what I had come to understand about my relationship with my ex-guru; what I had witnessed and experienced as a follower of this guru fell at the extreme end of abusiveness. By contrast, my family of origin, for all our difficulties, had been a far more benign environment.

As my analytic training progressed, I read voraciously—first Kohut, then Winnicott, Fairbairn, Balint, and eventually Ferenczi and Fromm—among many others of the analytic forebears. Soon the contemporary relational theorists beckoned to me, and Mitchell, Aron, Benjamin, Ghent, Harris, Hoffman, Bromberg, Davies—and many others—influenced me deeply. The common theme of all the authors I was drawn to was, in a word, relationality. The more I sought to make use of the relational sensibility in my work and in my life, the more I became acutely aware of the narcissistic bubble my prior so-called spiritual life had occupied.

So the study of relationality led me to the study of narcissism. What I read spoke mostly of narcissism as either healthy or pathological, with the pathological aspects viewed as innate, arising from genetic disposition more than environment. In Kohut's work (1984) I found more understanding of how environment played a role in narcissism, but I still wondered: What about the kind of narcissism that led a person to believe they were omnipotent, and thereby entitled to dictate the terms of other people's lives? What of those people (such as I had been) who submit themselves to such dictatorial contol? Most psychoanalytic case reports that spoke of a patient's narcissism seemed to me to be talking about people who had been traumatized by a narcissist; their trust in others and in themselves had been battered, often from within their families. These patients often showed narcissistic features—unstable self-esteem in two modes, either grandiose superiority or self-loathing—but once their family of origin histories were elaborated, a parent or parents, grandparents or siblings were invariably discovered who were over-inflated narcissists (Bach, 1985, 1994, 2006). It made sense to me to think of this kind of abusing other as pathologically narcissistic—but was the tormented, depressed patient in my office who told me of these traumatic abuses also supposed to be thought of as pathologically narcissistic?

I take this theme up in Chapter 1, in which I argue that the clinical phenomena typically thought of as constituting "pathological narcissism" are quite varied, and that dividing narcissists up into overt or inverted categories does not capture what to me is the most important thing to know about narcissism: how deeply rooted narcissism is in relational trauma. I encountered little theorization about how predominantly over-inflated narcissistic people traumatize significant others—by attacking the other's subjectivity. I wanted to know why some adult children of narcissists become traumatizers themselves, while others live in the painful grip of relational post-traumatic stress. I was most helped in my thinking about this by the work of Jessica Benjamin (1988, 1995, 1998, 1999, 2004, 2009a, 2009b), whose theory of intersubjectivity, understood as the process of developing the capacity for mutual recognition, immediately spoke to me. Benjamin's use of the term "complementarity" to stand for the breakdown of intersubjective relatedness into domination/submission strategies for control was exactly the link I was looking for in thinking about traumatic narcissism. These narcissists seek hegemonic subjectivity, the opposite of intersubjectivity. The victim of the traumatizing narcissist, I argue, is often mistakenly identified as the deflated pathological narcissist, when she would be more usefully understood as a victim of cumulative relational trauma. What is developmentally traumatic is the narcissist caregiver's rejection of the child's subjectivity, and the caregiver's refusal to allow intersubjective recognition to be mutual. The traumatizing narcissist seeks to abolish intersubjectivity, and to freeze a complementary dynamic in the relationship, allowing recognition in one direction only—toward himself.[1]

In Chapter 2, the traumatizing narcissist concept is further elaborated, and the concept of the "complementary moral defense," a relational elaboration of Fairbairn's "moral defense" concept, is introduced. The chapter begins with a study of the life of the playwright Eugene O'Neill, whose play *Long Day's Journey Into Night* (2002) is, from a psychological perspective, an extraordinarily insightful portrayal of the devastating effects of narcissism in a family—in this case, O'Neill's own family. I go on to present my clinical work with an adult child of traumatizing narcissist parents with whom I worked for many years. Aside from demonstrating the enactments and impasses that often arise with these patients, I also want to give life to the horribly traumatic damage done when the subjectivity of the other, and especially of the developing child, is the target of the traumatizing narcissist's destructive need for dominance. The first two chapters taken together serve to define specifically what I am calling traumatic narcissism; the nature of the traumatizing narcissist's relational system; and the destructive impact the traumatizing narcissist has on his or her significant others. I am making a case for an expansion of the psychoanalytic understanding of narcissism that would bring traumatic narcissism more fully into the relational realms of developmental theory, attachment theory, trauma theory, intersubjective theory, and clinical theory.

Chapters 3 and 4 bring the concept of the traumatizing narcissist's relational system, beyond the family and the clinic, into the area of authoritarian groups and institutions. Over the years, I have read a few too many commentaries on how the new social media phenomenon, and reality television, were making narcissists of us all. By way of example, a Google search for "social media and narcissists" brings up hundreds of links to essays on that subject. This way of thinking about narcissism has become pervasive, and, unfortunately, it trivializes the concept. The last several decades in the U.S. of nationalistic jingoism and war-mongering; of fundamentalist theocratic rhetoric and activism; of the corporate sponsored denial of the dangers of climate change; of the unregulation of duplicity and greed on Wall Street; and of the power of corporate money to buy and own politicians are trends of narcissistic self-interest and abuse of power of far more concern than any harmless showing off on Facebook about children's accomplishments, dates, parties, and family vacations.

While I touch on some of these graver concerns in Chapter 3, I do not attempt a full-scale cultural/political analysis of the destructive impact of traumatic narcissism at these broader levels. I must leave that to the historians, economists, and journalists who are far better equipped than I to tell that story.[2] Instead, I have chosen to view religious and therapeutic cultic groups through the lens of the traumatizing narcissist's relational system, focusing on the story of a notorious psychotherapy group that has been described by many former members as a cult. The Sullivan Institute led originally by Jane Pearce and Saul Newton was an experiment in creating a psychoanalytic ideology and applying it in a communal setting. The Sullivanians, as they were known, drew many patients over the last decades of the 20th Century. Headquartered in New York's Upper West Side and summering in the Hamptons, Sullivanian therapists were often former patients of the inner circle around Newton, who were personally "trained" by him, many of them unlicensed and with no qualifying degree. Newton and his group of therapists were reported to have flouted professional ethics and controlled, exploited, and violated patients, until the community finally dissolved upon Newton's death. Ideological, authoritarian, highly controlling, and demanding groups, sometimes referred to as cults (or in Canada and Europe as sects), illustrate the traumatizing narcissist's relational system as it functions beyond the dyad, in groups that can become as large as nations and coalitions of nations. I begin this chapter by describing my own experience of following and working for an Indian guru for more than a decade, prior to entering the mental health field. I end the chapter reflecting on how traumatizing narcissism takes its most potentially dangerous form in ideologies of nationalistic exceptionalism.

Chapter 4 explores ways in which lingering traces of authoritarianism in psychoanalysis can be found in the process of psychoanalytic supervision. As with Chapter 3, this chapter explores the ways that traumatic narcissism and authoritarianism are linked. I use some of my experiences as a candidate in psychoanalytic training, particularly instances in which I felt called upon to over-idealize and submit to a supervisor, or belittled or shamed by a supervisor, to reflect on ways of being watchful for the legacy of narcissistic authoritarianism of previous generations of analysts. I speak about the importance for analytic supervisors to support the development of the candidate's unique, personal idiom (Bollas) as an analyst.

In chapters 5 and 6, I return to the exploration of traumatic narcissism in the clinical setting. Chapter 5 examines clinical work with couples, or with individuals focusing on problems in relationships, looking specifically at the destructive impact of traumatic narcissism on intimate relationships. Chapter 6 addresses the phase of analytic work with the adult children of the traumatizing narcissist, in which analyst and patient have together achieved powerfully meaningful insights about the nature of the trauma and its impact. For many patients, the initial reaction to these insights is panic—understanding what happened does not immediately translate into what will happen next. I explore what this crucial struggle looks like clinically, and how the process of starting fresh unfolds—discovering what it means to live from a subjective orientation when one has lived one's life powerfully and adhesively identified as the object of others.

The final two chapters, 7 and 8, explore the meaning of the term "analytic love." Chapter 7 traces the history of the concept, beginning with tensions and disagreements between Freud and Ferenczi around the analyst's attitude toward the patient. Among those qualities of being an analyst thought of as making up the experience of analytic love, what is always implicit, if not explicit, in any description is the effort on the analyst's part to be aware of and able to regulate her narcissistic vulnerabilities. I expand on this theme in Chapter 8, in which I describe how my work with adult children of traumatizing narcissist parents has led to a deeper appreciation of the possibilities of analytic love. The concept of analytic love has been articulated beautifully by many psychoanalytic authors; most notably by Loewald (1960), who wrote of the pivotal phase in analytic work in which the patient has worked through the old to the point of being ready for the new. "The newness consists," wrote Loewald,

> in the patient's rediscovery of the early paths of development of object-relations leading to *a new way of relating to objects and of being oneself.* Through all the transference distortions, the patient reveals rudiments at least of that core (of himself and 'objects') which has been distorted. It is this core, rudimentary and vague as it may be, to which the analyst has reference when he interprets transferences and defences, and not some abstract concept of reality or normality, if he is to reach the patient. If the analyst keeps his central focus on this emerging core he avoids moulding the patient in the analyst's own image or imposing on the patient his own concept of what the patient should become. It requires an objectivity and neutrality, the essence of which is love and respect for the individual and for individual development. This love and respect represent that counterpart in 'reality,' in interaction with which the organization and reorganization of ego and psychic apparatus take place.
>
> (p. 20, italics mine)

Stephen Mitchell explained why much of his book *Relationality* (2000a) was devoted to exegesis of Loewald's work, when he wrote that Loewald's way of understanding analytic process contained within it "some of the most important facets of relationality developed in the analytic literature of recent decades" (p. xvi). What is particularly moving for me in the passage by Loewald is his implicit assertion that human love—parental, analytic, any and all—is most nurturing, most supportive of growth and the unfolding of our own unique human potentials, when the lover strives to be free of the narcissistic need to mold the beloved in one's own image; free of the need to impose on the other one's own definition of who the other should be. I understand Loewald to be speaking of the developmental trauma of objectification, the essence of the traumatizing narcissist's destructiveness. He links the healing of this trauma to the kind of analytic love he describes, which encourages the renaissance of the patient's subjectivity.

My hope in presenting my work on traumatic narcissism is that by exposing the profound instability at the core of the traumatizing narcissist's psyche, clinicians working with his or her victims, and victims themselves, can use their understanding of the traumatizing narcissist's relational system to find a pathway toward freedom, toward the restoration of their subjectivity, and toward the development of the capacity for intersubjective relatedness.

Notes

1 . . . or toward herself: gender pronouns when not speaking of a specific person are used interchangeably throughout the book.
2 These concerns have been extensively addressed by Hollander (2010) who is both an historian and a psychoanalyst; and in the work of Layton (2009, 2010, 2011, in press).

Acknowledgements

Let me begin by thanking the many patients I have been privileged to work with; you have taught me so much. In my clinical vignettes and processes included in this volume, I have in every case carefully disguised the identity of the patients (and of the supervisors in Chapter 4), and created a composite identity. What I describe in the vignettes happened, but material is combined and reorganized to protect privacy.

To those who read various chapters in various states of readiness, including some material that was published previously, my heartfelt gratitude and appreciation: Victoria Barlow, Philip Bromberg, Carolyn Clement, James Fosshage, Lorna and Bill Goldberg, Ruth Imber, Linda Jacobs, Peter Kaufman, Michael Langone, Peter Lessem, Tamsin Looker, Juliet Musso, Susan Obrecht, the late Valerie Oltarsh, Jill Salberg, Cynthia Shaw, Caryn Sherman-Meyer, Donnel Stern, Annie Stopford, Melanie Suchet, and the late Elisabeth Young-Bruehel. I needed much encouragement, and each of you gave it so generously, along with many helpful suggestions.

I am grateful for the love and support of my wife, Cynthia, throughout all this and for all the years leading up to it. To our children, Lila and Noah, who turned the sound on the television down many, many times when they would have preferred to have it booming—thank you.

To my editors at Taylor & Francis, my heartfelt thanks: Kate Hawes, Kirsten Buchanan, and Sarah Hudson.

Finally, I cannot possibly thank my psychoanalytic editors enough. Adrienne Harris, your astute suggestions were always constructive, and indispensably helpful. Lew Aron, my special thanks to you, going back to my first published paper, for always being an encourager and an inspirer. I could not and would not have written this book without your generous support.

Permission has been granted for the following material with thanks:

Excerpts from Some Hope from *The Patrick Melrose Novels* by Edward St. Aubyn. Copyright © 2012 by Edward St. Aubyn. Reprinted by permission of Picador.

Excerpt from *At Last* by Edward St. Aubyn. Copyright © 2011 by Edward St. Aubyn. Reprinted by permission of Picador.

Excerpts from Traumatic abuse in cults: A psychoanalytic perspective. *Cultic Studies Review*, 2003, (2)2:101–129. Reprinted by permission of International Cultic Studies Association.

Acknowledgements

Chapter 1

The Relationality of Narcissism[1]

A student attempting a thorough review of the psychoanalytic literature on narcissism might be reminded of the parable of the blind men and their encounter with an elephant: holding its tail, one of the blind men says the elephant is like a long thick rope. Holding its lower leg, another says the elephant is like a tree trunk. Holding . . . and so on. In a similar vein, analysts of different schools have their particular ways of thinking about narcissism, and they dispatch highly conflicting accounts from the different regions of the same animal they are observing. We need only invoke Kernberg and Kohut to illustrate the point when it comes to narcissism, though many others could be cited.

Narcissism today is a public word in common parlance. When most people talk about narcissism, they are referring to self-centered, vain, exhibitionistic people, people who seek admiration from others, and who make everything about themselves. An astonishing amount of popular psychology and internet chat is devoted to the topic—especially to the ways that narcissists exploit and abuse others and how one can best deal with them, protect one's self from them, and/or get them out of one's life.

When psychoanalysts talk about narcissism, however, we have to take pains to define our terms, of which there are many, and bushwhack our way through a jungle of complexity and contradiction. Are we talking about "healthy," "normal," or "pathological" narcissism? Is a narcissist deflated, overinflated, thick- or thin-skinned, overt or inverted? Is narcissism characterized by entitled grandiosity, or by primitive idealization, or both? Is it a line of development of the self, leading in maturity to empathy, wisdom, and humor; or a primitive infantile developmental stage to which schizophrenics regress? Is narcissism more broadly the dimension of mental activity concerned with maintenance of self-esteem? A pathology caused by an excessive endowment of aggression, or envy, or an extraordinary vulnerability to shame, or by traumatic impingements at crucial developmental stages? What about problems with making fluid transitions from subjective to objective states, and back—isn't that characteristic of the narcissist as well? All of the above is the answer, and a great deal more, when we go by the rich, complex, and sometimes contradictory psychoanalytic literature. Another parable, the one about the Tower of Babel, comes to mind.

Seeking to bring clarity and coherence to the subject, at least for psychoanalysts, Stephen Mitchell (1988) rejected the premise that narcissism was simply the result of intrapsychic developmental processes gone wrong. As he did with every psychoanalytic idea he addressed, Mitchell located the origin of narcissistic disturbances firmly in the relational matrix, as a set of personality features influenced by: 1) exposure to cumulative not-good-enough parental responses to the child's developmental needs—particularly those associated with the consolidation of good enough self-esteem; and 2) the not-regulated-well-enough narcissistic vulnerabilities and blind spots of the caregivers. What we experience with our patients that we have traditionally thought of as their narcissistic pathology is more productively understood, according to Mitchell, as repetition of entrenched relational patterns established in development—relational patterns that are very much at the root of the constricted, frustrating scenarios in which our patients are repeatedly finding themselves trapped, and which we and they enact in analytic work.

Grandiosity, the sense of omnipotence, and the tendency toward idealization are the innate human traits which, when severely exaggerated in the personality, are considered by psychoanalysts to be diagnostic of pathological narcissism. Mitchell saw these traits not merely as clinical phenomena on a health/pathology spectrum, but rather as components of universal existential illusions—as needed responses, however illusory, to the vastness of the universe, to our impermanence and unknowable significance within it. If held in flexible, playful contact with reality, these grand illusions could inspire creative, vital modes of living and relating. Rigidly fixed narcissistic illusions, on the other hand, would lead to constricted modes of relating that would interfere with the potential for more real, fuller engagement with real others. How parents, or others equally significant, managed their own narcissistic vulnerabilities, and how they responded to those of their children, would powerfully influence the flexibility or rigidity of the narcissistic tendencies in the developing child.

Mitchell's chapters (1988, pp. 175–234) on narcissism described people wounded by the narcissistic behaviors of their parents, and struggling as adults with painful difficulties of various kinds in work and love. He managed to sidestep the debated-to-death issues of etiology, and empathy vs. confrontation in clinical treatment, and went straight to the purposes narcissistic traits might serve in human development; and to how developmental derailments of self-regulating capacities in this area would create lasting relational difficulties in adult life. Without yet using this language, Mitchell described patients who had experienced cumulative developmental trauma from exposure to the narcissistic tendencies of their caretakers.

In a paper following the publication of Mitchell's work, Emmanuel Ghent (1989) moved further in the direction to which Mitchell had pointed. Ghent wondered:

> whether, perhaps, the roots of clinical narcissism lie in some failure to integrate adequately the mode of intersubjective relatedness, a wholly two-person

> psychological experience, either because the significant others were misattuned, underattuned or unpredictably attuned to this mode of relating. Could it be that people we encounter as patients may, despite being highly experienced in intellectual intercourse or sexual conjunction, nonetheless feel like frightened virgins when it comes to encountering this area of deeply longed for, yet warded off, intersubjectivity? Is it perhaps the deficit in this type of two-person experience that has even led to naming the phenomenon narcissism, an infelicitous term which carries the implication that a one-person psychology is at work? I believe, rather, that the phenomena of narcissism are largely rooted in a two-person psychology, derived in part from earlier senses of self, and in part from defensive operations designed to compensate for deficits in a coherent sense of self.
>
> (pp. 199–200)

In speaking of intersubjectivity, Ghent refers here to the infant research work of Daniel Stern (1985), work that has greatly influenced the rise to prominence of the "relational turn" (Greenberg & Mitchell, 1983) in psychoanalysis—a revolution that has kept the concept of intersubjectivity at the forefront of psychoanalytic theory, at the time of this writing, for more than 30 years. The many pioneering contributors to our understanding of the centrality of intersubjectivity, both in human development and in psychoanalytic treatment, are too numerous to mention here. Those contemporary authors whose work has most influenced my own thinking on intersubjectivity include, but are by no means limited to, Aron (1996), Benjamin (1988, 1995, 1998, 1999, 2004), Bromberg (1998, 2006, 2011), Ghent (1989, 1990), Hoffman (1998), and Mitchell (1988, 1993, 1997, 2000a, 2003a, 2003b).[2]

As Auerbach (1993) definitively observes, the old paradigm—of narcissism as an infantile developmental stage that hopefully evolves into relatedness to others—no longer applies, once we take into account the findings of modern infant research: the infant is related from the beginning, and seeks relationship from the beginning. By identifying "clinical narcissism" as a developmental deficit, arising from "deficits in a coherent sense of self," Ghent does not specifiy the cause of these deficits; but I believe he is suggesting that what has traditionally been referred to as narcissistic pathology originates in developmental trauma. I have come to think of "clinical narcissism" in exactly this way: as the result of cumulative developmental trauma to the capacity for intersubjective relatedness, particularly in the area of mutual recognition. What this means is that from a relational psychoanalytic perspective, narcissism can be understood as both traumatic and traumatizing, as follows:

- the developmental traumas that engender narcissism are transmitted intergenerationally;
- the central trauma in the genesis of narcissism is chronic, insufficiently repaired failures on the part of caregivers to support the developing child's needs for recognition as a separate subject;

- these chronic failures of recognition thwart the child's achievement of the capacity for intersubjective relatedness;
- most often, these chronic failures arise as a result of narcissistic disturbances in the parent.

Intergenerational Relational Trauma

One of the many gifts psychoanalysis has received from the prolific post-Bowlby wave of attachment theory research was a key finding of Fonagy et al. (1991), a finding bolstered by painstaking research, beginning with Main et al. (1985). They demonstrated that mothers and fathers who were able to be reflective and coherent in relating the narrative of their own attachment experience were three to four times more likely to raise securely attached children than were those parents whose narratives were unexamined and dissociative. This means that if one's own attachment trauma is dissociated, the chances of passing along insecure or disorganized attachment experience to one's own child are high. If, however, one's attachment experience was traumatic but is not dissociated, one is much less likely to pass along insecure attachment to the next generation.

This finding is a gift in many ways. For example, it has been a comfort to many an expectant parent I have worked with who was frightened about traumatizing her child, in the same ways she was traumatized as a child, to learn that her efforts to retrieve her own attachment narrative from dissociation could make it much less likely that her own child would not be able to attach securely. For analysts, the findings of Fonagy et al. provide compelling evidence confirming that trauma theory applies to *developmental, or relational trauma, which can be transmitted intergenerationally, especially if dissociated.*

Even without the illuminating benefits of modern infant and attachment research, among the original group of Freud's followers, no one recognized the centrality of relational trauma in understanding psychopathology more keenly than Ferenczi. In his long suppressed, extraordinary final paper, "Confusion of Tongues" (Ferenczi, 1933/1980), Ferenczi did much more than point to adult sexualization of children, rather than infantile sexuality and fantasy, as a cause of serious psychological damage the child carries into adulthood. Ferenczi went further, identifying the complex, cumulative emotional trauma the child who is neglected and/or abused experiences in the context of the developmental relationship. He went on to describe how parents project their disavowed guilt (and shame) on to the child; and how resentful they were, no matter how well masked, of the child's dependence on them—because of their own disavowed wishes to be the focus of attention and care. He recognized that such parents dissociatively take advantage of the child's instinctive willingness to "introject" the guilt and shame the parent disavows. The child, Ferenczi understood, does this by becoming self-blaming, self-loathing, and self-sacrificing. He becomes the caretaker of the parent, while dissociating the awareness of his own needs, along with his concomitant grief and rage about feeling abandoned and exploited.

Pretty much everything we know about attachment trauma and its lasting impact is there, in root form, in Ferenczi's final paper. He also describes the narcissist parent, to a tee, though not by that name. The confusion of tongues Ferenczi observed, when the boundaries differentiating adult passion from childhood tenderness are violated by adult caregivers, is one of the grossest possible examples of parental narcissism. Aside from understanding the profoundly confusing, exciting, humiliating, and terrifying feelings of the child who is sexually abused by an adult, Ferenczi points to another layer of trauma involved in such violations: the utter failure of the parent to *recognize* who his child actually is and what the child actually needs. Instead, the child is sexualized and told that it is she, the child, who has caused the sexualization. This catastrophic misrecognition and misattribution is an extremely destructive and cruel rejection and betrayal of the actual child—the child whose links to her own subjectivity are being destroyed, and replaced by the projections of the abuser.[3]

Recognition and Intersubjectivity

Recognition is another word in common parlance, which in relational psychoanalytic theory takes on depth and complexity from its link to the fundamental developmental processes observed in contemporary infant research. In one of Jessica Benjamin's[4] earliest seminal writings on the subject of recognition, she offers a list of near synonyms that capture what she means by the term:

> to affirm, validate, acknowledge, know, accept, understand, empathize, take in, tolerate, appreciate, see, identify with, find familiar, . . . love . . . What I call *mutual recognition* includes a number of experiences commonly described in the research on mother-infant interaction: emotional attunement, mutual influence, affective mutuality, sharing states of mind.
>
> (1988, pp. 15–16)

Benjamin asks, in her elaboration of concepts drawn in part from Hegel and Winnicott, how do two people "make known their own subjectivity and recognize the other's?" (1998, p. xii). Bringing the importance of this deceptively simple question into sharper focus, she cites philosopher Richard Bernstein:

> Reciprocity must . . . be preserved as a condition of conceiving the ethical relationship, in which, as Bernstein (1992) says, both self and other "stand under the reciprocal obligation to seek to transcend their narcissistic egoism." For "without a *mutual* recognition of the *Aufgabe* [task/obligation] of searching for the commonalities and precise points of difference, without a self-conscious sensitivity of the need always to do justice to the other's *singularity* . . . we are in danger of obliterating the radical plurality of the human condition" (p. 75).
>
> (Benjamin, 1998, p. 100.)

In this model of mutuality, there is an understanding that both parties are supported and enhanced when they consciously attend to striking a reciprocal balance between giving and taking. But mutuality is not a simple achievement, nor is it easy to sustain without effort. As Benjamin shows, the "shadow" of intersubjective recognition and relating is complementarity: the sadomasochistic, domination-submission dynamic of "doer—done to" (Benjamin, 2004). Relating in this mode, each person fears the loss of superior power, and insists on the supremacy of their own subjectivity. Each becomes locked in to the conviction that they are the victim of the other, each feeling they must negate the other, or be negated. One dominates, the other submits, then the other one dominates, and the other one submits . . . ad nauseaum. Giving and taking is now based not on good will and gratitude, but on strategic calculations aimed at maintaining dominance, and, at the deepest level, aimed at preventing being destroyed by the other—being the destroyer, not the destroyed. Failure of mutual recognition represents a collapse of intersubjectivity that Benjamin likens to a kind of death. "Just as Freud posited an inherent conflict in intrapsychic life between eros and death," Benjamin (1999) wrote,

> so [we can] posit an inherent conflict in intersubjective life between eros and narcissism, recognition and omnipotence. The tension that we ideally imagine between these continually breaks down and has to be accomplished over and over (p. 202) . . . It is the constantly renewed commitment to restoring . . . intersubjectivity that allows us to get beyond a struggle of your meaning versus my meaning, to a sense of working together to transcend complementarity in favor of mutual recognition.
>
> (p. 208)

Benjamin is careful to highlight here that we cannot perfect an ideally intersubjective position and then live happily ever after in a Utopian relational world. Recognition is a "constantly renewed commitment" we make, working together, creating a dialogue with our others—parents with children, spouses, siblings, colleagues, teachers with students, analysts with patients—that moves us toward mutual liberation from the tendency to seek power and control through negation of the other, out of fear of otherness.

Where the capacity for intersubjective relatedness has failed to thrive, traumatic exposure to parental narcissism has often been a key factor. Narcissist parents, as Miller (1981) pointed out in work that was groundbreaking at the time, relate to children with the expectation that the child will serve more or less exclusively as a gratifying object, for which the child is rewarded. But the child is punished—i.e., unrecognized—for her efforts to assert her separate subjectivity. The development of the mode of intersubjective relatedness can become a site of trauma as a result of the narcissist's pervasive negation of the child's sense of being a subject in her own right, and the system of rewarding the child's willingness to serve as the parent's object, while punishing the child's emerging subjectivity. For the developing child, the absence of recognition as a separate subject is felt as the presence of negation. Fairbairn expressed this indelibly:

> [T]he greatest need of a child is to obtain conclusive assurance (a) that he is genuinely loved as a person by his parents, and (b) that his parents genuinely accept his love. It is only in so far as such assurance is forthcoming in a form sufficiently convincing to enable him to depend safely upon his real objects that he is able gradually to renounce infantile dependence without misgiving . . . *Frustration of his desire to be loved as a person and to have his love accepted is the greatest trauma that a child can experience.*
>
> (1952, pp. 39–40, italics mine)

Recognition is an essential component of love, and it is equally as traumatic in development to feel unrecognized as a person as it is to have one's desire to give love to the parent go unrecognized, or, in the case of parental sexual abuse, grotesquely misrecognized. To love the parent means to recognize the parent as the source of love, and in doing so, to discover one's own love, love that wants to be given, exchanged, shared.

Unfortunately, narcissist parents demand their child's love in a way that already contains within it resentment and rejection of the child—because the narcissist can only give love conditionally. The child's expectation of being loved is already experienced by this parent as an unreasonable, selfish demand, and as an accusation by the child that the parent isn't giving enough. Most good enough parents feel a degree of inadequacy in terms of what they are giving their children, and they are constantly trying to juggle competing sets of needs, hoping to get their parenting somewhere in the good enough range. However, narcissist parents cannot bear to acknowledge any deficiency in themselves, and so justify their resentment of being asked to give love by making it the child's own fault that love is being withheld.

As Fairbairn understood (1952), children will go to great lengths to keep their parents good, and as Winnicott (1965) understood, they will often present themselves to the parent as what the parent wants them to be. Some of the children raised by narcissist parents become unable to feel a sense of validity other than by attempting to be a gratifying object for the other. From this position, the sense of personal agency and desire is atrophied, replaced instead with anxiety, and underlying resentment, about satisfying the demands and expectations of the other. These children and later adults have become oriented to the known and/or imagined perceptions of others, not to a trusted internal "voice" of their own. This constricted orientation to the judgments and conditions of others can leave one feeling chronically depleted and resentful, as though one is endlessly being "done to" (Benjamin, 2004). These people typically experience significant depressive symptoms, which are actually post-traumatic symptoms of cumulative developmental, or relational, trauma—symptoms that are often expressed in the form of painful lifelong longing for love that can never be requited. In development, to be recognized primarily as object—in other words, to be rigidly objectified—is to be cumulatively traumatized in one's efforts to consolidate the sense of subjectivity.

As with all forms of trauma, dissociation becomes a central survival mode for the adult child of the traumatizing narcissism. Trauma theorists describe a common aspect of dissociation as the formation of a "protector/persecutor self" (Howell, 2005; Kalsched, 1996). In essence, this is the part of the self that can be said to represent the adoption of the moral defense. The voice of the protector/persecutor says: "No. Do not believe in yourself, do not hope, do not dare. You'll only be hurt again." As the voice becomes more fearful of retraumatization, it becomes more laden with rejection and hostility, dissociatively identified with and mimicking the traumatizing narcissist caregiver: "You nothing, you loser! No one could or would ever love you, you're disgusting! Give up!" Like Fairbairn's internal saboteur, the undercover operations of the protector/persecutor self effectively discourage the hopeful, creative, and loving part of the self. I will refer in subsequent chapters to clinical work that uses the "protector/persecutor" framework.

There is a different route taken by some children of traumatizing narcissists—involving externalization, rather than internalization, of the hostile projections of the narcissist parents. People in this group, the "externalizers," might come to disdain needs altogether, and imagine that they themselves have no needs, that only others are weak and needy. This sort of person could become fixed in a subjective orientation, paving the way toward manic grandiosity and contempt for others, with a sense of entitlement and self-justification. The same cumulative traumatization to the sense of subjectivity as with the objectified child has taken place, but this child, rather than succumbing to a sense of helplessness and despairing of being able to feel recognized, instead develops as an adult into someone who arranges to wield the power to bestow, or not bestow, recognition upon others. He has defended against depression by the use of manic reversal—as if to say, "it doesn't matter that you don't recognize me; you are not important, and *I* don't recognize *you*." Another way to think about this is to posit that the traumatized, thwarted subjective self of this child morphs into a protector self, which succeeds in preventing the internalization of shame and badness. Instead, this super-defended self locates badness only in others—never in the self. Rather than persecute the self, this dissociated protector is quick to detect inferiority in others, and able to maintain the sense of superiority quite consistently.

I have often observed that in families with more than one child and at least one narcissist parent, it is not uncommon for one or more of the children to be depressive (objectified), and another(s) to be more manic, and rigidly subjectively oriented. It is also my impression that some children will show signs of narcissistic grandiosity and entitlement from a young age, and grow into their character more deeply as they get older. In other cases, many extremely grandiose narcissists can be discovered to have spent a good deal of life, even into adulthood, displaying their deflated, depressive side, before transforming themselves, Incredible Hulk-like, into their ultimate, floridly grandiose character type.

Sheldon Bach, in his influential work on narcissism (1985, 1994, 2006), sees fixity either in the objective or in the subjective position as an underlying condition for much of what we have called narcissistic and borderline pathology. Bach recognized that the nature of parental responsiveness to the child's emerging subjectivity—the presence of a facilitating environment that could engender basic trust—would powerfully influence whether or not fluidity between experience of oneself as subject and also as object could be achieved. From my perspective, rigid orientation to either the subjective or objective position is best understood as the result of the cumulative developmental trauma of unrecognition. *The trauma of unrecognition could lead one to desperately seek connection through subjugation, and self-objectification; or unrecognition could lead one to hyper-idealize oneself and hold others in contempt.*

The recognition of significant and empathic others is the means by which we become able to experience ourselves as subjects, while at the same time learning to recognize the subjectivity of others. It is the capacity for mutual recognition that allows for the flexibility in moving between subjective and objective perspectives to which Bach refers.[5] The experience of recognition—i.e., to feel seen, understood, cared about, paid attention to, affirmed, supported, and, with one's most significant others, lovingly cherished—is crucial to development, to the enlivening and the embodiment of the self. In its absence, shame, the devaluation of the self, fills the void. Recognition needs are basic human needs that are with us throughout the life span, as essential for real health and growth as food and water. Borrowing a turn of phrase of Winnicott's, there is no such thing as a baby who needs recognition and a parent who does not; the same holds for any significant other dyad, analyst and patient included, of course.

Unfortunately for many of our patients, their developmentally traumatic experiences have solidified into a tenaciously repetitive paradigm in which it now appears to them that only one person in any relationship is going to be entitled to recognition. The other has to find a way to manage without it—which, in fact, isn't possible. By the time the unrecognized adult child of an objectifying parent gets into therapy, she has typically experienced a long trajectory of failed attempts at connection, and of painfully broken and unrepaired connections. These patients' unconscious identifications with their disconnected, rejecting parents have led them to experience a painfully dissociated conflict between their shame and self-contempt about needs and desires, and their intense longing for recognition and connection. This is a conflict that can make an "intersubjective enough" intimate relationship in later life very difficult to achieve and sustain. A withholding parent, consciously sadistic or not, can go a long way toward bringing up a masochistic child, who would then have a strong chance of becoming an adult "looking for love in all the wrong places"[6]—in constant search of recognition from others who cannot or will not provide it.

Developmental Trauma or Pathology?

The different kinds of narcissistic problems I have been describing so far would typically be placed under the umbrella diagnosis of "pathological narcissism." I have been circumventing the use of this term because I find it problematic.

Patients described as pathologically narcissistic are often those whose self-esteem is terribly fragile; who easily feel insulted, attacked, and humiliated by expressions of the analyst's separate subjectivity; who may come to masochistically depend on idealized others, yet who dread the suffocating submission they feel required to proffer. These patients are trapped in the narrow space between preserving ties to others on the basis of accommodation on the one hand, and on the other, striving to preserve their own subjectivity—while dreading that to do so will mean they must lose any reliable ties to others. This person is often referred to as a "deflated narcissist" (Bach), a "shame-prone" (Kohut), covert, or "thin-skinned narcissist" (Rosenfeld, 1965, 1987).

At the same time, exactly the opposite sort of person is described, especially in Kernberg's (1975) work, but also in several lesser known papers of Kohut's (1990a, 1990b), as a pathological narcissist, referred to as the overinflated (Bach), grandiose, overt, or thick-skinned (Rosenfeld) type. Cunning manipulators of others, grandiose, envious, aggressive, exploiting, and controlling, these narcissists are users, who can be charismatic, seductive, and intensely attentive. Yet they ultimately prove to be concerned only with their own needs, feelings, and desires. If their significant others (spouses, siblings, children) attempt to assert their needs, this sort of narcissist is skilled at making such efforts out to be shameful, hurtful, and selfish.

Finally, people who oscillate from inflated to deflated narcissistic states are also called pathological narcissists.

I have never been comfortable with calling all of these kinds of people pathological. The patient who is labeled the deflated, thin-skinned pathological narcissist is usually someone who in development has suffered severe damage to their self-esteem system, and whose self-esteem regulation is therefore inconsistent and precarious, subject to the internal persecution of the split-off protector self. In my view, this person is more aptly deemed a sufferer of cumulative, developmental, post-traumatic stress. These patients are inhabited and often tormented by the ghosts of their traumatizers. To struggle desperately to regulate one's self-esteem, to become lost and hopeless about being loved and desired, to fear that only by subjugating oneself to seemingly more powerful others can one hope to be able to rely on human connection—these are survival attempts for people whose sense of subjectivity has been traumatically co-opted, who cannot confer legitimacy upon themselves, but must go begging for it from others. Speaking of these developmentally traumatized patients as pathological is sharply discordant to the ways that most psychoanalysts speak of any other traumatized patients.

The overinflated narcissist is often someone much more like the original Narcissus of Ovid's *Metamorphoses*, as I understand the Narcissus myth: reveling in being wanted and adored by others, contemptuously deeming no one good enough; reinforcing his grandiose overvaluation of himself by sadistically negating the value and worth of others; and ultimately trapped and destroyed by his delusional obsession with what he perceives to be his own perfection. This narcissist in real life, a myth in his own mind, is so well defended against his developmental trauma, so skillful a disavower of the dependency and inadequacy that is so shameful to him, that he creates a delusional world in which he is a superior being in need of nothing he cannot provide for himself. To remain persuaded of his own perfection, he uses significant others whom he can subjugate. These spouses, siblings, children, or followers of the inflated narcissist strive anxiously to be what the narcissist wants them to be, for fear of being banished from his exalted presence. He is compelled to use those who depend on him to serve as hosts for his own disavowed and projected dependency, which for him signifies profound inadequacy and is laden with shame and humiliation. To the extent that he succeeds in keeping inadequacy and dependency external, he can sustain in his internal world his delusions of shame-free, self-sufficient superiority.

When we say "pathological," what do we really mean? When this term is used by psychoanalysts, it seems to me that some level of psychopathy is what is really being implied. However, the narcissist who seduces others in order to control and exploit them, who attacks and negates the other's subjectivity in order to create hegemony for his own, and who does so while being firmly convinced of his unquestionable entitlement and righteousness, does not fit the meaning of psychopath as I understand it. The difference is that the psychopath knows he breaks the law and behaves with no regard or empathy for others. The narcissist I am describing is very firmly convinced of his righteousness. This kind of narcissism involves a delusional sense of omnipotence, buttressed by the paranoid belief that all who question the narcissist's perfection are merely envious and malicious (paranoid in the sense that the malice and envy are disavowed and projected). The term "pathological narcissist," often used to describe this set of character structures, is also used, problematically, to label and describe the people he typically exploits and victimizes, whose sense of self-esteem he has traumatically destabilized.

This problem may be understood, at least in part, as stemming from limitations in the original myth itself. As narcissism continued to be theorized after Freud's initial foray, the Narcissus myth proved somewhat one-dimensional and insufficiently explanatory. The myth did not elaborate, as psychoanalysts did, the ways that deflated and overinflated narcissistic traits always occur together, dialectically (Aron, personal conversation). Psychoanalysts observed that when entitled grandiosity is in the foreground of the personality, then over-idealization is somewhere in the background, and vice versa. The film *All About Eve* (1950, written and directed by J.L. Mankiewicz) vividly captures this dialectic in the character of starry eyed, fawning, servile Eve Harrington (portrayed by Anne Baxter), desperately eager to serve the great theater actress Margo Channing (played by Bette Davis), with the most slavish possible devotion. As the film builds to a climax, Eve has metamorphosed into the epitome of the entitled, grandiose, ruthless egomaniac narcissist. Compared to Eve's despicable narcissism, Davis' Margo Channing makes being hysterical, histrionic, and orally fixated look kind of appealing. Though Eve reaches her goal of artistic triumph, narrowly missing destroying the marriages of the two women who have helped her the most, she learns at the same time that she will nevertheless always be held as the virtual prisoner of the critic Addison DeWitt (played by George Sanders), who actually knows all about Eve, and views the two of them, himself and Eve, as equally rotten.

While it is common enough to find both aspects of narcissism in one person, it is often true that in any particularly narcissistic person, one of these aspects, let's say grandiosity, comes to the fore and predominates. The more entitled grandiose person is likely to enter into significant relationships with people whose predominant narcissistic trait is on the other side of the dialectic—someone who is struggling with deflation, who tries to stabilize his shaky self-esteem by attaching himself to someone with perceived power and prestige whom he over-idealizes. Unlike the back-stabbing Eve, whose relationships would always teeter on the seesaw of sadomasochism, with one of the dyad up, and the other down, many people are in relationships where one tends more toward the manic grandiose side of the spectrum, the other more to the depressive idealizing side, and a good enough balance can be struck between them.

The Traumatizing Narcissist

Here and throughout this book, I am especially focusing on a particular type of the predominantly overinflated, entitled, grandiose narcissist, and the way in which this person characteristically organizes relationships. I call this person the "traumatizing narcissist." In what I (Shaw, 2010) have previously termed "the pathological narcissist's relational system," I describe the narcissist who seeks hegemony for his subjectivity by weakening and suppressing the subjectivity of the other for the purpose of control and exploitation. The other is then left in grave doubt about the validity and even the reality of their own subjectivity. This sadistic, abusive aspect of narcissism stems from the belief, often held unconsciously, that the separate subjectivity of the other is a threat to the survival, literally and/or figuratively, of one's own subjectivity—and the other must therefore be captured and kept under control. Though I have used the terms "pathological narcissist" and "malignant narcissist" in the past, to more accurately reflect my current thinking, and to be more clear about which type of narcissist I am describing, I will instead refer to this pattern of relational behavior as belonging to the "traumatizing narcissist."

Suggesting yet another way of understanding narcissism may risk placing the last straw on the camel's back where defining narcissism is concerned. Nevertheless, the need for the new term arises from the paradigmatic shift in psychoanalysis brought about by the emergence of the "relational turn" (Greenberg & Mitchell, 1983). Seen from this perspective, narcissism is not simply a set of character traits that some people express, some of or all of the time—either in healthy or pathological ways. Narcissism that is traumatic describes a kind of relationship, in which the traumatizing narcissist relates in particular ways toward others, for particular purposes.

What is most characteristic of the traumatizing narcissist as I am defining him is his compelling need to suppress subjectivity in the other, so that the narcissist's subjectivity is always the exclusively important and only valid focus in any dyad or group. He creates fixed complementarity in his relationships, with himself in the dominant position, as subject, and the other as his object to use. Unconsciously, he is using the other to identify with and internalize the disavowed, shameful dependency he projects onto others. In the case of a traumatizing narcissist parent, the child's subjectivity is attacked, suppressed, and shattered. In this situation, the developing child's ability to self-regulate and balance the innate narcissistic tendencies is not just unsupported, but actively derailed by the parent.

The traumatizing narcissist's relational system consists of at least one traumatizing narcissist, and at least one other, a person who is vulnerable enough to succumb to the traumatizing narcissist's hostile takeover of their subjectivity. The traumatizing narcissist recruits others—her child, spouse, sibling, friend, patient, and so on—into a relationship that seductively offers the promise of the bestowal of special gifts—love, prestige, power, adoration. However, the traumatizing narcissist will soon find cause to accuse the other of insufficient concern and of selfishness. The other will then come to be ashamed of and disconnected from his own needs, other than his need to stave off disapproval from and rejection by the traumatizing narcissist. Most crucially, the traumatizing narcissist's goal is to corrupt and debilitate the subjectivity of the other—a form of dehumanization that is the very essence of traumatic abuse. If this other presents for treatment, the impression they give is of being deflated, depressed, masochistic. This sufferer of cumulative, relational trauma brought on by exposure to the traumatizing narcissist is thought of diagnostically, by some, as the deflated narcissist. I have found it more useful clinically to understand this person as having been significantly traumatized, cumulatively and relationally, and as one who is struggling with the pain and terror of her sense of aloneness and lovelessness.

The heightened sadistic tendencies of the traumatizing narcissist may be masked in some cases by charisma and seductive charm. She has successfully dissociated the need to depend on idealized others by achieving a complete super-idealization of herself. She is overt in her need for superiority and domination, successful in seducing others into dependence on her, and cruel and exploitative as she arranges to keep the other in a subjugated position. I refer to dyads or groups dominated by the traumatizing narcissist as being organized according to "the traumatizing narcissist's relational system."

I have chosen this term carefully, so as to emphasize that the child of a traumatizing narcissist parent is not the initiator of the relational dynamics we see as that relationship progresses. I am not talking about an infant or a developing child as a pathological or traumatizing narcissist, not at some particular developmental stage, nor as a result of extraordinary constitutional endowments. In the case of parent/child relationships, children naturally, not pathologically, seek to feel accepted by and made a part of the idealized parent and the parent's world—observations with which I believe Ferenczi, Suttie, Fairbairn, Winnicott, Balint, Bowlby, Kohut, among others, would readily agree. Children also naturally seek to be admired and applauded as they spread their wings and express their exhibitionistic, grandiose tendencies (as especially emphasized by Kohut). I think of developmental grandiosity as self-idealization, something most children do naturally, if allowed, as they dance all around the house like ballerinas, sing like American Idols, stare at the mirror waiting to see if they have washboard abs yet, and so on. They are naturally developing, if allowed to, their "love affair with the world," as stormy as that affair can become, especially during adolescence. I take this felicitous phrase of Greenacre's (1957), also associated with Mahler et al. (1975), to refer to the child's pleasure and excitement with herself, her world, and herself in the world—both as a creative agent (subject) and as an admired and loved, affiliated person (object). Given a chance, such children will develop good enough self-esteem, and good enough self-esteem regulation. A child exposed to parental traumatizing narcissism, however, will have much greater difficulty finding the "good enough" point for their self-esteem.

Traumatizer or Traumatized?

Rosenfeld's (1971) work on narcissism, drawn from his training with Melanie Klein and influenced by Karl Abraham as well (see Britton, 2004), has had an enduring influence on our psychoanalytic thinking on the subject. He is especially known for his descriptions of destructive narcissism in analytic patients, his identification of their omnipotent superiority, and his recognition of their aversion to dependence. His patients, as described in his clinical vignettes, would seem to have much in common with the overinflated, traumatizing narcissists I am describing. In this extended clinical vignette, Rosenfeld presents the essence of his original formulation, in which he describes the extremely frustrating behavior of the patient he identifies as a destructive narcissist. As I read his account, I see this patient quite differently—as someone likely to be the adult, post-traumatic child of a traumatizing narcissist.

Here, at length, is Rosenfeld's account:

Rosenfeld's Vignette

> One narcissistic patient, who kept relations to external objects and the analyst dead and empty by constantly deadening any part of his self that attempted object relations, dreamt of a small boy who was in a comatose condition, dying from some kind of poisoning. He was lying on a bed in the courtyard and was endangered by the hot midday sun which was beginning to shine on him. The patient was standing near to the boy but did nothing to move or protect him. He only felt critical and superior to the doctor treating the child, since it was he who should have seen that the child was moved into the shade. The patient's previous behaviour and associations made it clear that the dying boy stood for his dependent libidinal self which he kept in a dying condition by preventing it from getting help and nourishment from the analyst. I showed him that even when he came close to realizing the seriousness of his mental state, experienced as a dying condition, he did not lift a finger to help himself or to help the analyst to make a move towards saving him, because he was

using the killing of his infantile dependent self to triumph over the analyst and to show him up as a failure. The dream illustrates clearly that the destructive narcissistic state is maintained in power by keeping the libidinal infantile self in a constant dead or dying condition.

Occasionally the analytic interpretations penetrated the narcissistic shell and the patient felt more alive. He then admitted that he would like to improve but soon he felt his mind drifting away from the consulting room and became so detached and sleepy that he could scarcely keep awake. There was an enormous resistance, almost like a stone wall, which prevented any examination of the situation, but gradually it became clear that the patient felt pulled away from any closer contact with the analyst, because as soon as he felt helped there was not only the danger that he might experience a greater need for the analyst but he feared that he would attack him with sneering and belittling thoughts. Contact with the analyst meant a weakening of the narcissistic omnipotent superiority of the patient and the experience of a conscious feeling of overwhelming envy which was strictly avoided by the detachment.

The destructive narcissism of these patients appears often highly organized, as if one were dealing with a powerful gang dominated by a leader, who controls all the members of the gang to see that they support one another in making the criminal destructive work more effective and powerful. However, the narcissistic organization not only increases the strength of the destructive narcissism, but it has a defensive purpose to keep itself in power and so maintain the status quo. The main aim seems to be to prevent the weakening of the organization and to control the members of the gang so that they will not desert the destructive organization and join the positive parts of the self or betray the secrets of the gang to the police, the protecting superego, standing for the helpful analyst, who might be able to save the patient. Frequently when a patient of this kind makes progress in the analysis and wants to change he dreams of being attacked by members of the Mafia or adolescent delinquents and a negative therapeutic reaction sets in. This narcissistic organization is in my experience not primarily directed against guilt and anxiety, but seems to have the purpose of maintaining the idealization and superior power of the destructive narcissism. To change, to receive help, implies weakness and is experienced as wrong or as failure by the destructive narcissistic organization which provides the patient with his sense of superiority. In cases of this kind there is a most determined chronic resistance to analysis and only the very detailed exposure of the system enables analysis to make some progress.
(1971, p. 174)

Discussion of Rosenfeld's Vignette

Rosenfeld does a bravura job here of describing what the patient's behaviors and motivations *appear* to be about, and how he, Rosenfeld, experiences the patient.

I am sure many readers, myself included, can relate to Rosenfeld's conclusions if we think of some of our least gratifying patients, whose suffering seems intractable and unyielding. However, Rosenfeld, following Melanie Klein, is deeply committed to Freud's death instinct as a means of understanding narcissism, and there is the rub. The idiosyncratic overabundance of aggression connected to the death instinct in this type of patient is, for Rosenfeld, the only way to explain the phenomena he is observing. The patient's failure to thrive under the analyst's care is viewed as the aggressive workings of the death instinct, fueling the patient's determination to triumph over the analyst by not taking his help.

Not considered is the possibility that the patient cannot thrive because of devastating developmental trauma; and that there is impasse because the patient now finds himself in an analytic environment in which the traumatic situation is being enacted, with an analyst who can't see his own part in the enactment, thus leaving the patient to feel unsafe and traumatically restimulated.

In the dream, Rosenfeld understands the dying boy's libidinal, dependent self as having been attacked intrapsychically by the part of the patient that adopts a superior, contemptuous, omnipotent attitude—toward his own dependency, and toward the analyst he seeks to render impotent. I have no doubt that this patient would have done a good job of pushing the buttons of my narcissistic vulnerabilities and my need for validation, but I hope that I might nevertheless have heard this dream differently—as a vivid depiction of the enactment in which my patient and I had become stuck. I hope, as I was coming out of my own dissociation, that I would wonder if the dying part of the patient represented a child part of this patient carrying profound attachment trauma, poisoned by the absence of recognition he had experienced developmentally, which he was now experiencing with me, his analyst. I would wonder if the incompetent doctor wasn't me, the analyst, failing to realize that this child part of the patient needs to be "moved into the shade," out of the unsafe, retraumatizing "hot sun" of the analyst's intensely penetrating, condemnatory interpretations. I would hope that I could find a way, probably with much difficulty and much hanging in there on both our parts, for the patient and I to talk about how our enactment became organized along the lines of the patient's genetic developmental trauma. I hope he and I could both see how his restimulation stemmed in part from my own dissociative lapses in my struggle to fight off my sense of therapeutic impotence and narcissistic deflation; and that I was so determined to get him to submit to my version of reality that I was not able to recognize and care about the pain evoked in him by my interpretations. I would hope that we could find a way to feel safe enough to acknowledge and make sense of the destructiveness we were both caught up in and enacting. Out of all of it, I would hope we could both feel that a good repair had been made, and that we had achieved an experience of intersubjective relatedness that we could continue to develop and grow together.

It would be unfair not to mention that Rosenfeld had a late-career change of heart (1987, pp. 270–271). He ultimately put much greater emphasis on the role of developmental trauma for the narcissistic patient, and took a more sensitive, less confrontational clinical approach. Influenced by Rosenfeld, Britton (2004) has explicitly recognized that parental narcissism can result in childhood trauma that plays a major part in the development of narcissistic disorders. However, Britton retains the use of an intrapsychic genesis for narcissism, in the form of "an ego-destructive super-ego" (p. 486), and allows for an "excess of object-hostility in the infant" as a constitutional factor likely to produce narcissistic pathology. I find both the intrapsychic and constitutional explanations for narcissism unpersuasive.

While neo-Kleinian descriptions—such as those of Rosenfeld, Britton, and others[7]—of working with pathological narcissists are often extremely compelling, I find myself frustrated with the pejorative description of these patients as pathological, destructive narcissists, and the lack of recognition of the gravity and the extent of developmental trauma they have suffered. The overinflated, traumatizing narcissist is far less likely to present for treatment than the person that she has traumatized; and that traumatized person is often viewed as a narcissistic patient, when it would be clinically more accurate to recognize her as a trauma survivor. This patient, the victim of the traumatizing narcissist, can prove to be quite challenging to work with, can be quite masochistic, self-and-other-destructive, and intractably depressed. However, these phenomena cannot be unlinked from the developmental trauma, whether it be consciously known or dissociated, that is at the heart of the matter. The developmental trauma this patient has suffered has been at the hands of an overinflated, traumatizing narcissist parent, or significant other. We have a chance, with this deflated patient, to help her discover and define her own subjectivity, and to become freer from undue concern with and fear of the other's needs, expectations, and judgments.

Narcissism as Intergenerationally Transmitted Relational Trauma

As long as it was seen as necessary to comply with Freud's (and also with Melanie Klein's) wish to view narcissism and deal with it clinically as an exclusively intrapsychic matter, the understanding of narcissism as having a thoroughly relational origin, stemming from developmental trauma, and transmitted intergenerationally, could not fully take hold in the psychoanalytic literature. Alice Miller's (1981) first book on the subject of parental narcissism, and many of her subsequent books, have been best-sellers for years; Shengold (1989) made a very significant and enduring psychoanalytic contribution to the child abuse literature; and Davies and Frawley (1994) comprehensively illuminated, from a relational psychoanalytic perspective, the means of understanding and treating the adult survivor of sexual abuse. Nevertheless, the extent to which narcissism specifically can be relationally traumatizing, and how this trauma is transmitted intergenerationally, has not been as well elaborated.

As touched on earlier, research being done by contemporary attachment theorists provides powerful empirical evidence for the intergenerational transmission of cumulative developmental trauma, also referred to as relational trauma. Though Fraiburg et al. spoke long ago of the ghost-like presence of one's own attachment experience in the nursery—and its influence on how one relates to one's infant—empirical evidence of the transmission of attachment trauma has now been provided in numerous studies, beginning in 1985 with the work of Mary Main, who was able to clearly demonstrate the intergenerational correlation between the child's Strange Situation behavior, and the parent's "state of mind with respect to attachment" (as cited in Wallin, 2007, pp. 30–42). The parents' state of mind with respect to attachment will be profoundly influenced by whatever developmental traumas were most significant for them—including developmental experiences of parental traumatizing narcissism. If the parent who as a child was objectified and exploited by a traumatizing narcissist parent has not developed coherent understanding of their traumatic experience, this parent stands an excellent chance of bequeathing this trauma to her own child. The parent who comprehends his own traumatization has a far better chance of being a "de-contaminated" parent, more likely to raise his children without bequeathing them the inheritance of trauma.[8] As Bromberg (2011) has written,

> Developmental trauma (sometimes called *relational trauma*) is always part of what shapes early attachment patterns (including "secure attachment"), which in turn establish what Bowlby (1969, 1973, 1980) calls "internal working models." The internal working models include procedural memories which organize the core self and its relative degree of vulnerability to destabilization. Developmental trauma is thus an inevitable aspect of early life to varying degrees, *and is of significance in all analytic work*. That is, attachment-related trauma is part of everyone's past and a factor in every treatment experience, but for some patients it has led to a dissociative mental structure that virtually takes over personality functioning and mental life and thereby dictates the "Truth" about the present and the future.
>
> (p. 99, italics mine)

Traumatic narcissism is a particular form of attachment-related trauma. We see the impact of the traumatic narcissist as developmental trauma in our patients' absence of desire and in the absence of the sense of agency; in fear of subjugation, fear of not being enough for the other; in the longing for a surrender (Ghent, 1990) that can never be, because surrender must always degenerate into submission, or so it seems. These are deficits and fears that stem from developmental trauma to the sense of subjectivity. If one has been persistently objectified in development, meaningful love and work can be tormenting and elusive goals, because one has become unable, sometimes permanently, to have a good enough, consistent enough experience of oneself as a subject.

The Restoration of Subjectivity and the Construction of Intersubjective Relatedness

What does it mean to experience oneself as a subject? Throughout the life span, the effort to consolidate and express one's subjectivity means to have a consistent enough sense of one's intrinsic worth and value, to know what one thinks and feels, what one wants and doesn't want; to feel permitted, or free, to assert the legitimacy of one's own point of view, without having either to deny the reality of others, or to adopt the other's reality for fear of being isolated, or at worst, annihilated. A sense of one's own self as a subject means knowing desire, and experiencing oneself as an agent capable of meaningful and productive action. The struggle to maintain the integrity of one's own subjectivity, while remaining flexible and porous enough to negotiate mutuality, resisting both demands for submission and the need to demand it of others, is the theme I encounter again and again in my clinical work. One of the most important ways psychoanalytic work can be therapeutic is in the mutual discernment, negotiated in real time between analyst and analysand, of the difference between objectification as the means of subjugation—the mode of the traumatizing narcissist's relational system—and intersubjective relatedness. Acknowledging the developmental need for recognition, and the need for competence in constructing and regularly maintaining and repairing mutual recognition in relationships, is also very much at the heart of the means and the ends of relational psychoanalysis.

Relationships that can be less prone to subjugation struggles, and more encouraging of mutuality and recognition, are oases in human life. These are the relationships that provide respite from vulnerability to and vigilant defensiveness against narcissistic injuries; from anxious fears, isolation, and aloneness; from emptiness, and inexorable mortality—from all those inevitables that shadow our human existence. "The central dynamic struggle throughout life," Stephen Mitchell wrote,

> is between the powerful need to establish, maintain, and protect intimate bonds with others and various efforts to escape the pains and dangers of those bonds, the sense of vulnerability, the threat of disappointment, engulfment, exploitation, and loss.
>
> (1988, p. 29)

The struggle Mitchell identified is all the more arduous when one's formative relational experiences have made it seem hopelessly unsafe to develop and grow the sense of being a subject, a person in one's own right. Our ability as analysts to open ourselves to the experience of intersubjective relatedness with our patients, and our willingness to recognize, regulate, and, when appropriate, to talk about and be accountable for the ways in which our own often dissociated narcissism may be causing harm is, by my definition, the means by which we express "analytic love" (Shaw, 2003a, 2007; also see chapters 7 and 8, this book). If in our work we are able to allow the experience of intersubjective relatedness to come alive; if our patients can experience with us the possibilities for aliveness, creativity, and freedom in relationships that are not organized on the basis of subjugation, but which support the potentials of intersubjective relatedness, then we will have gone a long way toward meeting the goals and the promise of relational psychoanalysis, for both our patients and ourselves.

I will end this chapter by quoting Erich Fromm (1964), neglected and rejected by much of the psychoanalytic profession in his own time (see Philipson, 2011), but hugely popular with the reading public for decades. I find myself in deep accord with his views on narcissism, which for Fromm was the opposite of love. Fromm, like Freud, was a European Jew who saw first-hand the devastation of World War I and the rise of Nazism, followed by yet another World War. Fromm lived on to see the Cold War and the rise of the consumer culture. Perhaps nothing shaped Fromm's interests and ideas more than the horror of witnessing nations of civilized people fervently embracing the insanity and unspeakable cruelty of the Nazi ideology. For Fromm, the essence of man's cruelty to man was not a death instinct, as Freud or Melanie Klein might conceptualize, but narcissism, the malignant narcissism, as he called it, of a person or a group that refuses to recognize, that despises and seeks to destroy, the other. "The significance of the phenomenon of narcissism from the ethical-spiritual viewpoint," wrote Fromm, who did not find an ethical-spiritual viewpoint antithetical to a psychoanalytic viewpoint,

> becomes very clear if we consider that the essential teachings of all the great humanist religions can be summarized in one sentence: *It is the goal of man to overcome one's narcissism* . . .[9] The Old Testament says: "Love thy neighbor as thyself." Here the demand is to overcome one's narcissism at least to the point where one's neighbor becomes as important as oneself. But the Old Testament goes much further than this in demanding love for the "stranger." (You know the soul of the stranger, for strangers have you been in the land of Egypt.) The stranger is precisely the person who is not part of my clan, my family, my nation; he is not part of the group to which I am narcissistically attached. He is nothing other than human . . . In the love for the stranger narcissistic love has vanished . . . If the stranger has become fully human to you, there is no longer an enemy, because you have become truly human. To love the stranger and the enemy is possible only if narcissism has been overcome, if "I am thou."
>
> (1964: pp. 85–86)

Notes

1 Some portions of Chapters 1 and 2 have appeared previously in Shaw, 2010.

2 See Aron (1996) and also Wallin (2007), whose books comprehensively survey the intersubjectivity literature. Also see Aron (2000) for a review of many of the contributions to intersubjectivity theory.

3 Psychoanalytic authors and attachment and infant researchers too numerous to mention have observed and described the intergenerational transmission of relational trauma. It is implied, if not referenced specifically, in Fairbairn's theory of Object Relations (1952); in Sullivan's Interpersonal Theory (1953); and in Kohut's psychology of the Self (1984). Other papers and books relevant to the themes I develop here include those by Abraham and Torok (1984); Coates and Moore (1997); Faimberg (1988); Fraiberg et al. (1975); and Grand (2000).

4 My attempt to summarize some of Benjamin's thinking about recognition is necessarily brief and incomplete. I refer the reader to her publications (Benjamin, 1988, 1995, 1998, 2004).

5 Aron (2000), building on Bach's formulation, refers to self-reflexivity as encompassing the ability to flexibly move between subjective and objective orientations; he notes the relationship of these concepts to other facets of intersubjectivity, including the dialectics of self and mutual regulation (Beebe & Lachmann, 1998) and mentalization (Fonagy & Target, 1996, 1998; Target & Fonagy, 1996).
6 *Lookin' for Love* is the title of a song written by Wanda Mallette, Bob Morrison, and Patti Ryan, for the film *Urban Cowboy*.
7 See Segal (1997), and Steiner (1987).
8 While there are certainly strong links in my conceptualization of the traumatizing narcissist to the work of Abraham and Torok (1984) and Faimberg (1988), I was not aware of their work until finishing a first draft of this volume. Interestingly, these authors describe patients whose parents were narcissistically traumatized by their parents. Although I am referring specifically to my clinical work with adult children of traumatizing narcissists, there are a number of instances where it has been possible to identify their grandparents as traumatizing narcissists. In some of these cases, the grandparents were more abusive than the parents—in others, the parents had become more severely narcissistic than the grandparents.
9 Fromm's use of the verb "to overcome" reflects, I think, a loose understanding of what overcoming would mean: humans rarely, if ever completely, "overcome" their narcissism. Kohut (1966) would use the verb "to transform" to describe how raw narcissistic impulses can, under good environmental conditions, either during development or later in analysis, be transformed and put to constructive, creative uses.

Chapter 2

The Adult Child of the Traumatizing Narcissist

Enter Ghosts![1]

In this chapter, I illustrate the workings of the traumatizing narcissist's relational system through an extended clinical vignette of my work with Alice, the adult child of traumatizing narcissist parents. Alice is an example of the person in this system that I think of as the victim, not the perpetrator, of traumatic narcissism. It is usually the people who are or who have been in significant relationships with the traumatizing narcissist, people like Alice, who become our patients. Their narcissistic vulnerabilities stem from cumulative relational trauma, and the analytic work with these patients crucially includes the illumination and the witnessing of that trauma.

I would also like to be able to present clinical work with someone I could identify as a traumatizing narcissist—but in my experience, the most rigidly traumatizing narcissists rarely last very long in therapy, if they present for therapy at all. If they should enter treatment, they are unlikely to be seeking help to deepen self-knowledge for the purpose of changing and growing. Rather, this patient is typically seeking an alliance with the therapist that will buttress his self-justification. Presenting himself as a victim of his children, a friend, his spouse, etc., this patient can be found to have succeeded in making these others feel exploited to the point that they have divorced him, emotionally if not legally. I acknowledge that others may see this type of patient more than I, and might even have a practice full of them, but I don't hear such patients presented by colleagues very often, not in groups, not at conferences, not in classrooms—except when they are mentioned as the significant others of the patient.

If we ourselves have not been connected to a traumatizing narcissist, our traumatized patients are usually the best channels for getting to know the mind and the behavior of these traumatizers. However, I discovered another means of knowing more about the traumatizing narcissist, a discovery that was accidental and unexpected. So before turning to Alice, I would like to tell the story of someone who is no longer living, and whom I never met. This is the story of the great American play, *Long Day's Journey Into Night*, which is the story, fictionalized, of its playwright, Eugene O'Neill, and his family. The play brilliantly depicts a family desperately trapped in the madness of traumatic narcissism; but it is O'Neill's life as he lived it, after the events depicted in his play, that illustrate most vividly the worst potential for destructiveness in families where traumatic narcissism has taken root.

Long Day's Journey into Night

When Eugene O'Neill had finished his masterpiece, the autobiographical play *Long Day's Journey Into Night* (2002), he gave it to his wife Carlotta with this note:

> Dearest: I give you the original script of this play of old sorrow, written in tears and blood . . . I mean it as a tribute to your love and tenderness which gave me the faith in love that enabled me to face my dead at last and write this play—write it with deep pity and understanding and forgiveness for all the four haunted Tyrones . . .
>
> (O'Neill, 2002, p. 7)

He instructed Carlotta not to allow the play to be produced until after his death. It stunned audiences when it was first performed in 1956, and it stunned me as a college student when I first saw the film version; but never more so than when I attended a Broadway production in 2003. That night on Broadway, some four hours after the curtain went up, the brilliant cast took their bows. Both the actors on stage and the standing audience were ashen faced, many weeping. Outstanding performances by masterful actors were being applauded, as the shattered lives of the tortured souls they portrayed were being mourned in the audience's acknowledgment. Had Eugene O'Neill been alive to take a bow for the writing of his autobiographical play, I imagine he would have been greeted with even greater adulation.

O'Neill's *Long Day's Journey Into Night* tells the story of his own family, called the Tyrones in the play—his morphine-addicted mother, whose only girlhood dream had been to become a nun; his miserly, broken father, once an actor considered a genius, who had ended instead a redundant hack; the charismatic, brilliant older brother who could neither work nor love, nor stop from drinking himself to death; and O'Neill himself, the youngest, ill with tuberculosis, recovering from a year-long drunken binge that had brought him to the brink of suicide.

The play comes to its unbearable end. Now almost dawn, the sleepless family is gathered together. Mother is lost in a morphine rapture, recalling her girlhood dream of becoming a nun. As she croons of the only happiness she can remember—the golden days before she ever met her husband, or had her children—her sons and her husband listen: exhausted, devastated, brokenhearted beyond mending. The question of who is to blame for mother's addiction, and for the misery of them all, is still unanswered, though each member of the family blames every other member, and all most deeply blame themselves. O'Neill—named Edmund in the play, after his brother who had died of childhood illness before O'Neill was born—will leave that morning for the sanitarium, where he hopes to sober up and cure his tuberculosis. As the curtain falls, each member of the family has in some measure been forgiven by the playwright, yet no one has been spared.

Or so it seems. If we take a closer look at what O'Neill left out of his autobiographical play, written toward the end of his life, a very different, untold story is revealed. Virtually everything about young Edmund that we learn in the play exactly matches O'Neill's personal history, except for one omitted detail. The sea voyage O'Neill returned from prior to the action of the play (a voyage he memorialized in *The Moon of the Caribees* (1919) and the other short plays he wrote at the beginning of his career) was embarked upon almost immediately after the birth of his first son, whom O'Neill promptly abandoned and did not lay eyes on until the boy was 11 years old. O'Neill faithfully transcribed his autobiography in his first sea plays and in *Long Day's Journey Into Night*, but his son and the wife who gave birth to him were redacted, disappeared.

Reading O'Neill's biographies (Black, 1999; Gelb & Gelb, 2000; Sheaffer, 1968, 1973) shortly after experiencing the thrilling performance I've described, I found myself shocked and disturbed by the story he never told in any of his writing: the story of his three children, all of whom he was barely willing to see for more than a few weeks a year, never all of them together; and each of whom he eventually erased from his awareness (and his grandchildren along with them), all of whom he disowned and disinherited. One by one, he nursed his bitter contempt for each of them, and he let each of them know it in the cruelest of terms. As adults, his two sons ended their lives by suicide, one by slashing his wrists, the other, a long-time heroin addict, by jumping out a window. His daughter Oona, who married 56-year-old Charles Chaplin when she was barely 18 years old, was 66 years old when she died after years of depressive alcoholism. One person in this autobiographical long day's journey was, in fact, spared: O'Neill himself, its author. He presents himself as lost, searching, longing, despairing—but not as the self-absorbed deserter of his first wife and child, whose contempt for them was all he felt they deserved. O'Neill's portrayal of himself as a tragic hero could not hold up if the inconvenient truth of his traumatizing narcissism in regard to his children were acknowledged.

O'Neill expressed repeatedly, in plays, letters, and reported conversations, the persistent longing throughout his life and into old age to collapse in the arms of an ideally tender woman and find, with his head nestled at her bosom, a desperately sought relief from aloneness and pain, a paradise long-lost and finally found. The climactic scene of another of O'Neill's later masterpieces, *A Moon for the Misbegotten* (1952), portrays the male lead sobbing and confessing extensively while being held to the breast of the female lead. O'Neill took pains to specify in his stage directions that she was to have a deep chest, and large firm breasts. O'Neill's lifelong yearning for peace at the breast is extensively documented in two papers by Hamilton (1976, 1979). The intensity of O'Neill's fantasy of peace and redemption at the breast—an experience he was surely deprived of with his mother, who, in the throes of severe postpartum depression, retreated into morphine addiction soon after his birth—certainly makes sense in the context of his lifelong melancholia. Karl Abraham (1942) first noted this intense oral longing and considered it pathognomonic for melancholia. This longing may also offer a way to explain the contempt and disgust O'Neill felt toward his own children. If there was a breast to be had, O'Neill as father seemed to want it for himself alone; he did not want to have to share it. In "the battle for the breast," he came to view his children as his mortal enemies. In denial of his profound competitive envy of them, he contrived justifications for holding them in utter contempt—the more so as they began to achieve any kind of success or recognition for their independent professional accomplishments. He defeated their attempts to know and love him with the cruelest weapon a parent can employ—the withholding of love. By attributing his withholding of love to what he defined as their inexcusable deficiencies, he deepened the wounds.

Once O'Neill had decided his children were worthless, it was for him as if they had never existed. His marriage to Carlotta, his third wife, was his most successful, and Carlotta fully supported his abandonment of his children. Carlotta had in fact abandoned her only child, Cynthia, shortly after giving birth. She reunited with her daughter some years later, and the adult daughter, Cynthia, developed a fond relationship with O'Neill. Not surprisingly, Carlotta soon found reason to denounce and disown Cynthia; and then Carlotta helped to persuade O'Neill to denounce and disinherit his own children as well. With Carlotta's and O'Neill's adult children out of the picture, Carlotta had no competition for the complete control of O'Neill, and he submitted to her completely.

Many believe that *Long Day's Journey Into Night* is America's greatest play, and I have found it to be extraordinarily insightful and profoundly moving. Kohut was particularly fond of O'Neill's plays, and offered his own thoughts about O'Neill's biography:

> In contrast to most of the students of O'Neill's life, I would not regard his actions as being "selfish" in the derogatory sense in which this word is customarily employed but rather as being undertaken in the service of his creativity, i.e., as enabling him to reach conditions in which he could simultaneously live out the pattern of his self most fully *and* give to others the best he had to give . . .
>
> (1990a, p. 575)

The story of O'Neill's family of origin, and especially the narcissism of his parents, certainly helps us understand his drinking, his desperate yearning for the mending of his brokenness, his search for comfort in the arms of a devoted woman, who would be both wife and mother to him. Kohut is correct about what it took for O'Neill to be able to write as powerfully as he did. I suspect, though, that Kohut may not have been fully aware of the extent of O'Neill's abandonment and cruel condemnation of his children, and that he would be less likely to applaud unambiguously his adaptive use of playwrighting as his personal lifeboat if he had known that O'Neill had in essence pushed all three of his children overboard, leaving them to drown!

O'Neill was treated psychoanalytically for a brief time,[2] mainly for his alcoholism. He gave up alcohol for the most part, but lived out the rest of his life addicted to sedatives. His biographies do not say if the subject of his children was ever raised in his analysis, but it appears that it was not. As is well known, the traumatizing narcissist can be charismatic and gifted, he can produce great works of art, he can even demonstrate acts of courage and wisdom; but I do not think we as analysts can ever really know these people as patients in the same way that their children know them as parents. According to Aristotle, "the family is the most tragic site for drama because the greatest horror arises when cruelty is done where the presence of love is assumed" (cited in Davis, 1994, p. 154). The tragedy of O'Neill's family, his family of origin and the broken family he went on to create, is a tragedy in many families: where a parent's love is expected, a child instead finds pervasive rejection, exploitation, and cruelty. In extreme cases, the traumatizing narcissist can convince his own children that they have no reason to live.[3] In spite of how damaged O'Neill felt having grown up with such terribly traumatizing narcissist parents, he was able to survive his own suicide attempt. Two out of three of his children did not.

O'Neill's story, and the fate of his children, gives a grim portrait of the intergenerational nature of traumatic narcissism and its tragically destructive impact. Alice, the patient I mentioned at the beginning of this chapter, has fortunately survived her traumatizing narcissist parents, but it has been a long, painful struggle, and she has wondered many times if she had the strength to go on living. In describing her struggle, I am also describing mine, as her analyst. As is the case with survivors of any kind of trauma, the analyst's work is complicated, often confusing, often painful. Just a few of the many challenges in working with the adult child of traumatizing narcissists include living through and working out of the enactments; recognizing mutual dissociation and working to break loose; holding hope for long periods of time when the patient has none; struggling to find a way to understand and accept being identified by the patient as a "bad object." Alice's parents were particularly destructive, and their destructiveness haunted my work with Alice for many years.

Alice

Alice is the 40-something daughter of a now deceased, once very prominent psychoanalyst father; her mother was a notable figure in the mental health profession as well. Alice tells a story of unrelenting misery, in a glittering home with famous artists' paintings hung on the walls, her parents at the center of a group of distinguished friends who gather for sumptuous, sophisticated dinner parties. In private, father is depressed and passive, the target of his wife's searing contempt, especially when he tries to defend Alice from her mother's unabating criticism and disapproval. At regular intervals, father loses control and rages, smashing glasses against walls, screaming: "Fuck you all, I hate you, I wish you had never been born!" The outbursts alternate with retreats to near catatonic depressions, with father slumping in his chair, staring into space.

In spite of these periodic grotesque and terrifying episodes, father shows some tenderness toward Alice. In some ways, he is her ally in misery, as they sit at dinner while her mother and her older sisters chatter away, ignoring them. But father's attention becomes sexualized in ways that sicken and terrify her—where he stares when he looks at her, his unannounced intrusions into her bedroom, and unwanted comments about her body. Alice learns to suppress the impulse to turn to father for comfort and protection; turning to mother for protection from father is simply out of the question.

Alice cannot remember a time when she was able to elicit anything other than contempt from her mother. For example, they are in the car en route to the summer house, the air conditioning on so that the windows are closed. Alice is preadolescent. Mother lights up a cigarette, and Alice gets increasingly nauseous. She asks mother not to smoke, it's making her feel sick, and is told to stop whining and being so selfish, so demanding. Alice eventually throws up. Mother silently stops the car, angrily throws open the doors and tells Alice through clenched teeth to clean herself and the car up. Since Alice does not do a very good clean-up job, her mother grabs the towel from her and does it herself. Back in the car, there is silence, until Alice finally apologizes.

Alice describes her mother as a person who categorically refuses to admit to any imperfection in herself—of character, speech, motivation, or action. If Alice is unhappy, according to mother, it's her own fault—Alice is malingering, she's crazy, she's bad. Unfortunately, battling all her life to reject mother's judgments has not prevented Alice from internalizing them. By the time Alice comes to see me, she is 40 and has abandoned her nursing career, in which she was quite competent. Her initial idealistic enthusiasm collapsed as she came to feel more and more depleted by her work with patients, and battered by supervisors she saw as abusive and crazy. Hoping to nurture her creative talents and aesthetic sensibilities, she took a retail job in a crafts store, where she barely earns enough to live. Instead of feeling enriched by being in an artistic milieu, she has come to see herself as a shameful underachiever. On top of all this, she is dating a man she describes to me as paranoid and obsessive compulsive, and living in an unsafe neighborhood with a roommate she mostly avoids, who gets up early and cooks eggs, the smell of which makes her feel nauseous and persecuted. Resolutely defining her values as antithetical to her mother's, she has nevertheless found herself trapped in a life that seems to confirm her mother's contemptuously low expectations.

I call this patient Alice, in part because of my association to Alice Miller, whose *Prisoners of Childhood* (Miller, 1981) first opened the eyes of the wider public, including many mental health professionals, to the problem of parental narcissism. My other association to the name Alice arises because my patient's mother, as I know her through Alice's memory and contemporary experience, reminds me of Lewis Carroll's Red Queen, who ruled the grotesque Orwellian world through the looking glass that was in the original Alice's parlor.

The Complementary Moral Defense

While each traumatizing narcissist parent and traumatized child couple has its own uniquely complex story, one bottom line is that patients such as Alice, who have been brought up in the traumatizing narcissist's relational system, have been taught to believe that they are always wrong and cannot win, by a parent or parents who claim unyielding infallibility. The justice system in such families has become rotten, corrupt. Any opposition from the child is characterized by the parent as signifying the child's moral failure, punishable by the withdrawal of the parent's love and the administration of contempt. For Alice, it was as though she were perpetually on trial before a kangaroo court, on charges of moral turpitude. At the age of eight, she dreamed that a favorite toy, her beloved stuffed guinea pig, was suddenly staring at her, and as she watched in terror, it said: "You can say one thing before you die." Her last word, before waking, was "Me."

With a traumatizing narcissist parent, the child's "me" can become a matter of life or death. At stake is her psychic survival: i.e., her ability to experience herself as a subject, rather than as the depersonalized, dehumanized object of the other's requirements, demands, and judgments.[4]

Fairbairn's work, most especially his elaboration of the "moral defence" (sic) (1952), is crucial to my understanding of the relational dynamics of the traumatizing narcissist. Fairbairn's formulation of the moral defense is worth citing at length:

> the child would rather be bad himself than have bad objects . . . In becoming bad he is really taking upon himself the burden of badness which appears to reside in his objects. By this means he seeks to purge them of their badness; and, in proportion as he succeeds in doing so, he is rewarded by that sense of security which an environment of good objects so characteristically confers. To say that the child takes upon himself the burden of badness which appears to reside in his objects is, of course, the same thing as to say that he internalizes bad objects. The sense of outer security resulting from this process of internalization is, however, liable to be seriously compromised by the resulting presence within him of internalized bad objects. Outer security is thus purchased at the price of inner insecurity . . .
>
> (1952, p. 64)

In this quintessential passage, Fairbairn focuses on what the child does: she internalizes bad objects. In light of our contemporary recognition of the impact of cumulative relational trauma, what, we might ask, are the parents doing? In Alice's case, both parents were incapable of adequate provision, and of course this intensifies the destructive impact of parental narcissism on the child, more so than when at least one parent is good enough. Yet Alice's mother stands out to us as the more destructive parent, having adopted what I term, in an extension of Fairbairn's conceptualization, the *complementary moral defense*: i.e., the assertion on the part of the parent or other adult authority figure, usually implicit and sometimes explicit, that one owns exclusive rights to "the goodness," to innocence, purity, and perfection—and that the child therefore is the locus of any "badness" that arises. The parent who locks into this position, the complementary moral defense, has seized the upper hand, creating fixed complementarity, and destroying the possibility of intersubjectivity, with the child *who is now coercively driven to adopt the moral defense*. The child is overwhelmingly dependent on the parent, and has no choice but to adopt the moral defense, or face banishment—an unimaginably unbearable breach of attachment. To feel unlovable, undesirable, defective, disgusting, incapable of eliciting love—these are the psychic scars of the moral defense. Granted, the moral defense, taking on the burden of the badness, is to some degree a universal developmental phenomenon, with greater or lesser influence on the personality; but when a parent rigidly and consistently adopts the complementary moral defense, the child is likely to live with the sense that a crucial part of herself has been permanently destroyed. She may as an adult try valiantly to believe that she didn't bring the destruction on herself, but she will be hard put not to succumb to the dreadful belief that it was all her own fault.

The rigid employment of the complementary moral defense is an essential defining characteristic of the traumatizing narcissist, who maintains narcissistic inflation by belittling, invalidating, and thereby defeating others.

Relational Trauma, Dissociation, and Enactment

Fairbairn's (1952) structural theory of development can be seen as a kind of trauma theory, with the various splits in the ego he describes representing the dissociation that follows trauma. As discussed previously, the splitting off of a part of the self that becomes a "protector/persecutor," referred to in trauma theory (Howell, 2005; Kalsched, 1996), bears a striking resemblance to Fairbairn's moral defense, the taking on of the badness that would rightfully belong to the other. This is the part of the self, which Fairbairn termed the anti-libidinal ego, that will seek to "protect" the traumatized person from being fully alive, so as not to risk being retraumatized when wanting and hoping is met with frustration and disappointment. The protector/persecutor self will take on the negating aspect of the traumatizer and turn it against the part of the self that still wants to live, love, create, enjoy. The fear of disappointment (protector) is made impossible to ignore by the enforced conviction of one's absolute worthlessness (persecutor). I suspect that Eugene O'Neill's contempt for his children took root in each of them as this persecutor self, persuading his two sons to commit suicide, and his daughter to turn to addiction, just as he, and his mother before him, had done.

As desperately as the adult child of the traumatizing narcissist presenting for therapy may wish to trust and be helped, fear of retraumatization is so persistent that it can become difficult for the analyst to feel effective in any way. The revival of the patient's hopes for recognition creates more vulnerability for the patient than he can tolerate; better just to give up, to shut down. Suddenly, the analyst, who thought her connection with the patient was growing stronger, is shut out, not to be trusted—just another traumatizer, acting empathetic without really being so. The analyst attempts to make sense of what has happened; the patient will have none of it. Impasse.

In Jody Davies' groundbreaking work with Mary Gail Frawley on the treatment of survivors of sexual abuse (Davies & Frawley, 1994), and in a series of subsequent papers (e.g., Davies, 2003, 2004) that illustrate the coercive, introjective–projective push and pull of clinical enactment and impasse, Davies has evocatively portrayed the pain, the rage, and the frustration for analyst and analysand, of the breakdown of intersubjectivity into complementarity. Davies (2003) evokes the essence of this "no exit" experience—"Hell is other people," as Sartre (1946) so succinctly put it—in this way:

> patient and analyst become prisoners of the coercive projective power of each other's vision; each becomes hopelessly defined by the other and incapable of escaping the force of the interactive pull to act in creative and fully agentic ways.
>
> (pp. 15–16)

Davies' description perfectly captures my experience of repeated enactment in my work with Alice—which in turn very much captures Alice's experience of being the child of her destructive, narcissistic, always right, always perfect mother. Alice's longing for recognition was almost unbearably poignant, but her terror of being negated was easily and quickly triggered. If it was I who triggered her—the wrong smile, not smiling, the wrong words, the wrong intonation, the wrong silence—she would express intense aggrieved anger toward me. Even when she spoke her angry feelings more softly, I often felt held to an impossibly high standard, expected to behave myself according to Alice's stipulations—or else. At the same time she would anxiously struggle to deny what terrified her the most—that what she perceived as my badness might be her own internalized badness, projected—which meant to her that not only would she be bad, she would also be crazy. It was easy to understand that recognizing the validity of Alice's perception of my badness was important if we were to find our way out of our complementarity-prone dynamic. However, I often found it easier to understand intellectually than it was to recognize actually.

One day, a few months into our work, Alice informs me that she needs to put some food she has brought with her in the small refrigerator I have in the bathroom of my office. I sense immediately that there is danger in the room—the edge in her voice, which sounds to me like the anticipation of an attack, but with a matter-of-factness that seemed to dare me to say no; then the knot in my stomach and tensing of my shoulders. As Shakespeare put it in *Hamlet*, in what is probably the most famous stage direction of all time, "*Enter Ghost.*" Trying to sound neither annoyed nor guilty, both of which I am already feeling, I inform Alice that I share the refrigerator with the other therapists in the suite, and it is not for the use of patients. This is true, but I am also aware that I don't feel comfortable with her seeing what's in there—it's nothing embarrassing, really, but it's mine and it's private. Moreover, I just don't feel like sharing. Everything is happening too quickly.

I try not to let my resentment of what I perceive as her sense of entitlement show in my tone of voice—she seems to me to presume that I would have no objection. I feel like a bad therapist—like a bad person, judgmental and withholding. Quickly, she begins to sob, louder and louder . . . She is horrified, embarrassed . . . I must hate her; or, no, she hates me, my stinginess, my lack of generosity, my rigidity; she needs someone who is caring, whom she can trust, she has been too hurt all her life; maybe she is just a miserably awkward, thoughtless, selfish person to have asked; but her food, she's working so hard to eat healthy food and not junk, now the food will spoil, it won't stay fresh, she'll have to eat junk; life is too unbearably hard, nothing ever works, no one ever takes care of her . . . The panic and the sobbing have crescendoed, and she is unclear as to whether she hates me or herself or both.

Feeling somewhat dazed and quite confused—ashamed of my incompetence, guilty about my selfishness, and way too resentful of Alice—I falter, fearing that anything I say will be experienced as wounding, will just make matters worse for her, and will only subject my already withered self to further decimation. I am aware that I hate her right now. So I just try to breathe. I think about our complementarity, how quickly and thoroughly each of us has become convinced that we are the victim of the other, and I remind myself that it is unlikely that I am completely right and Alice is completely wrong. It dawns on me that I have not been entirely honest with Alice, and finally I say:

> Alice, I was irritated by how you seemed to assume you could use the refrigerator, and I was trying to pretend I was not. But I don't think either of us is monstrous. I have a rule that I'm a little rigid about, and I was a little annoyed and guilty and tried to hide it; you made an assumption, incorrectly, it turned out, that it would not be a problem. Neither of us is really so *bad*, are we?

We manage to get to the end of the session as I assure Alice that we will repair our connection and find our way forward. Over the next days and weeks, I come to understand that Alice needs to be able to be enraged with me, to be able to tell me how I have hurt and failed her; but she also needs me not to leave her emotionally, and not to retaliate. Initially, there is considerable defensiveness on my part—and some intellectualization; some unpleasant raising of voices on both our parts; the feeling on both sides of being abused; Alice questioning if I am the right therapist for her, me wondering if she might be correct to think I am not; and the wish on my part to shut down and give up. As we talk about what happened, I am eventually able to get more consciously in touch with the parts of myself that cannot bear the humiliation of feeling forced into submission. It becomes clear to me from what Alice has reported about so many interactions with her mother that feeling forced into submission, seething with resentment, and drowning in despair was the prolonged, constantly repeated experience of her childhood. As I become able to more fully feel a connection to the terrified, emotionally battered, and abandoned parts of Alice, I realize that I become invested in getting Alice to submit to my rightness and goodness, even when what I say is too painful for her to hear. I become more aware of how I frighten Alice, when I think I understand her but actually don't, and how I get defensive about her reaction, before I finally understand what frightened her. As I become clearer about all this, I feel able to express genuine remorse, and that helps Alice become a bit more calm. Alice seems to be able to tolerate my fallibility somewhat, to have some faith in my commitment to her, but we both struggle with fear and anger as we proceed.

After disruptions like the one described above, which have happened more often than I would like, and have tended over the years to be spread further apart but seem more intense when they recur, the repair usually takes weeks, sometimes months. During these times there are often significant setbacks for Alice: weeks of agoraphobia, a few weekends of suicidal ideation, a good deal of depersonalization, panic, and mistrust of me and of what will happen in our sessions. For my part, I experience dread of the subsequent sessions as well: Will she quit? Will she upbraid me so harshly that I will be unable to stop myself from becoming defensive and ragefully retaliatory? Will she, because of my incompetence, drop into psychotic depression and not come out?

Outbursts like these did not happen only in my office. From time to time, Alice spoke of her interactions with others, socially, in stores, on the street, with her few remaining friends. There were times when she was touched by an act of kindness, as when a stranger noticed she was ill on the subway and gave her a seat. More often, though, she spoke with varying degrees of contempt, horror, or outrage of the sickening insults and injuries she suffered when she ventured out of her apartment, or when she spent time with other people. I often had great difficulty sharing her feelings or remaining empathetic, because I heard in her descriptions that she was not simply reacting to others, but that she could also be provocative toward others. If I tried in any way to wonder about her behavior, or the other person's point of view, she was often shocked, and devastated, to think that I could imagine any other point of view except her own. She would become tearful, enraged, self-loathing, completely undone if she felt that I had even the slightest question about whether she played any kind of role in the co-construction of these incidents. I should add that I did not venture to even hint at those ideas until we were many years into our work.

One day she arrived in my office looking utterly wretched. She reported that she was having coffee in a crowded Starbuck's, and she took a seat at a large table where a couple were already seated. The man at the table told her that he was having an important conversation and that the table was not available. She told him that it was the only comfortable place to sit, and that he couldn't keep the whole table to himself. He disagreed, they argued, and she would not budge. They raised their voices; he became very insulting; people in the shop were looking; a barrista came over and, bizarrely, I thought, upheld the man's position and asked Alice to move. She refused, and now she was sobbing. The couple got up angrily and left, shouting hostile words at Alice. Alice sat alone, now loudly sobbing. One older woman came over to her and was kind, offering tissues, asking if she could help. Finally, Alice left, and came to my office for her session.

I felt compassion for Alice; I was genuinely saddened by the pain and humiliation she had experienced. However, I could not silence the question in my mind, though I did not speak it: "Why on earth would you not just get up and go somewhere else, instead of letting yourself be abused and humiliated like that? And why did this happen now, just when you were feeling excited and happy about your new art project?" I tried my best to suppress the frustration I felt. From years of experience, I expected that this incident would send Alice into a depressive tailspin that would take months to come out of. However, Alice felt proud of what she had done; she would write a scathing letter to the manager of that Starbuck's; she would never ever go there again. As I suspected, though, Alice spent months after this incident feeling completely shattered. I was able to tell Alice that she seemed, unwittingly, to be keeping her childhood abuse scenarios alive, by using any outer stimulus she could focus on to become completely retraumatized. She seemed to recognize that this was especially true at times when she felt on the verge of feeling revitalized and confident in herself. But Alice's sensitivity to restimulation was acute, and moving out of victimization and self-loathing in a lasting way seemed a long way off. What was happening, I often wondered, that made it so difficult for Alice to progress?

The Traumatizing Narcissist's Relational System: Objectification and the Destruction of Intersubjectivity

One step along the way toward attaining freedom from emotional enslavement to the traumatizer can be the demystification of the traumatizer's power. Demystification can help the adult child of the traumatizing narcissist free herself from the punishing grip of the moral defense, and the concomitant tie to the abuser, which is among the most daunting tasks in any analytic therapy with traumatized patients. The awareness of both loving and hating the traumatizing narcissist parent is typically dissociated for the adult child, so that her conflict about the parent is intensely disorganizing and painfully unresolved, with much of the hate side turned inward against herself. For this patient to retrieve and strengthen her subjectivity, the conflict must be made conscious, and for this to be achieved, it will eventually be important for both the analyst and the patient to formulate an understanding of the inner world of the traumatizing narcissist, to recognize more clearly the irrationality and the cruelty of the parent's complementary moral defense—and to recognize, when possible, the developmental factors that were traumatic for the traumatizer. With complex understanding, one's grief can be recognized as complex; mourning can commence; and the possibility emerges of compassion—of becoming free from the shame of feeling at fault for being unloved, and free of the prison of inconsolability. The choices one makes about one's ongoing feelings about and relationship with the traumatizing narcissist parent can then be choices that are made consciously and voluntarily. It cannot be emphasized enough that reaching these emotional turning points after traumatization can take a very, very long time. There is rarely, if ever, a perfect resolution for the adult child of the traumatizing narcissist; but feelings that were unbearable can become bearable, and life energy that was tied up in trauma can be freed up and invested in a life of one's own.

For the sake of clarity, in the following I summarize my understanding of the workings of the traumatizing narcissist's relational system. I am describing how the traumatizing narcissist parent impacts his and her children—in some cases, leading the child to develop into a newer model of the parent; in other cases, leading the developing child toward a life of post-traumatic self-negation.

1 **Intergenerational Trauma.** The traumatizing narcissist has typically been exposed to cumulative relational trauma throughout the developmental years, in the form of chronic shaming at the hands of parents and/or other significant caregivers who are severely narcissistically disturbed. The traumatizing narcissist parent envies and resents the child's right to dependency, and demands, covertly or overtly, that the child recognize the exclusive validity of the parent's needs and wishes—which means of course that the child is to be ashamed of her own needs and desires and view them as the parent does—as irrelevant, or as contemptible; i.e., greedy, selfish, weak, morally abhorrent. This parent assumes the posture of viewing dependency in others as contemptible, delusionally imagining himself to have transcended dependency. The traumatized child who has been successfully indoctrinated to view dependency as shamefully contemptible, and who as an adult has renounced (but actually disavowed) dependency, and erected rigid, manic defenses against shame, can now become the traumatizing narcissist—and as such, he may or may not be on good terms with the parental narcissist. He may even despise the parental narcissist—and still be unconsciously identified with the abuser, going on to perpetuate the legacy of the relational traumatizing of others, for yet another generation.
2 **Delusional Infallibility and Entitlement.** The adult traumatizing narcissist is obsessed with maintaining a rigid sense of omnipotent superiority and perfection—of infallibility, self-sufficiency, and entitlement. He defends his conviction of righteousness and justification vigilantly. In other words, he has adopted the complementary moral defense, the externalization of all badness. The psychotic nature of this delusion of righteousness should not be

overlooked or minimized: the traumatizing narcissist is often intelligent, socially adept and highly functioning, convinced of his own sanity and skilled at making others feel crazy. His protector self helps him keep himself hyperinflated; the persecutor dimension of the protector is turned outward (externalized), viewing others who do not recognize his superiority as inferior. For the traumatizing narcissist, maintaining a sense of omnipotent superiority—delusionally believing that one needs nothing that one cannot provide for oneself—defends against disavowed insufficiency of any and all varieties. Since, for the traumatizing narcissist, insufficiency is equated with mortifying dependency and the ensuing sense of impotence and inferiority, it is crucial for him to keep the destabilizing shame of these repudiated aspects of self from being released into consciousness.

3 **Externalization of Shame.** Rather than feel self-loathing and the helplessness of unrequited dependency needs, the traumatizing narcissist arranges for dependency and its accompanying shame to be kept external, assigned to belong only to others, so as to protect himself from self-loathing and ultimately from decompensation—literally, mortification, or (psychic) death by shame.[5] Contemptible, shameful dependency/weakness/badness must be continually demonstrated to be "out there," not "in here." Bach (1994) has observed this as well, stating that "the overinflated narcissist can experience himself as cohesive and alive only at the expense of devitalizing his objects" (p. 32). To achieve this goal of "devitalization," the traumatizing narcissist virtually colonizes others, using the other as a host, as it were, onto whom to project and control his unwanted and disavowed affects and self states connected to dependency—especially the shameful sense of neediness and inferiority.

4 **Suppression of the Subjectivity of the Other.** The traumatizing narcissist's child is, unfortunately, an optimal target for the reception of these projections, especially the projection of shame regarding dependency. The traumatizing narcissist parent sees only her own needs as valid—and characterizes the child who tries to express her needs as needy, selfish, and dependent. At the same time, the traumatizing narcissist parent cannot bear the possibility of being surpassed and not needed by the child, and so must undermine the child's efforts toward independence. This is of course a perfect double bind (Bateson et al., 1956). Unable to be anything but dependent, yet still attempting independence, the child of the traumatizing narcissist parent is condemned either way. She comes to associate dependency with shame and humiliation, and independence with rejection and abandonment. Unless she can adopt the counter-dependent, shameless stance of the traumatizing narcissist, she lives instead in a post-traumatic state in which her sense of inescapable badness is cemented.

To put all this in the simplest possible terms: the developing child of the traumatizing narcissist takes one of two possible paths for survival in the face of being raised by the traumatizing narcissist: 1) *externalization* of shameful dependency (the badness) through the subjugation of others; and 2) *internalization* of the badness the traumatizing narcissist parent has projected. Number 1 becomes much like his traumatizer—the traumatizing narcissist. Number 2 becomes the post-traumatic, objectified, and self-objectifying person who repetitively finds himself in relationships in which he is subjugated by the other.

What I want to emphasize in spelling out these four organizing principles of the essential dynamics of the traumatizing narcissist's relational system, is that the abused child who is his object is not, to say the least, being recognized as a subject in her own right. Her role in the construction of her sense of self is now forcibly taken out of her hands and appropriated by the traumatizing narcissist parent. Her sense of being the object of, and being defined by, the other is joined with her sense of shameful badness. She is stripped of agency and objectified. The fate of adult children of traumatizing narcissists, who, like Alice, fall within the post-cumulative relational trauma spectrum rather than the traumatizing narcissist spectrum, is to struggle again and again to know themselves and be recognized as subjects, against the powerfully reflexive pull to identify as the object of the other, as the one who is "done to" (Benjamin, 2004).

I see the moral defense in adult children of traumatizing narcissist parents not only as an attempt to create an illusion of safety by denying the badness of the parents, and making oneself the bad one instead, but also as a badge of defeat in a lost battle to develop and assert one's subjectivity; a testimonial to forced objectification; a submission, not a surrender[6] (Ghent, 1990), of one's own subjectivity to the subjectivity of the other.

Dissociation à Deux

Given the traumatic, assaultive situation of being designated as the source of all "the badness"—the "doer" of all the wrong—that Alice experienced in development, her sense of badness has proven to be difficult to disconfirm. As is so often the case when working with adult children of traumatizing narcissists, she and I have been highly prone to repetitive, dissociative interactions in the analytic situation, in which we find ourselves locked down, each in our complementary corner: Alice enraged and devastated over a failure of empathy on my part; me feeling attacked and/or controlled, helpless; Alice fearing that I will hate and abandon her if she complains about me. During these times, I feel the ghostly presence of the destructive, narcissistic, attacking parents emerging, sucking all the intersubjective air out of the room, leading each member of the dyad to feel like the victim of the other. Faimberg (1988) referred to this experience as "the telescoping of generations," discovered in "the unconscious identifications revealed in the transference" (p. 105). These ghosts are so powerful that, at times, it feels as though we are both holding our breath, in dreadful anticipation of a (figurative) visitation.[7] Davies (2004) put it this way:

> The presence of a psychotic parent—of one who forced the acceptance of an insane reality as the precondition for a loving relationship onto and into a vulnerable child—hovers around the consulting room, exuding a malignant and sulfurous stench, fueling the game of projective–introjective hot potato from which the patient and I struggle to emerge intact.
>
> (p. 719)

The central aspect for me of the working through of these impasse episodes—as has been elaborated in great detail by Bromberg (1991; and 2006, pp. 85–107 and 140–145), and by Stern (2004)—has involved finding a way out of the dissociative state one enters when one's subjectivity is perceived to be under assault. Initially when I feel under attack, I cannot see my own badness, I want to deny it completely. The dissociation dissolves for me when I become able to see in myself what I do not want to see. Most often with Alice, what I can't see is that sometimes when I think I am helping her, I am actually hurting her, and instead of being willing to recognize it and acknowledge it, I get mad at her for being hurt when I think that what she *should* feel is helped. Whatever I said that triggered her or that made her shut down or panic may have been right, but my rightness is not as important as the pain I am evoking in her. If I can recognize the shame and pain I evoke in her by doing what I do, that is, by being her analyst, and let myself feel my own shame about the pain I inflict, we can get somewhere. I am trying to articulate my version of a point made by Bromberg (2011), which I think could not be more crucial:

> despite its instability and "messiness," patient and analyst are typically able to "hang in" during an enactment and make therapeutic progress as long as the analyst's own dissociated shame does not lead, unreflectively, to an indefinitely long period in which his patient's distress is experienced as though it were a wish for him to give up his efforts rather than as an expression of her need for him to recognize her pain and to *care* about it. Enactments are always dyadic, which is why the analyst's ability to experience his own dissociation and his own shame are as intrinsic to the work as the patient's dissociated experience. During the reliving, a patient is scared not just because of what was frightening in the past, but because its enactment in the present *with the therapist* is itself frightening. Consequently, the coconstruction of new self-meaning always involves some self-destabilization, and it is thus of paramount importance that the analyst communicate his ongoing attention to the patient's safety while doing the "work."
>
> (p. 80)

Having identified that there is badness—mine, Alice's, our ghosts'—the question is, can I, the analyst, survive my shame about being fallible, about having badness, and still esteem myself as a good enough analyst? This is a crucial question for patients who are adult children of traumatizing narcissists—will their analyst be accountable in a conflict, or will his shame be so intolerable to him that he will seek to minimize the situation? Or even more retraumatizing, will he duck the blame and pass it to the patient? What I have said to Alice in the wake of our disturbing disruptions is that while we both recognize that what happens between us restimulates Alice's traumatic experience of annihilation in her family, I also recognize that I too regress, that I fail to resist the pull toward complementarity, and that I fail her, however involuntarily, in ways that feel like the ways she was traumatically failed as a child. I have also stated to Alice that just as I believe in the possibility for her of ongoing healing and growth, I believe that I too can grow to be the analyst that she can use, more reliably and effectively, for her growth—and that I will try my very best.

A relationship in which one member is expected to change and grow, and the other considers himself exempt from those processes, is a relationship in which the one expected to change is being subjugated, to one degree or another, by the one claiming exemption. Gurus who make the claim that they have arrived at a state of infallible perfection may or may not be charlatans, using their charismatic power for the purpose of exploiting others; but analysts who imagine that only their patients need to change and grow over the course of an analytic therapy are unwittingly, and in some cases knowingly, keeping their patients dependent—by implicitly or explicitly asserting that there is a state of being "fully analyzed" that the analyst has reached and the patient has not. When the analysand is forbidden to know that the analyst is also struggling to change and grow, or when the analyst believes he has no need to change and grow, the analysand may easily, and justifiably, feel subjugated, envious, and resentful—but at the same time, frightened to challenge the analyst and thereby lose their tie. For the adult child of the traumatizing narcissist, being in such a position is bound to be retraumatizing.[8]

With Alice, these acknowledgments of fallibility on my part (Bollas, 1983; Orange, 1995), and the process of repair we engage in after disruptions, have made it safer for her to hear me say the difficult things that need to be said. I have been able to point out to Alice how she repeatedly snatches defeat from the jaws of success, both in her life and in our work. We are able to talk about her ways of being contemptuous, and about her envious attacks on me and what I have to offer. Knowing that she can rely on my willingness to acknowledge my fallibility has given Alice greater courage to be able to recognize and confront the hateful, destructive parts of herself she feels most ashamed to expose.

Objectifying, Subjectifying

The process of repairing disruptions in a relational bond—acknowledging fallibility, being accountable for doing harm, apologizing, making amends, forgiving, expressing and receiving gratitude—can potentially be profound, shame diminishing, "subjectifying" processes. Repair processes are subjective processes that dissolve complementarity. They stand in contradistinction to the objectifying, narcissistic processes of coercive projection and belittling diminishment, the underlying purposes of which are to induce shame and establish domination. The objectifying processes are often employed covertly, in ways that are unconscious or disavowed. Repair processes, on the other hand, are "subjectifying" processes, and are usually more effective when overtly employed. The reparative processes can instill hope, and perhaps even faith, in the possibility that disruptions do not have to be catastrophic or terminal, but can be meaningfully repaired; and that one's badness, and the badness in others, can exist along with and not override and destroy goodness. I intend "goodness" as I use it here to have the same meaning as "lawful relating" (Benjamin, 2009a, 2009b), the justice system that stems from what Benjamin terms "the moral third."

Alice's developmental trauma was severe and unrelenting throughout childhood and adolescence. Both parents were destructive in their narcissism, one utterly rejecting, the other exploiting. As with all trauma, Alice was prone as an adult to extended periods of diffuse dissociation as well as acutely terrifying, more discrete dissociative episodes, within and outside of analytic sessions. There were many years when Alice seemed barely able to function, not able to work, often unable to leave her apartment, speaking from a place of terror and rage in session after session, reporting hideous dreams of dismemberment and torture, ruminating unceasingly on her mother's cruelty and hatred.

At other times, Alice seemed to come alive. She met a supportive and loving man whom she eventually married, she developed a better professional life, and found ways to express her considerable artistic abilities. Our struggles increasingly centered around her intense conflict between her adult, competent self, and the destroyed baby part of herself. How could I support the growth of her adult self, if for her that meant forgetting about and betraying her baby self? Sadly, neither of us were satisfied that the question was answered when our work ended. It was a terribly difficult conflict to resolve.

The Pain of Re-entry

Over the course of many years, any exciting progressive move Alice made, personally or professionally, and in therapy too, when she would become sharper, clearer, less dissociative, more emotionally alive, more connected, were always followed eventually by these precipitous drops back to hopeless, agonized despair. I would toy with the idea that Alice was enviously trying to ensure that I would not succeed as her therapist, cutting off her nose to spite her face, so to speak; but that never seemed quite right. I wondered if progress and success meant losing me, because then she would feel better and she wouldn't have to come any more—I would be done with her. And so she kept advancing, and then collapsing. Most compelling and explanatory to me was that for Alice to fully embrace her alive, creative self was terrifying, opening up the possibility of fresher, even greater disappointments than those she had already known. Her protector self was also a persecutor, regularly convincing her that no effort she made could ever succeed. She spent many, many hours of her days and nights in a shadowy limbo, shopping online, playing computer games, lying in bed awake but not awake. Nights were often spent in fevered dreams, full of violent terror. Bromberg (1993) explains the daunting challenge for the trauma survivor of coming out of dissociation:

> Putnam (1992) called dissociation "the escape when there is no escape" (p. 104). It is a defense against trauma, which, unlike defenses against internal conflict, does not simply deny the self access to potentially threatening feelings, thoughts, and memories; it effectively obliterates, at least temporarily, the existence of that self to whom the trauma could occur, and it is in that sense like a "quasi-death." The rebuilding of linkages, the reentry into life, involves pain not unlike that of mourning. The return to life means the recognition and facing of death; not simply the death of one's early objects as real people, but the death of those aspects of self with which those objects have been united. At the point the patient begins to abandon the instant and absolute "truth" of dissociative reality in favor of internal conflict and human relatedness, the patient discovers that there is no path without pain. Russell (1993), in a recent article, speaks to the experience of the patient's recognition and processing of trauma as requiring the capacity for a particular kind of grief. "We have to presume," he writes, "that the pain accompanying this grief is extreme, among the most painful of life's experiences. We make this assumption because of the enormous psychological price that is paid to continue to avoid it."
>
> (p. 154)

As profoundly depressed as Alice was, she only rarely expressed the kind of grief Bromberg and Russell reference above. This kind of grief has within it, I believe, the sense of a possible life that is freer from obsession with the trauma and from emotional enslavement to the traumatizer. This kind of grieving can evoke the working of an internal self-consoler, something I believe is potentially available to all. This self-consoling mechanism is what protects the mourner from melancholia. While consolation was not something Alice experienced from her mother, she did in certain ways know that experience with her father, before he betrayed her trust by sexualizing her; and she felt that at least one of her sisters had been kind to her. However, whatever consolation Alice could feel, whether from external or internal sources, did not last for long.

Sometimes, I was the best therapist Alice ever had, kind, gentle, and fatherly; or I was a man she was sexually attracted to and hoping I felt the same toward her. At other times, I was an insensitive, incompetent, intellectualized therapist who had nothing in common with her, who just wanted to control her and get her to feel good so that I could feel good about myself, who repeatedly said hurtful, untrue things to her that caused her to give up all hope of ever being able to stop living in excruciating psychic pain. I am pretty confident I was mostly somewhere in the middle—sometimes great, sometimes obtuse and inept, and mostly good enough—which is what Alice's mother had not allowed her to feel, and which is what I hope someday Alice will feel more steadily, with greater conviction—mostly good enough.

Conclusion

Working with adult children of traumatizing narcissist parents inevitably entails enactments of relational traumas that are painful and difficult for analyst and patient alike. When the ghosts of the traumatizing narcissists in the object worlds of our patients enter the transference/countertransference matrix, it is inevitable that at some point, the analyst's ghosts will manage to get loose and join in as well. At moments like these, we have reached the point at which Fairbairn (1952, p. 70) wryly suggested that exorcism might be the indicated treatment modality.

To be able to help our patients lift the curse that blights the expansion of freedom in their relational world, we will need not only to help them discover a path away from their bad object ties; we will also need to be able to recognize, as Davies (2004) reminds us, the emergence of our own bad objects in the analytic space. The stakes are quite high. In some cases, psychotherapy may be the patient's last hope for being able to find a reason to go on living. The child part of the adult child of the traumatizing narcissist is terribly susceptible to "failure to thrive," in spite of whatever the adult part has been able to accomplish. Patience and kindness can wear thin, when the angry ghosts of the traumatizing narcissist cast their shadows on the analytic couple. The analyst who can successfully regulate shame in working through disruption—not by disavowing it and projecting it, but by owning it and bearing it—can provide a crucially reparative experience for the adult child of the traumatizing narcissist. It can be a "subjectifying" experience, in which the patient is not required to hold the analyst's projected shame, and thereby not conscripted into being the object of the analyst. If analyst and analysand can successfully co-construct these and other acts of mutual recognition, there is good reason to hope that the patient's engagement in the compulsive, nightmarish game of projection/introjection—doer-done to, hot potato—can be greatly diminished, perhaps even laid to rest. The present can become something alive, and not an eternally haunted, endless reenactment of a traumatic relational past. *Exit Ghosts.*

Notes

1 Portions of this chapter have appeared previously in Shaw, 2010.
2 See Sheaffer (1973), pp. 188–205.
3 See Ferenczi's paper entitled "The Unwelcome Child and His Death-Instinct" (1929). Additionally, the suicidal wishes of children of traumatizing narcissists are dramatized with extraordinary dramatic power and depth of insight in the mother–daughter relationship in Ingmar Bergman's *Autumn Sonata* (1978), and in the father–son relationship in Bergman's last film, *Saraband* (2003).

4 See Abraham and Torok (1984), their paper entitled: "The Lost Object—Me": Notes on Identifcation within the Crypt.
5 For a fascinating depiction of the fate of this character type at its most extreme, see Robert Jay Lifton's (2000a) account of the Japanese guru, Shoko Asahara, who led his follower group of accomplished professionals in the science fields to release sarin gas in the Tokyo subway system. Forced to appear in court and stand accused, Asahara quickly decompensated to florid schizophrenia.
6 Ghent's use of the word surrender refers to experiences of opening, to oneself, to others; in spiritual terms, to the sublime. Surrender is freeing. Submission, by contrast, may seem like this kind of surrender experience, but ultimately proves to be enslaving, obscuring, negating.
7 I use the term "ghost" here with appreciation for Fraiberg et al.'s (1975) application of the metaphor in the context of intergenerational trauma. Also see Bromberg (2003).
8 See Benjamin (2009a, 2009b), and Sedlak's (2009) discussion. Benjamin makes an eloquent case for the analyst's need to change (I would add "and grow") as essential to the analyst's ability to facilitate the patient's change.

Chapter 3

Traumatic Narcissism in Cults[1]

The damage caused by the traumatizing narcissist is not limited to the developmental context, or to the family or significant other context. Many kinds of groups, small and large, can become highly destructive when the top level leaders of those groups are traumatizing narcissists who become successful at bringing others into their relational system. In this chapter and in Chapter 4, I will look at the functioning of the traumatizing narcissist's relational system in groups, starting with a group I myself was deeply involved with, prior to entering the mental health field.

When I began graduate school in social work in September of 1994, it had been just two years since I moved out of the spiritual community, the ashram, I had lived and worked in for more than ten years, up until my 40th birthday. In the Hindu tradition, an ashram is a retreat compound that is the communal home of a guru, a teacher who is worshipped as a living saint, where followers come to pray, meditate, chant, and work together. My ex-guru maintained ashrams in India and in upstate New York, as well as in other locations in the U.S., and also toured extensively throughout the world. At the height of her popularity in the mid-1980s, thousands of visitors, swept up in the excitement of the growing New Age movement, flocked to weekend retreats at her ashrams to receive spiritual awakening. I worked over a period of more than ten years as a spokesperson, community manager, meditation teacher, public relations director, and director of educational programs, in the U.S. ashrams and in extensive travels to the group's many international centers all around the globe. I had been successful in strengthening and expanding the devotee communities I was sent to visit—organizational work for which I was praised by Guruji, the (fictionalized) name of my former guru. As a result, I was given more and more managerial responsibility in the last few years of my time in the ashram, and I became one of the relatively small group of followers who were granted extensive direct contact with the guru.

One day, some small thing I casually said while speaking with Guruji and some other staff members—I said a few words in defense of one of the monks, or Swamis, whom Guruji was berating—suddenly changed everything. From then on, Guruji began speaking to me with searing contempt and derision. After six months of being exposed to her relentless, caustic denigration—face to face, in written notes, and on the phone—and after almost daily episodes of public excoriation and humiliation, which included Guruji enlisting others to join her in the attacks against me, Guruji instructed me to leave the ashram and return to live and work in New York City. I had seen this happen to many others, many times. Part of me felt horrified that it was happening to me; and sadly, part of me felt special. In accordance with the mercurial way that Guruji typically behaved, I was still asked to do a good deal of work for the ashram after my expulsion. For two more years, I remained in good favor with the guru, and was even given a cherished front row seat at public satsangs, programs in which Guruji spoke to large audiences and accepted offerings.

In the next two years after moving out of the ashram, scrambling to make a living, still thinking of myself as a follower of Guruji, I did a good deal of soul searching, much of it through the process of psychotherapy. One of the uses I made of psychotherapy was to explore my career options. My work in the ashram had been at my own expense until my funds ran out, after which I lived on a very small stipend. My parents had passed away, there was no family money, and I was earning a living doing word processing as a temp at law firms. Inspired by the work I was doing in therapy, I eventually chose to seek the necessary education and training to become a psychotherapist myself.

In my first social work field placement, many of the clients I was assigned described terrible histories of physical, sexual, and emotional abuse in childhood, and in some cases were involved in ongoing abuse, either as perpetrators or victims. Many of these clients were struggling to recover from devastating addictions. Although my own life had been something of a bed of roses in comparison with the suffering these people had known—not without trauma, but certainly not with the poverty and violence my social work clients reported—I soon discovered I had a deeper connection to their experiences of trauma and abuse than I at first realized.

I had always portrayed my participation in Shakti Yoga (a fictionalized name), to myself and others, as an idealistic commitment to a noble spiritual path, dedicated to spiritual awakening and uplift in the world. Just after graduate school began, I learned of an incident concerning a friend of mine, a young woman just turned 21, who was sexually harassed in the ashram by one of its most powerful male leaders—a man in his late forties who was notoriously seductive, and who years ago had pled no contest to statutory rape in the one instance when the parents of a teenage girl he had seduced took action against him. When the young woman friend of mine sought help from Guruji regarding what had happened between her and the male leader, Guruji told her, through her secretary, that she had brought the harassment upon herself. Guruji warned the young woman: "Don't ever tell anyone about this, especially not your mother." The young woman's mother, an influential leader of the Shakti Yoga community in a large U.S. city, was a long-time devotee of Guruji's.

After two years of intense inner conflict, the young woman finally did tell her story. As a result, many others began to speak out, eventually contributing to an extensive exposé of Shakti Yoga in a well-respected national magazine. The article revealed a Pandora's box of well-documented abuses by the leaders of the group that had been going on for more than 20 years. I learned later that Shakti Yoga followers were chosen by Guruji to become Reiki practitioners specifically for the purpose of doing long-distance Reiki on the author of this article, in hopes of stopping it from being published (Szabo). When the magazine came out, followers from all around the New York area bought every copy off the newsstands they could find, brought them to the upstate ashram, and burned them in a huge ceremonial fire pit. Just to be sure all bases had been covered, followers around the world made a point of finding the magazine in libraries and tearing the article out.

In the two years prior to the publication of the article that I had spent living and working back in New York City, I had slowly and painfully begun to acknowledge to myself, my therapist, and my wife, herself a member of the group at that time (but no longer), that there were aspects of Shakti Yoga and its leaders that I found unethical and disturbing. In particular, I had personally experienced and also frequently witnessed Guruji verbally and emotionally abusing her followers—publicly shaming those with whom she was displeased in cruel and humiliating ways. I had heard her tell blatant lies and witnessed her deliberately deceiving others she wished to embarrass or harass, expressing pleasure in doing so. I witnessed her condoning and encouraging illegal and unethical business and labor practices, such as smuggling gold and U.S. dollars in and out of India, and exploiting workers without providing adequate housing, food, health care, or social security. I was aware that for many years, Guruji, and her predecessor, Sri Babaji (a fictionalized name), had been using spies, hidden cameras, and microphones to gather information about followers in the ashram, which was then used to embarrass them, often publicly. All of these behaviors were well known to those of us on the staff of the organization, but were much less familiar to the thousands of followers who did not live and work there in direct contact with Guruji. Staff members such as myself considered ourselves privileged to be exposed to the more private persona of Guruji, whose typical cruelty to and micro-control of her staff and many "special," (i.e., wealthy) followers, along with her expectation that no amount of money was too much to be spent on her, was always understood as "crazy wisdom," a term that refers to and celebrates the eccentric, mind-blowing, and paradoxical behaviors of spiritual leaders in various Eastern traditions. Aggression, greed, sexual predation, and other forms of cruelty are often among these behaviors in the stories of such leaders, who are understood to be, contrary to appearances, benignly breaking down the boundaries and defenses of followers, "liberating" them from their small, petty, unenlightened egos. Even revered spiritual leaders such as the Dalai Lama and Pema Chodron have been made fully aware of the sexual abuses of leaders in their Buddhist tradition, and airily dismissed abusive sexual predation by these so-called realized masters, such as Sogya and Trungpa Rinpoche, as trivial.

Ghent (1990) made an astute distinction between *surrender* and *submission*. He conceptualized surrender as a letting go of defenses, and an opening to the possibility of the sublime, both as internal state and as interpersonal experience; whereas he understood submission as the dehumanizing, sadomasochistic perversion of surrender. Although I was not aware of Ghent's work until some time after leaving Shakti Yoga, I was beginning to formulate similar ideas. I began to be aware that I had been deceived, and had deceived myself, in a classic bait and switch operation—the bait being surrender, the switch being masochistic submission to a cruel and controlling, yet idealized, leader.

Of all the dissociating I had been doing, to me the most shameful was that in order to continue to convince myself that I was making the best possible choices by devoting myself to Shakti Yoga, I suppressed my awareness of stories of sexual abuse in the ashram, stories it would be absolutely heretical to even mention to another follower. I had heard rumors that contrary to his claims of celibacy and renunciation, the predecessor guru, Sri Babaji, had up until his death in his seventies been relentless in sexually preying upon female followers, many of them girls who were not of legal age. When some followers exposed him publicly, he lied and attempted to cover up the scandal with threats of violence to the whistleblowers, threats made by Sri Babaji himself and by deputies he appointed and dispatched himself—one a former pro-footballer, the other a former Vietnam combat veteran.

I had deliberately chosen to disbelieve and deny this information, though a deeply buried part of me had kept mental notes on many whispers and hints. Later, after I severed all ties with Shakti Yoga in 1994, I came to learn of far more extensive sexual abuse of young girls as well as adult women, several of whom I met and spoke with. Without knowing each other, the women reported exactly similar details: a secret room with a specially built table, which allowed Sri Babji, then in his seventies, to stand while he raped them. I will spare the reader further, more specific details that all of these women who spoke out, again without access to each others' accounts, described. Guruji has continued to deny and cover up this aspect of her predecessor's behavior to this day. I also learned that many of the parents of the young girls whom Sri Babaji had molested had been proud that their daughters were "chosen," as though for a special, divine ritual. I knew some of these people well: before coming to live full-time in the ashram, one of the parents had been an Ivy League professor; another a once-prominent pscychoanalyst. After Sri Babaji's death, Guruji continued to defend and financially support the male leader who had abused the young woman I knew, who was also preying upon dozens of other women, many of them minors.

All my dissociated knowledge suddenly and dramatically broke fully into consciousness when I heard the story of the young woman I knew; I literally felt my body become enlivened, and could physically feel my mind—brain?—expanding, opening. In the phrase, "Don't ever tell anyone about this, especially not your mother," I heard a chilling echo of the voice of the incestuous father, the battering husband, the sexual harasser, the rapist. As Judith Herman says, in her seminal work *Trauma and Recovery* (1992), "secrecy and silence are the perpetrator's first line of defense" (p. 8). It was hearing these words, "Don't ever tell," that broke for me what Ernst Becker (1973) has called "the spell cast by persons—the nexus of unfreedom." I recognized in Guruji's behavior toward her followers the hallmarks of abuse: the use of power to intimidate, seduce, coerce, belittle, and humiliate others—not to strengthen, uplift, and enlighten, as advertised, but for the more base purposes of psychological enslavement and parasitic exploitation.

It should be noted that Shakti Yoga resembles in many ways a mainstream Hindu religion. In the U.S. and other major world capitals, it was successfully marketed to a population of highly educated, affluent professionals, and included quite a few internationally known celebrities in business, the arts, and in journalism. Once I had spoken out publicly about Shakti Yoga, in the early days of the internet, I was instantly, literally within hours, *persona non grata* in the community, so that the dozens of people I thought of as friends, and the hundreds of others from all over the world that were friendly acquaintances, immediately cut me off completely. Fortunately, there were enough members who left the community when I did for us to form an internet support group. I also began to attend conferences organized by what is now the International Cultic Studies Association (ICSA), where I have met hundreds of people over the years who identify either as having been in an abusive, authoritarian group, or who were concerned for loved ones in such groups.

At the first of these conferences I attended, I asked a cult expert there if he thought that people who became involved in these groups had some common psychological traits. His answer was a definite "no!" which surprised me, because I was pretty sure that there were. It seemed obvious to me at this point that for many if not most of the people I knew who became involved in this kind of group, the cult leader was like an idealized parental figure, and the group like an idealized family. Affiliating with the group, for many, was at least in part an attempt to compensate for some sense of lack in one's family of origin. At that time, however, this understanding was thought of as a form of blaming the victim. The line of thinking then, in 1994, about people who got into cults, was that cult followers were the victims of charismatic con artists who used "mind control" techniques, as defined by Robert Jay Lifton (1961) and by Singer and Lalich (1995), to entrap and control followers (see Appendix A at the end of this chapter). These techniques were essentially those identified by Lifton as used by Chinese Communists in prison camps. Those who got into cults, according to the thinking at this time, were people who just happened to be unlucky enough to get sucked in and exposed to mind control, also known as thought reform. Although I in fact recognized every one of Lifton's mind control techniques as integral to the authoritarian culture of the group I had been in, I was convinced that there was more to it than that, more than just accidental exposure to undue influence (Cialdini, 2008). I was convinced as well that my ex-guru had not studied the thought reform techniques of the Chinese Communists, but rather that these behaviors came naturally to her, and others like her, based on certain aspects of character shared by charismatic, authoritarian leaders.

Since becoming licensed as a clinical social worker in 1996, I have worked with dozens of cult-involved people, both in pro bono situations and in my private psychotherapy practice.[2] I have never met a former cult member who did not admit to entering the group willingly, fighting hard to maintain membership in the group, and, upon leaving, doing so with much confusion, fear, and grief. Much of my interest in and development of ideas about the relational system of the traumatizing narcissist stems from my interest in making sense of what for me, and for thousands of others who have experienced abuse in cults, was an enormously painful, life altering experience that began in an ecstasy of hope and possibility, and ultimately became an abyss of cumulative relational trauma.

In this chapter, I would like to use the cult situation to further amplify the concept of the traumatizing narcissist and his relational system. I must first explain that I use the word cult with some misgiving. On the one hand, "cult" is a term most people think of as describing a group with a charismatic leader or leaders. This group, in the public imagination, has followers who fanatically embrace an ideology dictated by the leader, which involve rituals of self-purification and a mission to eliminate impurities in the world; and in which followers adopt ritualized, idiosyncratic modes of speech, dress, and behaviors that are typical of the group as a whole. These ideas about cults are in fact more or less accurate. On the other hand, where the average person's image of a cult goes wrong is that most cults never gain much public attention, and only a very few gain tremendous size and involve bizarre displays such as mass weddings, or horrors such as mass suicides. Additionally, cults are not only religious groups, but are also found in political, therapeutic, business, academic, technology, art, and almost any other kinds of communities.

I will use the word cult here for the sake of expedience, but authoritarian ideological group, or abusive, exploitative high-demand group would be more accurate, albeit clumsier, terms. The use of the word cult can also be problematic for former member whistleblowers, and defenders and counselors of former members: larger and more wealthy groups accused of being cults think nothing of silencing critics with relentless harassment through unending lawsuits.

With these caveats in mind, I define this kind of group, sometimes referred to as a cult, as follows: any group, of at least one leader and one follower, in which the leader exhorts others to follow him and support his mission, and in which the leader can be identified as a traumatizing narcissist. In such a group, members are required to suppress their subjectivity and attempt to make themselves whatever kind of object the leader wants them to be. To clarify, I am not saying that charisma and missionary zeal in a group leader will always result in cult-like dynamics. In a group with a mission in which the leader is not a traumatizing narcissist, one might actually see meaningful work done toward the group's goals. In cults, however, the *stated*, typically grandiose goals of the group are not met, because the group's energies and resources are constantly directed toward the *actual* goal, which is always the self-aggrandizement of the leader and his organization through the subjugation and exploitation of his followers. This of course is precisely the same goal as that of the traumatizing narcissist.

In fact, cult leaders are invariably traumatizing narcissists, as defined in the preceding chapters: grandiose, overinflated narcissists who seek hegemony for their subjectivity by weakening and suppressing the subjectivity of others. They control and exploit followers by seductively dangling carrots—which in this context would be what purportedly could be achieved by becoming a follower—such as success, fulfillment, wealth, or enlightenment. Along with the carrots comes the relentless use of sticks, such as humiliating character assassination and threats of expulsion, meant to persuade the followers that their own subjectivity is inadequate and corrupt compared to the leader's, and therefore in need of extensive correction that only the group and its leader can provide.

For those not familiar with cult phenomena, it can be quite astonishing to learn how similar the relational dynamics of leader and follower are from group to group, regardless of how outwardly different the group, its ideology, leaders, and followers may be. The following are some of the most common dynamics:

1. **Purification of "Ego."** The follower's deficiencies are grouped under the umbrella of "the ego," the "monkey mind," or a similar idea using different words, which is regarded as a harmful appendage or blockage of the true self, and must therefore be "purified" by the leader for the follower to reach her potential. Purification in the case of cults typically means being subjected to various forms of sadistic belittling and humiliation, including in some cases accepting beatings. Purity may also be judged by one's willingness to give over most of any money one might have, and/or willingness to be subjected to sexual abuse. Leaders do not have to be grateful for anything they are given or for anything they take from followers—when taking, the leader is understood to actually be giving. George Orwell (1949) identified this sort of mental gymnastics as "Doublethink" and "Newspeak" in *1984*, his vision of a world ruled by Stalin-like leaders.
2. **Only Perfection is Good Enough.** One's "potential" is defined in any way the leader chooses, but in one form or another, cult leaders are always demanding perfection, in the form of devotion, loyalty, willingness to obey, and willingness and ability to recruit others. By demanding perfection, the leader makes it impossible for the follower to fully succeed at anything, including devotion, and therefore it is impossible for the follower to avoid the leader's abusive criticism. The follower's status can be raised, at least temporarily, when he demonstrates his willingness to act, abusively and criminally if need be, in accordance with the principle that whatever end is specified by the leader always justifies any means.
3. **Incessant Urgency.** The more successful and powerful a particular cult becomes, the greater the risk of public exposure, and, therefore, the more urgent and hysterical the culture becomes. The leadership of the group becomes

more shameless and without boundaries, demanding more and more time, money, and energy of the followers, defining enemies of the group to eventually include anyone not in the group, and becoming increasingly punitive of deviance within the ranks.

4 **Violation of Boundaries as a Norm.** As followers discover that no effort they make is ever good enough to earn the leader's full recognition, or to make them exempt from the leader's destructive attacks, they become more and more desperate to please the leader, becoming willing to let down their own boundaries, and to violate the boundaries of others at the leader's behest.

5 **Inner Deviance Must Be Eradicated.** Ultimately, followers act on the belief that only the leader's thoughts and feelings matter and have validity, and the follower must exist only to serve the leader's aims. The follower actively seeks to negate any aspect of his own subjectivity that the leader might disapprove of.

6 **Defend the Leader No Matter What.** To most outside observers, the leader's aims are clearly nothing more than self-aggrandizement. Insiders, however, in spite of little or no evidence on which to base their assertions, cling stubbornly to the belief that the leader is actually pursuing lofty and noble aims. Asked to do anything to enrich the leader, including, in the case of some notorious groups, prostituting themselves, followers obey and find a way to believe that whatever they do is righteous. By remaining loyal to the leader, the followers persuade themselves that their own existence is given meaning and validity by their support of the leader's mission.

A cult then can readily be understood as a variant of the traumatizing narcissist's relational system, in which the leader presents herself as the living embodiment and ultimate master of the principles of her own ideology. Her mission and her ideology are formalized in ways that will vary in the details from one group to another. The group's goals frequently shift, are proclaimed to the followers with grandiose pomposity, and are often connected to a demand for payment for the privilege of being granted access to the esoteric wisdom. The unstated and disavowed *actual* goal of any group led by a traumatizing narcissist is for the leader to keep herself in a state of narcissistic hyper-inflation; the *actual* job of the follower is to do whatever it takes to help the leader to achieve that aim.

Followers in cults are traumatized in various ways by the different kinds of abuse they are exposed to as they accept the leader's control over them. Abuse in these situations typically includes intimidation, belittling, and humiliation, and, more concretely, severe overwork and deprivation of sleep and proper nutrition. The follower's rewards, which are recognition from the leader and the ensuing prestige they gain within their group, are bestowed and rescinded at the leader's whim, keeping the follower in a state of instability and fear about displeasing the leader and thereby losing status and favor.

What is often most traumatic for followers who leave cults is the realization that what led them to blind themselves to the sadistic cruelty and the selfishness of the traumatizing narcissist leader was how desperately hungry they became—how willing they became to abandon their own subjectivity and allow themselves to be violated—for any bit of recognition they could get from the leader they idealized. One of the reasons why many of the people who leave cultic groups choose not to identify their own experience as abusive is because to do so would mean acknowledging an extraordinary degree of grief over the loss of a deeply cherished idealized attachment, connected to their most cherished hopes about themselves and about life. This is in addition to the unleashing of an extraordinary degree of shame about their own self-deception and gullibility, and shame and rage about the amount of abuse they were willing to endure for the sake of maintaining their tie to the leader. Eventually, the realization that their devotion and labor in the group led to no real personal growth, and to no significant contribution to society, will also become a source of deep shame and regret.

My cousin's wife is a psychiatrist, and a few years after I left Shakti Yoga, when I told her I was going into psychoanalytic training, she said, "Great! You left one cult and now you're joining another!" This is not an uncommon observation;[3] but my own analytic experience up to that point was quite the opposite of my cult experience. Living a life focused on idolization, as I had done for so many years as a guru worshipper, I had forgotten what it was like to experience myself as being worthy of kindness, encouragement, and empathy. Guruji's *modus operandi* had been to follow up any expression of praise or approval with brutally intense disparagement and rejection; so that those of us who dealt directly with her came to anticipate that the more kindness she offered, the more brutal it would be when the other shoe dropped. In therapy, the experience of my analyst being consistently empathetic with me and not suddenly switching to hostile attacks, and the experience of having my point of view and my subjectivity being respected and affirmed, was something I had almost forgotten was possible. It was also a great relief to experience that disruptions could be repaired, not through one of us submitting abjectly to the other, but through negotiation and mutual accountability. These experiences, plus reading psychoanalytic literature on my own all through social work school, convinced me that there was potential in psychoanalytic work for deep understanding, healing, and growth. These were the same goals that I, and so many others like me, thought would arise out of my dedication to Shakti Yoga and its leader. When it became clear that no such thing was possible there—and that idolization and self-negation, not self-realization, were the only real possibilities in that relationship—I was ready to start over. Better late than never.

I have described some of my own cult experience here as part of my effort to raise awareness within the mental health community, and particularly the psychoanalytic community, of the problem of traumatic abuse in cults.[4] I speak to many people who report not feeling understood, and even feeling doubted or blamed, when they have tried to describe their cult experience to a therapist. Many people have also reported to me that they were recruited into a cult while they were in therapy, and that they wondered why the therapist neglected to find out about the group and bring information to their attention. Perhaps most unfortunately, many people have reported being recruited into cultic groups by their therapists. Therapists may have signs of a particular group to which they are affiliated, such as photos of the leader, altars, books, recordings, incense, and other paraphernalia, on display in their offices, piquing the patients' curiosity. Or they may proselytize even more directly.

My colleagues at the ICSA and I are aware of a tremendous amount of abuse in cultic groups, world-wide, that never makes the headlines and goes unnoticed, even in the mental health community, in the same way that the sexual abuse of children, or rape, or the battering of women by violent partners, once went unnoticed. In fact, the experience of being abused in a cult is very often described by ex-members as akin to what it must be like to experience incest, rape, and/or battering. While the betrayal and violation that occurs in cults can be compared to some aspects of rape and incest, what truly corresponds is the lack of empathetic witnessing many ex-cultists experience with friends, family, and therapists as they make their way through post-cult recovery.

To bring the matter even closer to home, there have been a number of egregious examples of abusive, authoritarian psychoanalytic psychotherapy cults, which have received little if any attention from within the psychoanalytic community.[5] A particularly tragic case has been reported by Raubolt (2006), in which a group of analysts under the influence of a sadistic and controlling supervisor were only able to recognize what was happening to them over the course of many years of control and abuse, when a patient of the supervisor shot him to death. The story I will speak of in greater detail here is one of the most notorious cases of a psychoanalytic cult.

The Sullivan Institute

It begins in 1957, when Saul Newton and Jane Pearce started training therapists in what they called the Sullivan Institute for Research in Psychoanalysis, later described in their book, written primarily by Pearce, *The Conditions of Human Growth* (Pearce & Newton, 1963). Aside from a *New York* magazine article (Black, 1975) and a *Village Voice* article (Conason & McGarrahan, 1986), little has been written of the Sullivanians, until recently. Amy B. Siskind, raised within the Sullivanian community and now a sociologist, has adapted her Ph.D. dissertation into the first published book about the Sullivan Institute. Siskind (2003) does not provide a tell-all personal account of her own experience as the child of a Sullivanian patient, nor does she provide a psychological analysis of the dynamics of the group, its leaders, and followers. What she presents is a thorough sociological–historical account of the group, its leaders, and its practices, as well as excerpts of accounts of the experiences of former members.

Jane Pearce, a psychiatrist who studied with Harry Stack Sullivan in the late 1940s, met Saul Newton in the early 1950s at the William Alanson White Institute, where he worked in the bursar's office. Newton had no degree and no formal training. He was a charismatic confabulator, who convinced people who knew him that he had fought with the Abraham Lincoln Brigade in the Spanish Revolution. In fact, he had not been a soldier at all, but a payroll clerk. Newton and Pearce married, and together they sought to extend and elaborate Sullivan's ideas. They were particularly disappointed that Sullivan's critique of society and family norms hadn't gone far enough; dissatisfied with the White Institute and seeking full control of an institute of their own, they permanently severed their ties to the White Institute. At no point did the Sullivan Institute, as Newton and Pearce formally named their enterprise, have any kind of legal or financial ties to either Harry Stack Sullivan, or to the William Alanson White Institute.

Like many others swept up in the counterculture revolution of the 1960s, Newton and Pearce sought to create a community, like a Puritan city on a hill, whose members would disdain decadent bourgeois conformity and convention, and reach superior psychological status through radical processes of regression, corrective experience, and personality restructuring. The hidden problem with many of these kinds of personal growth and self-realization projects is that they can often degenerate into an attempt, for leaders and followers, to gain power so as to compensate for a sense of impotence. Things go very wrong in these groups when narcissism runs amok, and when omnipotence, as opposed to power, becomes the unconscious goal. To seek power and influence is always the aim of any group organized with some sort of social betterment in mind. However, when the leader of such a group is a traumatizing narcissist, the only true aim of the group is to persuade itself of the leader's omnipotence, and to persuade as many others as possible to believe and to join. These groups develop delusions of superiority, which are always accompanied by contempt and paranoid fear of those outside the group. The traumatizing narcissist's complete disavowal of any imperfection means that all that is "wrong" must always be placed outside of the leader. This means that within the group, deviants must be identified, punished, and purged on a regular basis, and enemies outside the group must be identified and demonized.

Before cataloging some of the practices of the Sullivanian community, and the particular ways that omnipotence and demonization were enacted, I want to emphasize, for those who may not know, that these things did not happen, for example, in a fundamentalist, apocalyptic, UFO, or other cultic group in the deep south or the remote west of the U.S., far from the reach of progressive contemporary cultural and intellectual influence, and from the culture of psychoanalysis. This story took place on the Upper West Side of New York City, involving a population of middle class, liberal, college-educated artists, professionals, academics, and intellectuals—many of whom were notable in their professions, and several quite famous. At the group's peak in the 1970s and 1980s, Siskind describes how hundreds of patients lived communally in large apartments and saw their therapists several times a week. The second-tier therapists were current and former patients of Newton and the other founding leaders. The patients saw the senior and junior therapists not just for therapy, but also at meetings, classes, legendary parties in the Hamptons with plenty of drugs and alcohol, and in bed. Patients were told to spend as little time as possible with anyone not in the group and to carefully schedule every minute of their time to be with other group members. They were encouraged to never sleep alone, to experiment and sleep with anyone and everyone in the group. They were taught that families, and especially mothers, are toxic. Pressured to cut off contact with families of origin, they were told that if they did not, they would likely become hopelessly mentally ill and end in suicide. Patients were discouraged from marriage, and some mothers in the group were persuaded to have their children raised by others in the group. In the 1970s, parents were expected to send their children to boarding school as soon as they could afford to, so as to have as little contact with their own children as possible, and thus not poison their child's development.

Much of this was justified on the theoretical premise, derived from Newton's idiosyncratic interpretation of Sullivan's work, that infants react to their mother's anxiety, viewed as being cultural in origin, by restricting their own development and splitting up the self into good me, bad me, and not me parts. Children raised by unconscious, overly anxious parents, according to Newton and Pearce, contributed to the endless perpetuation of a sick society, a culture of convention and malaise. One might agree or not with the social critique, but what made Newton and Pearce's execution of their theory particularly destructive was the quality of disavowed hatred and contempt in their scapegoating of parents, which they insisted their patients share, and they effectively disguised, even from themselves, as zeal for therapeutic transformation and social reform. Disavowing their hatred and rage, they were blinded by it, dissociatively unaware of the obvious: that planning to reform and liberate society at large by psychologically enslaving a group of people, calling them patients, exploiting them financially, emotionally, and sexually, and controlling and directing every move they make, is sheer madness, plain and simple.

As the group grew in size, Siskind chronicles how it became ever more paranoid and coercive. A former actress named Joan Harvey became Newton's wife after he divorced Pearce, and Harvey created a political theater group called the Fourth Wall, which became the chief activity of the group in its latter years. Now community members not only had to support the therapists, but to support a theater as well, and demands on members for contributing money and participating in group activities increased to the point that members barely had four hours a night for sleep. The Three Mile Island nuclear reactor crisis, and then the advent of AIDS, became flash points for further panic, demands, and restrictions. Siskind's portrayal of the group's reactions to these events is particularly chilling, as she describes how the typical dynamics of an apocalyptic cult came into play. As with apocalyptic groups in general, the failure of Newton and Harvey's dire predictions about nuclear devastation and germ warfare triggered a deepening of their paranoia and the florescence of their underlying psychosis. By the time it all started winding down for the Sullivanians, Newton was alleged to have attempted to seduce several children, including his own daughters, and to have regularly demanded that female patients have sex with him during their sessions. Splits among the leaders, now numbering even more ex-husbands and ex-wives, and finally Newton's death, were the last nails in the group's coffin.

As all this unfolded, especially throughout the 1980s, the Cult Clinic of the Jewish Board of Family and Children's Services in New York helped counsel traumatized members who left the group, and helped divorced spouses and family members of Sullivanian patients organize support groups. Beyond that, the professional mental health community was silent. As part of my own research into the Sullivanians, I was put in touch with a very senior, highly respected analyst who I was told had been familiar with the group and some of its leaders. It was not clear to me if he had actually been one of the Sullivanian therapists at any time, or what exactly his association had been. I did not ask, and he did not tell—clearly in retrospect, an enactment. I sent him a previous version of this chapter that focused on Siskind's book, and then contacted him to get his reaction. His answer, to my astonishment, was the following: "These accounts of abuses were greatly exaggerated, and were really only alleged by the most mentally unstable, low-functioning members of the group." I do not think it is a stretch to generalize from his statement that mass dissociation is possible in any group, at any time, anywhere—and tragically, dissociation is often most prevalent in those who witness abuse and could, but do not, attempt to stop it.[6]

While sexual violations in psychotherapy have been well studied by psychoanalysts (e.g., Celenza & Gabbard, 2003; Celenza, 2007), therapy cults have not. Perhaps the concreteness of sexual violation makes it easier to grasp and repudiate than the dynamics of sadistic control and domination between therapist and patient, which can be enacted more subtly and be therefore less obviously transgressive. Siskind quotes accounts from former followers of Newton and Harvey indicating they lived in constant fear that the psychological illness diagnosed by their therapists would never end unless they gave themselves over completely and allowed their therapists total control of their lives. Sullivanian/Fourth Wall followers were repeatedly bullied into believing their only hope for redemption was to allow therapists to control them completely, and therapists were able to sadistically leverage their power, keeping patients tied to them at the juncture where madness and evil intersect. The cruel therapy practiced in the Sullivanian/Fourth Wall community amounted to nothing less than mental torture.

Traumatizing narcissists (including those operating on a scale larger than the family, a commune, or a small business, whom Fromm (1964) labeled "malignant narcissists") create totalitarian systems in which their malignant envy and paranoid fears, defended against with delusional omnipotence and bolstered by self-righteous rage and hatred, merge to shape a contemptuous agenda to enslave, control, and annihilate others, if not literally then figuratively. They defend their projects as morally justified, for the greater good. The narcissist is convinced that his selfish, cruel agenda is in fact a generous, compassionate offer of enlightenment and liberation, conducted under his superior auspices for the benefit of the rest of the inferior world. With this kind of traumatizing narcissism, all is self-righteousness and sanctimony, but nothing is sacred, no boundaries are respected.

Nationalistic Exceptionalism

The story of the Sullivanians is one that psychoanalysts should know; but our interest need not be limited merely to how an understanding of cults can illuminate the personal and family dynamics of our individual patients. Psychoanalysts once believed that our theories could have a meaningful impact on society. Erich Fromm devoted himself again and again to the theme of authoritarianism and freedom, understanding both the mind and motives of the traumatizing, or in his words, the malignant narcissist (1964), as well as of the individual who escapes from freedom (1941) by idealizing and submitting to infantilizing, controlling others. Fromm reacted to World War I and II, the Korean War, the Cold War, the Cuban Missile Crisis, and the Vietnam War, and the public listened.

As I write this in the U.S., Fromm's ideas seem completely fresh, ready to be elaborated and used again to understand both the interpersonal world and the larger world we live in. For example, there is the notion of "American exceptionalism," which is a form of narcissism on a nationalist scale that is fundamental for today's politically conservative thinkers; it is a view shared as well by some political centrists and some on the left. Historically, American exceptionalism undergirds the rationale for the virtual eradication of the Native American aboriginal population, and the justification of the slave system. More recently, the belief in American exceptionalism deeply informed the sense of superiority and entitlement that prompted the G.W. Bush administration to invade Iraq. Iraq was unquestionably under the despotic rule of a cruel and vicious tyrant, but only the ideology of exceptionalism—narcissism on a national scale—could justify waging an unprovoked war. To try to persuade Americans and the international community that this act of aggression on the part of the U.S. was justified, false claims were asserted about the existence in Iraq of weapons of mass destruction, along with false claims that there was a direct link between Iraqi terrorists and the World Trade Center bombing of 2001. Political motives for attacking were rationalized as the moral duty of the exceptional American nation to address tyranny in another nation. I have no doubt that for the members of the Bush administration, the end justified the means. The end was understood as the liberation of Iraq; the plunder and economic exploitation of Iraq, characterized by Naomi Klein (2007) as "disaster capitalism," was denied as a secondary end of the invasion, but was carried out vigorously nonetheless. The Bush administration intimidated and bullied those who challenged their narrative, denying that the intelligence they presented had been falsified, suppressing the hard evidence that clearly refuted their claims, and recklessly vilifying those who attempted to challenge them. Such was most conspicuously the case with the outing of Valerie Plame as a CIA agent, because her husband, former ambassador Joe Wilson, publicly refuted claims made by the White House of evidence of the existence of weapons of mass destruction in Iraq. Plame's outing ended her CIA career, where she had been a deep cover agent with an outstanding career record (Plame, 2007; Wilson, 2004).

Another example is the Tea Party, purporting to be a grass roots movement representing the average citizen who is fed up with the grasping tentacles of "big government." In reality it is a front group, paid for, organized by, and representing the financial and political interests of some of the wealthiest hedge fund billionaires, corporate conglomerate tycoons, bankers, and media moguls in the world (Frank, 2012; Mayer, 2010). How can it be explained that working and middle-class people who feel oppressed are devoting themselves politically to the empowerment of the corporate ruling class—who represent nothing if not the ruthless undermining and exploitation of workers in those very same working and middle classes (e.g., union busting, paying below minimum wage, hiring part-time to avoid paying health benefits and pensions, shipping jobs overseas, etc.)? Ignorance is too simple an answer. Developing righteous loathing of an enemy who can be demonized—for the right wing in the U.S. that would be "liberals" and the minority groups they traditionally represent, including immigrants—has historically proven to be very appealing to those who are frustrated and embittered about losing whatever power and control they may once have felt they had. These are the people that largely comprise the Tea Party, people who are ripe for recruitment to serve and to be exploited by a radicalized, monied elite, aided by opportunistic, fact-free demagogues such as Rush Limbaugh, who enjoys exalted guru status among his followers, and who many critics believe to be the de facto leader of the Republican Party.

Many of today's radical elites are inspired by another famous guru, Ayn Rand, whose philosophy of "objectivism" was embodied in the contemptuous superiority, grandiosity, and entitlement of her fictional characters. These elites, such as Rupert Murdoch, Peter Peterson, the Koch Brothers, Mellon Scaife, and even the late billionaire Reverend Sun Myung Moon, to name just a few, have for many years been bankrolling think tanks and politicians who focus on influencing conservative, disgruntled white voters in the U.S.—a group that fears and resents the removal of barriers toward upward mobility for minorities, especially for people of color. Cannily uniting with orthodox and fundamentalist religious groups around social issues such as gay marriage and abortion, radical conservatives have built an activated base that can put into office those politicians who are most willing to do the bidding of the monied elites. The phenomenon of working-class and poor people actively supporting candidates who brazenly plan to strip away all or as much as possible of the social safety net the government provides, of which they themselves are in fact the chief beneficiaries, can only bring to mind to this former cult member the drinking of the Kool-Aid with Jim Jones in Guayana.[7]

The traumatizing narcissist as charismatic leader is a predator who presents his personal obsession with self-aggrandizement as the selfless pursuit of betterment for others, and he and she are alive and well, casting their spell all over the globe in the 21st Century. In elaborating a theory of the traumatizing narcissist's relational system, in which intersubjective relatedness and mutual recognition is suppressed and hegemonic subjectivity is established, one of my aims is to build on

Fromm's understanding of the importance of issues of freedom and authoritarian oppression in psychoanalytic work, and the importance of the capacity for mutual recognition in relationships—about which Fromm also wrote, in his own language, in his most popular work, *The Art of Loving* (1956). These are the issues taken up by relational psychoanalysis, possibly without conscious awareness of Fromm's influence, and restated in new language that has been significantly enriched by the renaissance of Bowlby's attachment theory and of interest in Ferenczi's and Fairbairn's work, by Winnicott's influence on North American psychoanalysis, by critics of modernism such as Foucault, feminist and queer theory, trauma theory, new theories of subjectivity and intersubjectivity, by infant research, and by the many other influences that have made the relational turn in psychoanalysis so robust.

For Fromm, authoritarianism was an expression of group narcissism, which he deemed malignant. Love, for Fromm, was the opposite of narcissism, the only hope for a "sane society" (1955). Throughout history, innumerable groups have proclaimed their superiority, and therefore deemed themselves entitled to control and exploit others—from the time of Biblical slavery, to serfdom, the Crusades, the Inquisitions, American slavery, the Holocaust, Apartheid, and beyond. Because my own perspective focuses on the impact of being exposed to and traumatized by those who exercise this kind of domination, control, and exploitation, I have chosen to speak of this narcissism not in the way Fromm did, as malignant (though indeed it is), but as traumatizing. Whether in the family, the workplace, the religion, the political party, the nation, a coalition of nations, or in any group of any size that some might identify as a cult, the traumatizing narcissist leader's program of seduction and exploitation results in a kind of rape of the personhood, the subjectivity, of the other. His relational system consists of transactions consistently organized by the sadomasochistic binary; his best followers are those who masochistically submit to his sadism, but who pass the sadism down the hierarchical chain. His is the only right, the wrong is always ascribed to the other; and the possibility of intersubjective relatedness and mutual recognition among members, or between the leader and the follower, is entirely foreclosed. The leader is always above, and the follower is always below. For followers, no attachment can ever be as important as one's attachment to the leader.

Traumatizing narcissism seems to have been with us since the dawn of humanity. It is the source of all the ways that humans have objectified, enslaved, and dehumanized other humans. It is the very essence of relational trauma.

Appendix A

Dr. Robert J. Lifton's Eight Criteria for Thought Reform

1 **Milieu Control.** This involves the control of information and communication both within the environment and, ultimately, within the individual, resulting in a significant degree of isolation from society at large.

2 **Mystical Manipulation.** There is manipulation of experiences that appear spontaneous but in fact were planned and orchestrated by the group or its leaders in order to demonstrate divine authority or spiritual advancement or some special gift or talent that will then allow the leader to reinterpret events, scripture, and experiences as he or she wishes.
3 **Demand for Purity.** The world is viewed as black and white and the members are constantly exhorted to conform to the ideology of the group and strive for perfection. The induction of guilt and/or shame is a powerful control device used here.
4 **Confession.** Sins, as defined by the group, are to be confessed either to a personal monitor or publicly to the group. There is no confidentiality; members' "sins," "attitudes," and "faults" are discussed and exploited by the leaders.
5 **Sacred Science.** The group's doctrine or ideology is considered to be the ultimate Truth, beyond all questioning or dispute. Truth is not to be found outside the group. The leader, as the spokesperson for God or for all humanity, is likewise above criticism.
6 **Loading the Language.** The group interprets or uses words and phrases in new ways so that often the outside world does not understand. This jargon consists of thought-terminating clichés, which serve to alter members' thought processes to conform to the group's way of thinking.
7 **Doctrine Over Person.** Member's personal experiences are subordinated to the sacred science and any contrary experiences must be denied or reinterpreted to fit the ideology of the group.
8 **Dispensing of Existence.** The group has the prerogative to decide who has the right to exist and who does not. This is usually not literal but means that those in the outside world are not saved, unenlightened, unconscious, and they must be converted to the group's ideology. If they do not join the group or are critical of the group, then they must be rejected by the members. Thus, the outside world loses all credibility. In conjunction, should any member leave the group, he or she must be rejected also (Lifton, 1989).

Notes

1 Portions of this chapter have appeared previously in Shaw, 2003b, and Shaw, 2005.
2 When people who have left Shakti Yoga contact me seeking counseling, I refer them to other cult experts, since we share the same abuser. My conversations in these cases are on a peer-to-peer basis. I only consult professionally with former members of other groups.
3 See Mitchell and Black (1995), p. xx, which includes the following tongue-in-cheek section heading: "Myth #4: Psychoanalysis Is an Esoteric Cult Requiring Both Conversion and Years of Study."
4 Ruth Stein (2010a) offered an excellent review of the literature on cults, including her own keen observations of ways in which the psychotherapy process can be perverted to become a form of mind control. Stein skillfully contrasts the effects of the generative psychotherapy process to the cultic psychotherapy process. I will take up many points

similar to Stein's in the next chapter on narcissistic authoritarianism in the supervisory situation.

5 For the purposes of this book, I speak here of psychoanalytic therapy cults, but many therapy cults exist outside of psychoanalytic culture, such as politically oriented therapy cults, New Age healer cults, spiritually oriented therapy cults, family and marital therapy cults, and so on. Some of the leaders of these kinds of groups are licensed mental health workers, while many others have no license or training, or have had licenses revoked and are continuing to do business. I will not address here the subject of large group awareness training (LGAT) seminars, which for some participants can also become a cult-like experience.

6 As of this writing, Jerry Sandusky has been convicted on 45 charges of molesting boys, whom he had selected over decades to be beneficiaries of the charitable foundation he established at Penn State University. The famous Penn State football coach, Joe Paterno, and half a dozen other college officials, after learning in 2001 of an eye-witness account of Sandusky anally raping a boy in the locker room shower, concluded that the "humane" thing to do was to forego reporting anything to the police, and simply ask Sandusky not to bring children on campus. Sandusky continued to rape young boys until his arrest in 2012 (Becker, 2012).

7 A *New York Times* article of February 11, 2012 entitled "Even Critics of Safety Net Increasingly Depend on It" persuasively documented the reliance on government aid that staunch Tea Party members compartmentalize when they express their support of measures to do away with government aid (Appelbaum & Gebeloff, 2012).

Chapter 4

Narcissistic Authoritarianism in Psychoanalysis[1]

So far, I have been focusing on the most egregious aspects of traumatic narcissism, in part to make the point that there is far more traumatic abuse by narcissists in families and in groups of various kinds than is commonly recognized. In this chapter, I will speak of certain more subtle ways that narcissism can have a destructive impact—in particular, in the context of psychoanalytic supervision; first, however, a brief introduction to the problem of narcissism and the psychoanalytic profession, from the beginning.

Some time ago I played, for a psychoanalytic study group of which I was a member, a comedy sketch recorded in the 1960s by Elaine May and Mike Nichols, in which they portray a psychoanalyst and her patient. Having had a good laugh each of the numerous times I have listened to this sketch over the years, I gleefully, and as I now know naively, imagined my typically serious and scholarly group uncharacteristically doubled over, wiping tears of laughter from their eyes, enjoying a good joke on us all. In the sketch, the patient (Nichols) informs May (his analyst), that in the following week he will have to miss the last of his five sessions per week, since it is Christmas Eve and he plans to be with his family that day. Instantly shattered by the news of her patient's plan to desert her, May attempts to maintain her analytic stance and mask her spiraling self-fragmentation by demanding that her patient explore, be curious about, reflect on, and associate to his need to miss his session. In the face of his insistence that he just wants to be with his family on Christmas Eve, the analyst begins to weep quietly, then to sob in despair, then to scream with rage. Unable to help her recompensate, the patient quietly retreats, wishing her a Merry Christmas, as the analyst continues to unravel. When I turned off the recording, I faced a silent group, with some members finally confessing to a sense of excruciating anxiety while listening. There was little further discussion. We moved on quickly to the material we had planned to discuss. In showbiz parlance, I had bombed. Though unable to articulate at the time why the sketch repeatedly cracks me up, I can now say that for me, it helps to laugh about the ever present, always not fully-analyzed narcissism of the psychoanalyst—that is, to laugh at it, but not to laugh it off.

Narcissism has shadowed the psychoanalytic profession from the beginning, as Freud's harshest critics never tire of reminding us, and it is a problem that our profession still struggles to address adequately. As analysts, we have long been concerned with our patients' narcissism, and as teachers and supervisors, with narcissism in psychoanalytic candidates (e.g., Brightman, 1984–85). With the ongoing influence of the relational school, which has been constructed from many post-Freudian sources (among them: feminist, queer, postmodern, postcolonial, gender, hermeneutics, and cultural theories), it is increasingly the case (e.g., Brenman, 2006; Cooper, 2004; Hoffman, 1998) that our narcissism as analysts, teachers, and supervisors has also come to occupy the field of our observation—not just in the form of community gossip, but in our literature. In this chapter, I will discuss the connection between narcissism and authoritarianism and explore aspects of the supervising analyst's narcissism.

Freud formulated his conceptualization of narcissism in 1914, and, unfortunately, proceeded to enact some of its more problematic aspects—by deeming himself the only analyst not in need of an analysis by another analyst; by setting up a book of rules for the analytic process, which he exempted himself from following; and by marginalizing innovative followers and favoring those whom he could more easily control. Freud's break with Ferenczi, the last and most extraordinary of his chief disciples, marked a turning point in the evolution of psychoanalysis. Ferenczi had begun his alliance with Freud as one of his most fervent acolytes, and was directly involved in helping Freud maintain near dictatorial control over the psychoanalytic movement for many years (see Fromm, 1959). As their relationship grew, Ferenczi's poignant efforts to be analyzed by Freud, in a deeper way that would have allowed for the expression and analysis of his negative transference, and Ferenczi's offer to analyze Freud, were both rejected with no small measure of scorn on Freud's part (see Aron and Harris, 1993). In language that would not have been available at the time, I believe, or perhaps I should say I have a fantasy, that Ferenczi was inviting Freud to join him in co-constructing an experience of intersubjective relatedness, in which not only the analysand, but also the analyst, within the context of the relationship they create, discover together how to put aside narcissistic tendencies toward domination and submission. Did Ferenczi intuit—as one by one, Freud banished his most independent-minded followers, Rank, Adler, and Jung—that if he could not help Freud to see his own narcissistic blind spots, that psychoanalysis itself would suffer from becoming too rigid, too dogmatic? Did Ferenczi expect to be the next disciple to be purged? I believe the answer is yes, Ferenczi must have known what was to come. If indeed he did, it is remarkable that he nevertheless continued to pursue his goal, which was to reinstate trauma theory as crucial to the understanding of human psychology, in spite of Freud's ban of the subject (see Breger, 2000, 2009).

Balint's (1968) portrayal of the banishing of Ferenczi from the analytic community as a trauma to the profession continues to resonate. Not simply about Ferenczi, the trauma is about the suppression and shaming of those mental health workers inspired by Freud who seek to evolve in ways that are not officially authorized by those who have, in the past and perhaps still, sought a monopoly on the profession. In the latter years of the 20th Century, a good fight has been waged by many, particularly by psychologists, against this once-entrenched situation. But the trauma still reverberates in a kind of collective unconscious, where a special superego police force for psychoanalysts sounds an internal bullhorn, in our offices and conferences, with the accusation that "You Are Not Psychoanalytic!" It is ironic and perhaps tragic that as Nazism, one of history's most atrocious examples of authoritarianism, spread throughout Europe, Freud was attempting to fortify and legitimize his psychoanalysis by the exercise of authoritarian control and suppression of dissent. This must have seemed like the necessary means to an urgent end, for Freud and those who felt compelled to maintain strict adherence to his views, but in the long run these methods have backfired, leading to insularity and unrealistic self-importance that has made the profession vulnerable to attacks from all sides—and especially from the health insurance companies. Although it is increasingly more likely in our professional publications and conferences to see rival psychoanalytic schools seeking common ground, years of rampant factionalism and internecine power struggles, along with authoritarian, incestuous training systems (see Levine & Reed, 2004), have substantially contributed to the embarrassing fact that the majority of the public here in the U.S. no longer has a clue as to what we mean when we say "psychoanalysis." We are, if we look from outside our profession, in many ways a legend in our own minds.

Has the relational turn, with its ongoing deconstruction of the analyst's authority, come on the scene just in the nick of time? Yes it has. However, the battle to re-legitimize psychoanalysis is far from won. The "relational turn" (Greenberg & Mitchell, 1983) is in many ways a return to and an embrace of Ferenczi's thwarted aspirations and realizations—in particular, his deep and hard-won understanding of the impact of the analyst's subjectivity, both the conscious and the dissociated aspects, on the patient.

It is in the spirit of joining that project of re-legitimization that I address here the touchy subject of the analyst's narcissism. Because the psychotherapist is a potent transference figure—not a parent, not an Oracle, not God Almighty, but, for many patients, potentially something like all three—the abuses of power therapists are capable of, in training and clinical situations, and the damage done to students and patients, should not be underestimated (see Stein, 2010a). Aside from some of the more gross boundary violations, such as the sexual violations studied by Celenza (2007) and Gabbard and Lester (1995), there have always been far too many situations in which analysts mask their need for narcissistic gratification, and their emotional and financial dependence on supervisees and patients, by coercive means of control and exploitation. We have a moral imperative to protect students and patients from abuse, to "do no harm," and this means that we must address these problems of narcissism in analysts and their institutions where they begin, in the training of our candidates, and in the training of our teachers and supervisors.

The Basis of Narcissism in Authoritarianism

Authoritarianism, as I am defining it, describes the organizing principles of an institution or group (e.g., government, school, profession, family, cult, etc.) that supports an elite individual (or group) who claims infallible, unquestionable power to rule over the institution and its members; who demands strict obedience; and who criminalizes subordinates who attempt to deviate or to assert their individual freedom. These behaviors are the same as those I have identified in previous chapters as employed by the particular type of overinflated, grandiose narcissist I refer to as "the traumatizing narcissist." His fullest potential for authoritarianism was articulated by Erich Fromm, writing from the perspective of one born in 1900 who, like Freud, was a Jew who witnessed the mass destruction of World War I, only to see it followed by the rise of fascism in Europe and an even more destructive war. Fromm introduced the term "malignant narcissism" (1964) to describe the ultimate form of traumatization, torture, and annihilation, as it was carried out by those like Hitler, Stalin, Mao tse Tung, and their followers. Twentieth-Century dictators presided over barbaric mass "purifications" of perceived enemies, for the purpose of "cleansing" society of those who were considered inferior and undesirable. Unfortunately, such malignant narcissism continues in the 21st Century, causing whole nations to suffer the trauma of engagement in unspeakable atrocities.[2]

In this chapter, however, I will speak of far milder forms of authoritarianism, which I think of as "everyday narcissistic authoritarianism," or "soft" narcissism, if you will. I focus on some examples of soft narcissism in clinical supervision[3] because I believe they are ubiquitous and not adequately examined. The examples I will give are meant to show how vestiges of narcissistic authoritarianism in psychoanalytic training continue to haunt our training situations, in spite of theoretical and cultural shifts away from authoritarianism. While the supervisors in the following examples were trained in the 1960s and 1970s, by the late 1990s they were known for their connections to contemporary self psychology, intersubjectivity, and relational theory, which is to say that their chosen theoretical schools are not associated with the more orthodox schools in which stricter authority might be expected and perhaps accepted. The incidents I will recount exemplify small moments of disruption that went unrepaired. When disruptions like these occurred for me and for my fellow candidates in training, they stood out sharply from what were otherwise more positive and supportive experiences. These kinds of disruptions reinforced whatever feelings of fear and insecurity we were attempting to grapple with, and left us confused, disconnected, intimidated, and ashamed. Unfortunately, there is a tradition in psychoanalysis, of shaming and intimidating (whether mildly or severely), and refusing to take responsibility and apologize for errors, with roots that go back at least as far as Freud and Dora, a treatment now widely perceived as grossly misattuned and insensitive (Appignanesi & Forrester, 1992; Mahony, 1996); and to the disagreements between Freud and Ferenczi (see Berman, 2004, Chapter 1). I believe my supervisors had taken far more of this sort of thing from their analysts and supervisors than they were dishing out. Now and then, however, the occasional flashback would surface, and I would then be treated to a narcissistic lapse, a taste of what it was like in the "olden days."

In addition to issues of trans-generational transmission of narcissistic behaviors, analysts of course bring their own history of narcissistic vulnerability to the situation. Analysts are often fulfilling deeply cherished, idealistic aspirations in choosing their profession, aspirations that transcend narcissistic concerns regarding power and prestige. The desire to help, to be loving, caring, understanding, and healing are expressions of altruism that many analysts value highly. Many of us are continually moved and grateful to be able to witness the growth and change process in those we help. Yet along with these kinds of motivations can be found more unconscious and selfish ones, which I believe are quite common, and which Hoffman (1998) has discussed in his elaboration of "the dark side of the analytic frame." Among these would be:

1 the use of our professional status as a means of establishing ourselves as "the sane, healthy one," usually in defense against a parent's or sibling's projections of craziness;
2 we may be driven to rescue people successfully either because rescuing a family member was impossible, or because we became preoccupied with making a depressed parent happy;
3 we may be seeking to gain the higher moral ground in a power struggle happening in real time with significant others and/or with archaic internal objects;
4 we may be seeking to acquire virtue as helpers in an effort to extinguish a sense of worthlessness.

Certainly the motives for our choice of profession are complex and overdetermined, and always include to some degree the fulfilling of our narcissistic needs. The acquisition of prestige, power, and control is usually somewhere in the mix, even in the face of highly effective assaults on our power, control, and prestige from the insurers and their beloved behavioralists (see Hoffman, 2009). Lewis Aron (personal communication) has suggested that as analysts have found themselves with less power in society, less authority with patients, lower status and remuneration than in previous decades, we may have become even more susceptible to the temptation to seek power over our students, with whom there is even more asymmetry than with patients.

Whatever they may be, our narcissistic vulnerabilities will determine where we fall on the authoritarian continuum in terms of our work. For sure, we cannot be professionals without assuming authority. Professional narcissism becomes problematic when it drives us to seek power and control by becoming authoritarian—i.e., infallibly righteous, demanding allegiance and punishing deviation, and controlling by means of seductiveness, intimidation, belittling, condescending, blaming, and shaming. The more narcissistically vulnerable one is, the more potential there is for authoritarian control to be employed defensively, or, on the other hand, to be submitted to as the price of acceptance.

As analysts, teachers, and supervisors, we all struggle, more or less, with (at least) the following four areas of narcissistic vulnerability, any one of which could lead to authoritarian control behaviors as we attempt to establish our authority as teachers and supervisors:

1. the temptation to exhibit our superior expertise and power so as to invite idealization and defend against our own anxieties about inadequacy;
2. envy, competitiveness, and the fear of being surpassed;
3. the need to be admired and to feel indispensable, along with the fear that we will be rejected (excruciatingly expressed by Elaine May in the comedy sketch); and
4. concerns about our reputation, especially in institutional situations.

Regardless of the supervisor's theoretical orientation, the potential always exists for these vulnerabilities to emerge in the supervisory process. Such vulnerabilities can be expressed by a supervisor in behaviors such as exhibitionism, intimidation, and/or shaming, which display the supervisor's sense of superiority and promote the supervisee's sense of inferiority and dependence. Whether the supervisor sees her role as that of an objective, didactic expert, as in the classical tradition, or as an embedded participant, as in the contemporary relational school (Frawley-O'Dea & Sarnat, 2001), the general narcissistic vulnerabilities outlined, and many that might be more individually idiosyncratic, will inevitably emerge in supervisory work, even if only to the mildest degree.

Let me offer two examples of what I think of as more or less typical, everyday kinds of authoritarian supervisory moments. I completed my MSW degree in 1996, and my analytic training in New York City in 2000, at one of the several psychoanalytic training institutes in New York that are attended primarily by social workers. I was a mid-life career changer, and my supervisors, though not much older than I, were very well seasoned compared to me. They were highly intelligent, sincerely dedicated psychoanalysts, with more or less the same narcissistic vulnerability as most humans. By no means would I consider either of the supervisors I allude to here (well disguised) to be traumatically narcissistic; nor would I consider them to be pervasively traumatizing to candidates. Nevertheless, I examine here moments in my work with them when the line between authority and authoritarianism was crossed, and the supervisor's narcissistic vulnerability became visible—to me.

Supervisor I

In my second year of analytic training, I spent most of a weekly supervision session bristling but accommodating to a supervisor I found condescending and didactic. "Speak in short, precise phrases," she told me one day, and she demonstrated, reminding me of Professor Henry Higgins, how she thought analysts should speak. I have never much cared for the stereotypical, essentially self-aggrandizing ways that analysts sometimes speak (sounding too much like Elaine May in the comedy sketch), and I wasn't planning to emulate such stereotypes. Additionally, I was reasonably certain that my supervisor didn't always practice what she preached, and that she probably prattled on and on too, at times. Saying nothing of any of this, I nodded my head. My personal idiom (Bollas, 1983), and the intersubjectively constructed idiom particular to my patient and I, was meant to be discarded as worthless; what I was being asked to do was parrot my supervisor. I didn't want to be, nor to be seen as, a resistant, narcissistic candidate—as candidates who are not sufficiently submissive are often labeled—so I attempted to be compliant.

We finally had a real argument in a later supervisory session where, in response to my disclosure of some countertransference difficulties I was having, she took out a book and read a whole page about analytic technique to me. Discouraged and angry that my countertransference struggles seemed of no interest to her other than as technical errors to be intellectually disposed of, I expressed my frustration. She was astonished, and admonished me for not taking in the bountiful good things she was giving me. A week later, I tried to patch things up by mentioning that I sometimes found it difficult to relate to authority figures. She responded with a nod, at most, and proceeded as though nothing had happened. We never discussed it further.

My chief impression of our work together over the course of a year was an internalized admonition about being long-winded, which I have not forgotten, and I sometimes experience as good to remember. Unfortunately, I had insulted my supervisor, who from that day forward carefully guarded her personal feelings about me, or us, and left it entirely up to me as to whether we would have any further dialogue on the subject. We did not.

The need to be admired, feared, and imitated is an expression of the supervisor's narcissism. A supervisor who presents herself as the model for how the supervisee should speak and think is assuming that the supervisee wants to be a clone. Of course, I as a supervisor, and most supervisors I know of, will offer ideas about what to say to a patient in this or that situation. To the extent that these suggestions are made in a collaborative spirit, and not as didactic instructions, or as a way for the supervisor to display superiority, these kinds of suggestions may be truly helpful. Today, however, speaking generally, attitudes of candidates in analytic institutes have changed, and hyper-idealization of senior analysts is somewhat less the norm—a shift that is in step with the 21st-Century diminishment in prestige of the psychoanalyst as compared to his position for most of the 20th Century. In line with this shift, I believe most supervisees are looking for support and encouragement to develop and grow as persons and analysts in their own right. While it was once the case that an analytic institute taught one school of theory only, today there are a number of analytic institutes that attempt to familiarize students with the various theoretical schools. A student is usually exposed to multiple supervisors in the course of training over four to six or more years, and each one may work quite differently from the others. Supervisees are doing a lot of picking and choosing, comparing different supervisors on multiple dimensions, from theoretical preferences to style of dress and décor of office. If we offer supervisees technical and theoretical models based on our own biases and preferences, and of course we always do, we owe it to them to acknowledge our biases and preferences, explain the basis for our preferences, and encourage them to form their own.

Many institutes now elicit evaluations of supervisors from supervisees, no doubt sincerely hoping to promote collegiality rather than indenture. Yet I believe it is rare for a supervisee to disclose their critique of a supervisor fully. Supervisees in this situation often feel themselves to be, and possibly actually are, at risk of being diagnosed as narcissistic (note the projection) and judged by their institute as difficult, in need of further analysis, and so on. Compliance is the safer route for many. Defiance risks punishment by tarnishing the supervisee's reputation within his institute, which could mean losing opportunities for referrals, and for playing significant roles in the institute after graduation, such as becoming a training analyst there, teaching, supervising, serving on the board of directors, etc.

Supervisor 2

I was presenting a patient, in my final year of training, whom I liked a great deal. I was speaking of a struggle I had been having with listening to her, connected to my sense that she was dealing with a great deal of shame that she was trying to keep at bay. As a result, she seemed to use at times a very contrived, theatrical persona when she communicated with me, a persona that stood in sharp contrast to what seemed like another aspect of her that emerged in some sessions, a more related, reflective, alive version of her. My patient and I had begun to be able to talk about this, and I was relating this to my supervisor. I repeated a remark I made to the patient, to the effect that I found myself more engaged and connected to the real person than to the theatrical persona. Without inquiring further of me, or waiting to learn how my patient reacted, my supervisor colored, stiffened, and said quite sharply, in a tone of rebuke I don't think I had heard since about the seventh grade: "And who do you think you are to have said that to her?"

I was a fourth-year candidate, and tired of being intimidated in general, no matter how much I was depending on the support of the institute, so I raised an eyebrow or two and looked quizzically into my supervisor's eyes, as if to say, "Seriously? You're taking that tone with me?" After a tense momentary standoff, he softened. The supervisor went on for the rest of our session that day to be more supportive and empathetic, but we did not return to or try to work through what happened until the following week. While reporting on the same patient, I let my supervisor know that I was aware, during my session with the patient subsequent to my supervision, of imagining my supervisor negatively judging all of my interventions, including "uh huh" and "mmm hmmm." Without hesitation, my supervisor said that he was having a stressful day the week before and that I should go ahead and work without imagining him disapproving of me. Although I was the one initiating all the processing of what had happened, I appreciated his concession, and we got on pretty well from there; yet, I would have to say that my trust was shaken from that point on.

This supervisor was willing to be accountable for his shaming, intimidating behavior, but only after I brought it up, and only nonchalantly, with no apology. Leaving the mess for the supervisee to clean up seems to stem from an era when the analyst's authority was not to be questioned, and the analysand's problem with the analyst was seen as resistance. The first problem with that is that it is dishonest. The analyst is using theory in self-defense, which is not necessarily what is best for the patient. The second problem is that even if one is committed to the model of the silent analyst who speaks only to interpret, the supervisee is not a patient and should not be treated as one. The supervisee is both a student and a colleague.

It is of course entirely expectable that one might slip up and err as a supervisor by being too didactic, or reacting hastily in a shaming way. As I see it, however, the supervisor then has the responsibility to notice her impact on the supervisee, and to process with the supervisee what has happened so as to repair the disruption. In the absence of such willingness to process, the supervisee, who is likely to be vulnerable to a shaming and intimidating supervisor, may develop more anxiety about disapproval than would already be normally present. His work as he presents it could then become organized around receiving the supervisor's approval, around meeting supervisory requirements that are subjectively biased toward the supervisor's particular theoretical and technical preferences, and are shaped by the supervisor's narcissistic concerns. To paraphrase a Winnicottian conceptualization, the supervisee learns to develop a "false supervisee self" based on compliance. In my view, this also greatly increases the chances that the supervisee will go on to elicit similar results with his patients.

Because candidates are typically investing so much in becoming analysts, it is easy for them to base their self-esteem as people on their performance as rated by their supervisors. This is especially true given the amount of power, both personal and professional, candidates typically perceive supervisors as having. The candidate's perceived and actual dependence on the supervisor for approval, certification, reputation, future referrals, etc., sets up a loaded situation for the candidate, who then may feel forced to "hold the hot potato" in a conflict because the supervisor is more powerful and therefore "right," and to contend otherwise would put the candidate at risk of being judged to be "narcissistic." Double bind! On the one hand, we set ourselves the goal of expanding the freedom of our patients, and on the other hand, we establish training methods that all too often lead to accommodation, compliance, and conformity in our trainees. Here is where supervisors and supervisees can learn to draw the line between authority and authoritarianism, or risk turning training into indoctrination. Suppressing individuality and creativity in candidates in favor of compliance and accommodation is the Orwellian version of psychoanalysis, of which we should all be very afraid.

Conclusion

Psychoanalysts have struggled since the beginning of the profession to understand their power, and to use their power responsibly and therapeutically. However, power is never a simple matter for humans to negotiate—it is always potentially corrupting. It is in no small measure the postmodern trend toward the interrogation of authority that has begun to resuscitate and reinvigorate the psychoanalytic profession. The willingness to level with ourselves, to confront our own professional narcissism and question all our assumptions about our authority and the use of our power, may yet rescue psychoanalysis from the brink of obsolescence—the perilous position our own professional narcissism has, to a great extent, helped to put us in.

As supervisors and teachers of psychoanalytic candidates, we have the opportunity, when called upon, to acknowledge and regulate our narcissistic vulnerabilities openly and with compassion. We can help to release supervisees from undue shame about and fear of their imperfections; we can aid them in their development of a sense of unique professional identity. By doing so, we protect ourselves, and our supervisees and patients, from the danger of authoritarian domination, indoctrination, and theoretical dogmaticism—always indicators of the kind of narcissism that leads to the degradation of intersubjective mutuality. Our students can be helped to join the psychoanalytic professional community with the expectation not only that they will be supported to learn and grow, but that they can make their own unique, personal, individual contributions to the progressive evolution of the profession.

In the remaining chapters that follow, I return to my focus on traumatic narcissism as it impacts the clinical situation. Chapter 5 explores problems that arise in couples therapy when the couple has become trapped in the traumatizing narcissist's relational system. In Chapter 6, I explore the challenging task the analyst and patient face when the adult child of the traumatizing narcissist recognizes more deeply how objectified he has been and how he continues to objectify and subjugate himself relationally. Patients want to know how they can change, how they can stop being what they have always been, who they are if they are a subject, not an object for the other's use. The clinical work I present in Chapter 6 illustrates the process of grappling with these questions.

Notes

1 An earlier version of this chapter appeared in Shaw, 2006.

2 Also studying and writing for many years about the psychoanalytic understanding of what Fromm would have referred to as the malignant narcissism of nationalism are Robert Jay Lifton (1961, 2000b), and Vamik Volkan (e.g., 1986); and, more recently, Ruth Stein (2010a, 2010b).

3 Supervision is the process in which candidates of psychoanalytic training institutes are supervised by senior analysts who then participate in the process of deciding if a given candidate is eligible for certification as a psychoanalyst by that particular institute. Graduates of such institutes also participate in peer supervision groups, or form small groups which hire a senior analyst for supervision.

Chapter 5

Traumatic Narcissism in Couples

Invisible Violence and Clinical Morality

Working with couples for more than a decade, I find the experience quite challenging, often rewarding, and sometimes quite painful. In seeking to make sense of why some people, in spite of very severe disagreements and emotional alienation, were nevertheless able to restore their love for and commitment to each other, and why others could not, no matter how hard they might try, I recognized a recurring theme. In many (but by no means all) of the couples that could not stay together, there was typically one member of the couple who took a significant share of responsibility for the problems they were having, while the other member entirely or almost entirely refused to accept responsibility for the problems.

I have come to see this configuration in a couple as a bright red flag, pointing to the strong possibility that this couple is engaged in the kind of relationship I think of as structured on the basis of the traumatizing narcissist's relational system (see chapters 1 and 2). Such relationships consist of a controlling, abusive partner who has adopted the complementary moral defense, thus fiercely defending her moral purity; and a subjugated and self-subjugating partner who, fearing the loss of the relationship, adopts the moral defense and thereby takes on the responsibility for the badness.

One thing that separates this type of relationship from the familiar model of the battering husband and the battered spouse, is that in the traumatizing narcissist's system, physical violence may or may not be present. What is always present is invisible, interior pain inflicted on the other, in the form of the negation of the other's subjectivity. Shengold (1989) called this interior violence "soul murder," which he defined as the "deliberate attempt to eradicate or compromise the separate identity of another person" (p. 2). I am with Shengold on this, except for the use of the word "deliberate." I have never met a traumatizing narcissist who thought for a moment that they were doing anything deliberately harmful to their partner. They are most likely to feel that it is they who are being wronged. The traumatizing narcissist is defended by his adoption of the complementary moral defense, and can only see his behavior as justifiable, morally correct, and directly caused by the moral failures of the other. His unconscious expectation is that the other will accept perpetual guilt.

Another distinction from the battering spouse model is that the traumatizing narcissist is not a gender specific category. Physical domination and violence, to which many men may be more physiologically, culturally, and hormonally inclined than women, is not required for the emotional and psychological pain that the traumatizing narcissist inflicts. With or without physical violence, the traumatizing narcissist is a perpetrator of abuse; the partner is a victim of abuse. The abuse consists of the narcissist's behaviors that cause the victim to feel ashamed of and afraid to give voice to her own subjectivity, and afraid of contempt and rejection should she fail to accommodate adequately to the narcissist's requirement that he be idealized/idolized. The traumatizing narcissist's delusional sense of perfection and infallibility is often what leads couples to therapy, to premature breaking off of the couple's therapy, and what leads couples to divorce. I am not saying it is impossible to lead the traumatizing narcissist to accountability, self-awareness, contrition, remorse, atonement, and empathy; I am saying that to do so is among the most challenging clinical problems we face. It is also one we rarely encounter: the traumatizing narcissist typically drives her significant others to therapy, but rarely submits to psychoanalytic therapy herself.

The moral dimension of working with intimate violence has been termed "clinical morality" by Goldner (2004), whose many years of experience working with abusive couples has greatly influenced her work as a psychoanalyst. Goldner points out that:

> sustaining moral clarity in a context of the psychological ambiguity of intimate relationships is crucial and yet is always elusive, requiring skills beyond those we typically associate with the art and craft of the [clinical] interview. . . . The introduction of the concept of morality into the clinical situation seems odd to many practitioners . . . It is not that we therapists *deserve* to be society's moral arbiters, but that, in this psychological culture, our expert position rightly or wrongly gives us a kind of moral authority in the sphere of personal life.
>
> (pp. 348–349)

Acknowledging that the assumption of moral authority by the analyst can be a dangerous move toward analytic authoritarianism, Goldner nevertheless urges the therapist to hold the line between moral and immoral when it comes to violence perpetrated by men against women. Mainstream Western society categorically agrees; and while psychoanalysts will mostly tend to seek complex ways of understanding traumatizing behavior, it is hard to imagine even the most conservative analyst applying a morally relativistic stance toward intimate violence.

Does the same bright line apply to our work with the traumatizing narcissist's relational system? Is there a moral obligation on our part as analysts to label behaviors and verbalizations far more subtle than a slap, a kick, a punch, as morally wrong? I have chosen to speak of the "traumatizing narcissist's relational system" precisely because these are relationships in which traumatic, abusive harm is done, not only by violent men, but by any human of any gender or sexual orientation—and the harm that is done is not necessarily visible to others.

As psychoanalytic therapists working with couples, we often find ourselves expanding our therapeutic engagement in many ways—arbitrating, mediating, negotiating, educating, and, yes, certainly where violence is concerned, defining moral principles and insisting on boundaries. We also know where we stand when it comes to rape and childhood sexual abuse. When it comes to recognizing and addressing the relational system of the traumatizing narcissist, however, we are dealing with a kind of violence for which no court will mandate treatment or punishment. It becomes our duty, in my view, to recognize and name this kind of abuse. We have the authority to attune to and recognize when invisible violence—violence inflicted upon the interior person—is being perpetrated. This is a moral line that the therapist must, in my view, be willing to clarify and instate.

Goldner makes the point that the violent perpetrator often tends to experience himself as completely overtaken, as not having a choice, and as forced to the point of violence by his partner. Goldner demonstrates the skillful ways in which it is possible to respond to the perpetrator with empathy and complex psychological recognition—and how that can be done without diluting the identification of the violence as morally wrong and unjustifiable. I believe it is even more challenging to accomplish this with the traumatizing narcissist—who is delusionally persuaded of his own moral rectitude. Violent perpetrators who are capable of acknowledging shame about their behavior can be helped to gain control and take responsibility. The traumatizing narcissist, on the other hand, defends against shame as if his life depends on warding it off; his assumption of moral superiority and perfection is his most powerful defense against the threat of an outbreak of his disavowed shame. Nothing is more important to the traumatizing narcissist than to be free of shame, which is why he uses significant others to carry shame—so he doesn't have to.

This situation is further complicated for the therapist by the fact that not only do people who are traumatizing resist seeing themselves that way, it is also the case that people who have been traumatized may not agree that they are traumatized, or that there is or was a traumatizer. We may see a patient as a victim of traumatization, but that person may only recognize himself as someone whose inadequacies and failures are his own fault, making him deserving of punishment. In some clinical situations, if we are too quick to explore the possibility that the patient has been traumatized by a narcissist partner (or for that matter, by traumatizing parents), we risk creating another version of a "confusion of tongues" (Ferenczi, 1933/1980): this time, between the therapist's language of trauma, and the patient's language of affiliation.

In the following, I will outline the typical personality features and dynamics of the intimate couple caught in the traumatizing narcissist's relational system. I will then provide clinical vignettes that illustrate a variety of ways that traumatizing narcissists and their partners organize relationships.

John and Mary

John and Mary are the names I will use to describe the different roles and behaviors taken up by the generic traumatizing narcissist and partner. I want to emphasize that "John" and "Mary" can both be either male or female, heterosexual, or LGBT.

John, the traumatizing narcissist, complains that Mary is not loving him enough, not keeping his needs in mind; he feels that his anger and belligerence that his partner complains about isn't that big a deal, and that it wouldn't be happening if she weren't repeatedly disappointing him. Mary is always trying to figure out how to avoid making John angry, jealous, and hurt. In our generic scenario, the couple comes to counseling when Mary is on the verge of giving up, often after a particularly upsetting fight. Mary feels unable to keep bearing the brunt of John's anger and taking the blame for their problems. John usually tries to get the therapist to see how wrong Mary is, and how it is he who is the victim, but eventually he appears to make some concessions, and he begins to try to persuade Mary to get back together again. Mary, needing to feel needed, will often give it another try or two, but eventually she may move on, with great pain and effort. I should note that it is almost always Mary who tries to get the couple into therapy, and almost always Mary who continues in individual therapy once John is out of the picture. John comes to therapy reluctantly, is quick to want to end the therapy, and is unlikely to continue in individual therapy, at least not for long. Mary often stays in therapy, but continues to get involved with unreliable or traumatizing partners for a while, before she eventually finds the strength to make better choices.

John, the traumatizing narcissist, is a person who is sufficiently inflated narcissistically to persuade himself that his self-esteem is stable, and that he is infallibly in the right. There is only one reason why he gets upset, and that is because Mary keeps upsetting him. John's disavowal of shame connected to his intense, anxious dependency leads him to externalize self-doubt and project it in a way that his significant other internalizes. In other words, he uses his partner as a host for these dissociated affects. I have encountered John (of any gender category)—the traumatizing narcissist in a relationship—in a number of variations, but there are some common threads:

"John"

1 "He" (or she) has a traumatic developmental history of deprivation of parental provision, whether because of parental narcissism or illness, mental and/or other, premature loss, etc.
2 Having failed to please a rejecting or absent parent, he has developed a strong, leonine personality, which masks his intense but disavowed dependence and vulnerability. He is rigidly subjective in his orientation. He can be charming, vulnerable, seductive, he expects to be accommodated to, and he succeeds in intimidating significant others into "walking on eggshells"

around him—an unconscious reversal of his relationship with the disappointed and disappointing parent. He is attracted to partners whom he senses to be more vulnerable than he.

3 He proclaims his love intensely, passionately, but soon makes it clear that he does not feel that what he gets in return is sufficient.
4 He is persuasive about this, so that his partner feels quite guilty, and becomes fearful about what she will do next that will trigger his accusations and reproaches.
5 He finds ways of isolating his partner, disparaging others she is close to, and he trivializes her work or other interests.
6 He will expect and receive many apologies from his partner, but he will not offer them reciprocally, and rarely, if ever, see a need to; or his pseudo-apologies will be carefully worded, along the lines of "I'm sorry you feel that way"—but *not* "I'm sorry I hurt you." It is rare for John to acknowledge or even to see his own part in the destruction of his relationships.

The other member of the couple—in this context, Mary—also has some distinguishing characteristics that can be outlined:

"Mary"

1 Just like John, "she" (or he) has a traumatic developmental history of deprivation of parental provision, whether because of parental narcissism or illness, mental and/or other.
2 Having been unable to please a disturbed parent, she feels guilt more strongly than resentment; and so as an adult she has become compliant and accommodating in relationships, bending over backwards to give unselfishly, experiencing herself most pronouncedly as the object of others' needs, judgments, and expectations. As the object of the other, she is oriented toward preoccupations with the feelings, needs, and desires of the other. She selects partners who are demanding, focused on their own needs, and dismissive of her needs. As much as she feels used, she puts herself in the position of the giver, not the taker.
3 She has tried to express her subjectivity in various ways (various art forms, academically, professionally) with much promise, but always with much frustration.
4 She may develop a "secret life" in adolescence that contrasts to her outward show of compliance; secret behaviors could include drug or drink abuse, precocious sexuality, cutting, etc. The more compliant she becomes in a relationship with a John type, the more she becomes prone to somatization.
5 She is quick to blame herself, and dissociate indignation and rage, which she may take out on herself in various ways—or which may become somatized, for example as skin or bowel disorders.
6 She is dissociative about time. For example, when Mary is a woman, she may only come to realize she wants to have children when she realizes that it may

> be too late to do so. When Mary is a straight man, he has been in numerous relationships that end, not because he actually wants the relationships to end, but because the girlfriend finally gives up and leaves when she realizes that he is frozen, and that she is too close to running out of time to have children.

John's narcissism is traumatizing. Mary, trying to get love by giving as selflessly as possible, trying assiduously to avoid seeming needy, very dissociated about her needs, is trapped in an unconscious repetition of her developmental trauma—trying to give love that will make the other happy and elicit the other's appreciation, and failing, again and again. She blames herself.

The presence of the traumatizing narcissist in an intimate relationship inevitably leads to relational impasse. As described in chapters 1 and 2, that is what traumatic narcissism does, and what the traumatizing narcissist seeks: to attack the subjectivity of a needed other; to keep the other dependent by using the other as a host for dissociated, disavowed, and projected shame; to foreclose intersubjective space; and to establish hegemonic subjectivity as the governing framework of the relationship. The unconscious goal of the traumatizing narcissist is to create a relationship that allows her to remain fixed in a position of superiority by destabilizing the other.

When I begin working with a couple, one of the things I am carefully trying to observe is if there seems to be one member who cannot and will not accept any measure of responsibility for the problems of the marriage. This is often complicated in various ways, and not always readily discernable. For one thing, one member of the couple may in fact be more problematic than the other: for example, a man with a secret gambling addiction; or a woman who exercises obsessively to the point of illness. However, the obviousness of that kind of concrete problem with one member of the couple should not lead to the assumption that the other member is not contributing to the problem. In most cases, careful exploration of the couple's dynamics will show that the problems are complicated and co-constructed. The angrier partner is not necessarily the only destructive partner: passivity and avoidance can be just as destructive, and is usually the perfect complement to the other's explosive tendencies.

Still, there are times when it could not be more obvious, where clearly Mary tries to communicate, and John is unmistakably belligerent, unyielding, and relentless in placing all blame on Mary. If it seems clear that John's behavior has been highly destructive, and if this situation persists and John cannot be budged, I see little hope for improvement. The couple may choose to stay together, but Mary will have to be doing a lot of dissociating to rationalize accepting the abuse of John. On the other hand, if we encounter Mary as an individual patient, and Mary tells us about John as characterized previously, we will have to listen carefully and explore fully the dynamic between them before determining if John is in fact a traumatizing narcissist.

In the vignettes that follow, I illustrate several of the ways I have been able to observe the traumatizing narcissist's impact on intimate relationships. I will first present treatments that ended prematurely, or that did not end with the couple's reconciliation. I will conclude with a vignette describing a happier outcome both for patient and therapist.

Anne

Anne (like "Mary") is struggling in a relationship with her older policeman boyfriend, Joe (like "John"). Anne is very petite, and she tells me that Joe is very big, gruff, and intimidating. She has moved into his apartment, she is upset that he won't yet ask her to marry him, and he says that she is much too needy. I learn that just as it was with her parents, there is never any chance of her point of view being validated, if she disagrees with Joe. He just talks her right down. It is now to the point where she can barely speak without the tears coming, her voice trembling and choking. She is unable to work on her art work, and she is unable to think about what she wants to be doing with her life, though she hates her current receptionist job. Joe had a rough life; he ran away from home at 16 when his fights with his parents became more and more violent. Now reconciled to his parents, he and Anne often spend time off with his or her family. He works nights, Anne works days, so they are somewhat isolated socially. Around their families, she needs to be careful of what she says. If she gets at all emotional, she starts to cry. She is depressed, and although I sense that she is very angry, she tries to convince me that what's happening in the relationship is really her fault. We work on things, and before too long she tells me that she was able to have a conversation with Joe about some feelings she was having without crying. This felt like an important breakthrough for her.

One day, Anne is telling me about her family, how she and her sister were often punished by her parents for being fresh, and I ask about the punishments. "Well, if it was not too bad an offense, we'd have to sit at the table, explain what we did and how it was wrong, and then hold a bar of soap in our mouths. If it was really bad, it would be liquid soap." Anne can see the shock on my face, which I'm actually trying not to show, and I can see she is now uncomfortable. I ask, "How do you feel about that kind of punishment?" "Well, I think my parents tried to be fair," she says. "Really?" I ask. "It sounds quite harsh to me." Silence. "Anne," I ask, "do you think you would punish your own children that way?" "I might," she says, with what seems to me like a touch of defiance.

Anne cancels her next session by email later that day, and though I make several efforts to contact her and reschedule, she denies that she was unhappy with anything about our work, and assures me that her schedule change at her job was the only reason she had to stop.

Anne claimed that she was seeking therapy because she was ruining her relationship by being needy and weak. The way I heard it, Joe was being very controlling and negating—like a traumatizing narcissist. However, before I was willing to make that judgment about Joe in my thinking about him—a judgment that would have indicated a negative prediction about his capacity for change—I tried to help Anne find ways to speak to Joe that would not break down into angry disputes. She seemed to be succeeding to some extent. Perhaps Joe could and would change in ways that reflected more empathy for Anne; and perhaps Anne could come to feel stronger and more connected to herself as subject—to her own needs, feelings, and desires—rather than be focused so much on trying to be the right kind of object for Joe.

It was when Anne described her parents' punishments with soap and liquid soap—to me her description of these childhood events sounded like ritual torture—that I could not hold back a spontaneous expression of shock and disapproval. When Anne told me that she might punish her future children in the same way, I found myself at a loss for words. I'm sure I could have handled this moment better, but at the time I felt she was expressing to me that her way of life—submission to authority, self-blame, and self-punishment—was not something I was authorized to question. I can now see how my reaction to the soap punishment was probably very shaming for her. Too much was exposed too quickly by my reaction. Though it may eventually have been possible for Anne to find parts of herself that did not condone being abused by others, that awareness would have had to develop more at her pace and less at mine.

Ted and Kelly

Ted and Kelly's relationship, as I came to understand it, was haunted by Ted's mother, a traumatizing narcissist. Unconscious of the destructive influence his mother had on the shaping of his personality, Ted's marriage was coming apart by the time he and his wife were referred to me.

Ted and Kelly are an attractive couple, he a professional engineer for a utility company and she a successful high-end real estate broker. He seems irritated, very quiet, and she very anxious, tearful. She tells me how wonderful Ted really is, how kind, sensitive, even-tempered, and loving. She has angry outbursts that make her feel so ugly and so ashamed, and she sobs as she speaks, so upset that she is hurting Ted; but she simply does not want him to touch her any more, and she feels horribly guilty, wondering if Ted should just find someone better for him, someone who can love him as he deserves to be loved. They have been together about ten years, and it was three years ago that Kelly finally broke down to the point where she pushed Ted to propose and marry her. They talked about having children, but it never went beyond talking. Ted had always said "we can if that's what you want," and now Kelly is really beyond the age she would have wanted to have children.

It takes a while for me to start to hear more about what is under the surface—that Ted apparently does not want anything. Only Kelly wants anything, and as far as Ted is concerned, whatever Kelly wants is fine. Ted feels fine all the time, it's only Kelly who doesn't feel fine. Kelly is patient and accommodating about Ted's passivity, until she is so frustrated that she blows up, and he gets really upset, because he just doesn't understand why Kelly is upset.

I also learn that Ted takes his time deciding about things. He needs a new car, his old one is actually dangerously in disrepair, but it's been more than a year since he's been looking into it, figuring out what's best, and he doesn't understand why Kelly gets so frustrated. He doesn't care which movie they see, which restaurant they could go to, what he'll order—whatever she wants is fine. If he wants hot sauce at a restaurant, instead of asking for it himself, he'll ask Kelly, "Do you want hot sauce?" Kelly doesn't want to always be the one that gets to hold the hot potato, the one who wants, when the other never wants because he is always fine. She feels like a selfish, greedy, opinionated bitch—because she has desires and preferences, and Ted does not.

Why not? Ted grew up with a silent, passive father (like "Mary") who allowed his traumatizing narcissist mother (like "John") to control everything, make every decision, and punish anyone who complained or disagreed with her through her angry tears and her well-developed sense of victimization. Ted's twin brother learned to ignore the mother and develop a strong sense of entitlement and authority, which Kelly was eventually able to describe as his acting like a pig in shit. Ted, unwilling to overtly reject his mother, learned to build a solid wall all around himself, and to keep his inner world very still, almost empty. In that way, his mother's intrusive, raging, controlling behavior didn't really register, nor did his brother's. He was fine, and everything was fine. His father had developed the same strategy with his mother.

Kelly had loved how gentle and mild Ted was, especially after she had spent a tumultuous adolescence bitterly fighting with her hyper-controlling mother. However, when she started feeling like she wanted to kill him if she heard one more, "I don't know, what do you want?" she put herself in therapy, trying to understand what was wrong with her. In couples work, she was stunned to realize that Ted's profoundly dissociated rage, stemming from his traumatic developmental experience of his mother's traumatizing narcissism, was finding expression within her; and that he simply could not find it or feel it in himself.

I was able to persuade Ted to go into individual therapy, and Kelly continued in hers, and they continued working hard in couples therapy as well. Ted made a tremendous effort to understand himself, and the dynamic between them, but he could not find a way to move out of his schizoid paralysis, even as he could see how much it shut Kelly out and how painful it would be to lose her, which seemed as though it was a real possibility.

Was Ted a traumatizing narcissist? It seemed quite clear that his mother fit the description, but Ted's gentleness and kindness did not jibe. Unfortunately, behind his kindness was a stone wall that rejected and returned any kind of aggression directed toward him, and kept anger, desire, and initiative locked down and deeply buried, hidden to himself within himself. Once Kelly stopped feeling like a monster for having desires and feelings, including aggressive feelings, she could no longer suppress her anger toward Ted. He could go along with whatever she wanted, but Ted would not, even if it meant losing her, take the risk of really committing to wanting. I thought that Ted was slowly making progress, going from what started out as a very shut-down place to a place of real affect and dawning understanding; but now that Kelly had found her anger, it seemed like no amount of change would be enough.

In this couple, the impact of Ted's traumatizing narcissist mother on Ted had led him to operate outwardly as the perfectly obliging, easy-going object of others. Ted's subjectivity was profoundly dissociated, kept in suspended animation. For Kelly, Ted was not domineering and intimidating, which helped her feel safe with him, the antidote to her angry, disapproving mother. Unfortunately, Kelly found herself becoming just like that angry mother with Ted: as his passivity grew deeper, Kelly grew more furious.

Kelly ended couples therapy at the point where she clearly stated she would also be leaving Ted. I only learned later that she left her therapist shortly after ending the couples therapy, furious that the therapist was unwilling to tell her what she thought was right, to stay with Ted, or to leave. Neither I nor Kelly's therapist know how the story ended.

Luke and Elizabeth

Luke (like "Mary"), an attractive, intelligent man in his late fifties, had been a social activist priest in a mainstream Protestant church for many years, and was particularly known for his excellent work with the mentally ill and the homeless. His wife, Elizabeth (like "John"), was also very active in the church and held an important paid position. Elizabeth came from a wealthy Southern family and it was her trust fund more than Luke's income that allowed them to live in Manhattan and send two talented, intelligent daughters to private schools. Luke was unhappy in his marriage, and as we talked, I began to hear about his "redneck" (his word) family and his abusive father who eventually committed suicide. Luke went through a period of alcoholism before joining the ministry, and this lapse proved to be a point Elizabeth frequently found cause to refer to when they were in disagreement. From her perspective, Luke's unhappiness with her was a sign of his instability and untrustworthiness. She made it clear that she had little faith in his ability to earn enough to sustain himself without her contribution. When they saw a couples counselor who suggested that Elizabeth might also have some responsibility for their problems, Elizabeth made it clear that there was no validity to that idea, and that if things were to work out for them, it would be because Luke was finally going to straighten himself out. She then declared the couples therapy terminated.

Luke initially presented for depression, but it did not take long for him to acknowledge that he was exhausted from trying to be all things to all people, but especially to his wife, who was somehow always disappointed, hurt, angry, and dissatisfied. Elizabeth always found a way to remind him of his shameful past as a means of deflecting all blame for conflict on to him. As he worked through his desires and fears, he gradually saw that the only thing stopping him from leaving Elizabeth, leaving the ministry, moving back to the part of the south he loved and

LIBRARY MAIL DMM: 173.5.0

FROM: INTERLIBRARY LOAN
MERCER COUNTY COMMUNITY COLLEGE LIBRARY
1200 OLD TRENTON ROAD
WEST WINDSOR NJ 08550

TO: INTERLIBRARY LOAN
TRAVERSE AREA DISTRICT LIBRARY
610 WOODMERE AVE
TRAVERSE CITY MI 49686

starting over, was his fear that Elizabeth would turn his daughters against him, which in fact she had long been doing in subtle ways.

Luke eventually made his move, and we continued working by phone. He had many connections in the mental health field and was able to get work quickly in his new location. He put a lot of effort into deepening connections with his daughters, and was patient when they were distant or angry. He persisted and succeeded in strengthening those bonds. Throughout the divorce process and beyond, Elizabeth took every opportunity to remind him of what she felt he should be ashamed about, but Luke resisted the pull, and eventually remarried, happily. He now enjoys a very successful career as a highly respected advocate for the mentally ill in his state.

Luke's individual work led him to recognize that he had turned over every stone, looking for a way to move to an intersubjectively constructed relationship with Elizabeth. Every effort led to the same insistence from Elizabeth: that she was the flawless, wounded innocent, and he was the selfish, shameful one. Once Luke understood how he had been trained to play this role throughout his life, he was determined to accept that role no longer. Freed from being the object of Elizabeth's projections, the subjective space he opened up within himself could be filled with the pride and the pleasure in his many accomplishments, professional and interpersonal, that he had long denied himself.

Therapeutic Goals with Couples Affected by Traumatizing Narcissism

Addressing the objectivism that is the historical legacy of mainstream psychoanalytic practice, Irwin Hoffman (2009) described a psychoanalysis based on "critical or 'dialectical' constructivism" (p. 1044), which:

> replaces a diagnostic, knowing, prescriptive psychoanalytic attitude with one that requires responsible, creative, improvised, and collaborative efforts on the parts of the participants *to make something* of the ambiguous, context-dependent reality that evolves in the course of their interaction. In this paradigm, the analyst embraces the existential uncertainty that accompanies the realization that there are multiple good ways to be, in the moment, and more generally in life, and that the choices he or she makes are always influenced by culture, by personal values, by countertransference, and by other factors in ways that can never be fully known.
>
> (pp. 1044–1045)

Hoffman's point here is essential to a relational perspective. There are "multiple good ways to be" for couples, too, even when the hurt and angry couple in our office has a relationship that differs in many respects from what we personally might think of as "healthy." With a battling couple, most therapists, relationally oriented or not, would be quick to observe the breakdown of intersubjective relatedness to complementarity, whether using that particular language or not. What I see as distinguishing a relational psychoanalytic approach in this context is the recognition that couples who unconsciously create domination/submission dynamics, and who are helped to see and understand those dynamics, can be offered the option to learn about and employ intersubjective modes of relating—*but it is an option.* Not everyone will want this enough to actually put in the work required for change to take place. Some may simply not be able to strengthen themselves enough to achieve it. Developing intersubjective relatedness, mutual recognition, and constructive repair processes as a couple is an option, not a mandate, and that choice is made by the couple. The therapist cannot make it for them.

Certainly these three capacities (intersubjective relatedness, mutual recognition, and constructive repair processes) are not the only factors necessary for an enduring, fulfilling relationship, but I think of them as basic relationship skills that are very useful when used well. The problem for some, though, with this kind of "good behavior" in a relationship is that there might not be enough chaos and drama to keep it interesting. It could become too safe, too vanilla. Be that as it may, for dramatic, chaotic couples who are screaming, and sometimes jumping up, arm-waving, threatening to throw up, or plotting tit-for-tat suicides in my office (yes, I've experienced all of the above and more), I tend to promote to them the idea of finding ways of feeling safe enough to be vulnerable and tender with each other, before worrying about things getting too safe.

Relationships that seem unhealthy and unhappy to me, that seem to be operating on the antithesis of recognition and intersubjectivity principles, are not necessarily going to be relationships that our patients will be able to, or actually want to, change or terminate. As with Anne and also Kelly in this chapter, many patients will leave their therapist before they leave their partner—whether their complaint was about narcissistic abuse, or any other kind of problem. The wife of the late George Harrison, Olivia Harrison, referring to the many ups and downs they experienced in the course of their marriage, and especially to George's attractiveness to other women with whom he fairly frequently strayed, put it pithily: "We stayed married because we didn't get divorced."[1] Many people stay married, don't really reconcile many of their problems, including some that may be quite serious, and in the end, they feel good enough about their marriage anyway. Then again, many who stay married do so in depression, despair, and/or deadness.

Even so, I do not see my function when working with couples as being a salesman or proselytizer for a particular kind of recognition-oriented, intersubjective marriage. There is really only one bottom line—physical violence can be understood, but never condoned. If I observe behavior that is not physically violent, but that I think of as abusive, and the patient denies being abusive, I think hard on my judgment before deciding to use the abuse label. I am concerned not to enable abuse by being too tentative in labeling it; however, I am also concerned about reductionist thinking—such as the couples therapist I was told about who reacted to a patient saying "bullshit" to her husband in a couples session. The couples therapist stated that she strictly forbade the use of any profanity in the sessions—and the couple promptly looked for a new couples therapist. Couples sometimes need to have fully expressive fights, lots of them, fights they have avoided for years, if they are to continue to go forward together. The couples therapist who is confused at all about the possibility of abuse should seek consultation sooner rather than later. We do not want to allow abuse; but we do not want to inhibit needed expressions of anger.

I see the therapist's function with a couple as helping them gain multiple perspectives on the structure of their relationship, and to see if it is possible to help them understand how that structure may relate to their own developmental issues and to those of their partner. I want to offer the possibility of change and growth that is enlivening and enriching, even though difficult and painful work will be involved in getting there. Of course I will intervene in ways that attempt to promote mutual recognition, and I will persist in those attempts as long as the couple is motivated to keep working on their relationship. Do I think and believe that people who want to stay together should try, as best they can, to recognize the pull and the grip of sadomasochistic complementarity in their relationship, and commit to strive instead toward mutual recognition and better ways of negotiating conflict? I absolutely do. However, those values are my bias, and at the appropriate time, I make my bias known.

If one or both members of a couple demonstrate that they cannot or will not budge out of complementarity, then at some point, if they haven't chosen to end the treatment themselves, I will ask them to carefully consider whether or not they really want to continue. I consider it very important to recognize that when one of the partners in a marriage has consistently displayed the behaviors of the traumatizing narcissist, the couples therapy rarely goes well; and unless the couple's therapist or the narcissist's individual therapist achieves a spectacular breakthrough with the narcissist partner, the couple either stays together in an essentially sadomasochistic dynamic, or the masochistic partner finds a way to change and grow and break free.

On the other hand, my experience with many couples where traumatizing narcissism is not a factor has been that when they are able to understand the difference between mutual recognition and doer-done to dynamics, and when they understand that conflicts and ruptures are inevitable but repairable, they can begin to move closer to each other, with less fear and greater willingness to be vulnerable. Many people aren't naturally good at intimate mutuality—maybe that's most people—but are still able and willing to change and grow, and find a level of mutuality that is, when all is said and done, good enough. What defines good enough for any given couple is, in the end, subjective. For example, how many times a day, week, month, or year people think of having sex as enough; or what kind of sex constitutes great sex vs. okay sex or bad sex; or what level of adventure is enough, and how much safety is too safe—these preferences vary quite extensively.

Couples who are capable of mutuality and aliveness, who are willing to change and grow as they age, have much in common and deal with many of the issues that concerned the people Mitchell (2003b) spoke of in his posthumously published book, *Can Love Last?*. Mitchell extensively contemplated, with numerous clinical vignettes, the complexity of relationships set against the backdrop of conflicting human needs for aloneness and connection, safety and adventure, closeness and distance, and the passing of time. Mitchell describes patients who for the most part are able to awaken a capacity for mutuality, and mobilize a willingness to grow.

It is just this capacity and willingness that is lacking in couples whose relationship has been organized on the basis of the traumatizing narcissist's relational system. The traumatizing narcissist cannot acknowledge any need to change or grow, for to do so would be to admit insufficiency. In this kind of couple, the narcissist's partner will be expected to do all the changing, in the form of accommodations that are in fact submissions. The traumatizing narcissist does not need to grow in her own view, because she is already always fully in the right, already in possession of the highest possible moral ground. The narcissist's partner cannot grow if he is determined to stay in the relationship, because growth would entail recognizing the extent of his subjugation, and the need to do something about it. Because a subjugated other is the only acceptable partner for the traumatizing narcissist, the narcissist partner's growth will either have to take place everywhere else but in his relationship, or he will eventually have to leave the narcissist.

Although I am pessimistic about the fate of relationships with a traumatizing narcissist partner, if I am asked by one or both partners in the relationship whether I think divorce is the right option, I always suggest that they consider very carefully if they feel they have turned over every stone. Have they fought hard enough to be seen and heard by their partner? Have they really tried to recognize and be recognized, as fully as they possibly can? It is hard for many people, especially when children are involved, to admit that they have done all they could, and that they are ready to divorce—even when the ideation has already become a plan. This is often especially true for the partner of a traumatizing narcissist, who has been told so often that everything is entirely their fault.

Working with couples, it is almost universally true that the change and growth they will both need to make, if there is the intention or even just the hope of staying together, is the development of ways of relating intersubjectively, where mutual recognition is the goal, and both are committed to finding ways of constructively repairing disruptions. Certainly there will be couples who are quite good at this, or who seem to be, who do not stay together, for whatever reasons. Couples who want to stay together, who want to be happier and more fulfilled (happy enough, fulfilled enough, at least), will have to learn to better empathize and recognize each other, to better shift self-reflexively between subjective and objective positions with greater fluidity. They will have to discover and break through their dissociation about their needs, and they will have to come to terms with the fact that they have to take responsibility for how their needs do and do not get met. Most importantly, they will have to tolerate greater levels of vulnerability and humility in offering contrition and forgiveness.

Contrition, Atonement, and Forgiveness

I am surprised by how often I discover that people I work with who appear to be highly intelligent and well educated become confused about the meaning of these words: contrition, atonement, and forgiveness. Here are some brief, simple definitions, cobbled together from various online dictionaries: contrition—feeling sincere remorse and guilt for hurting another; atonement—to seek redemption and forgiveness; forgiveness—the relinquishing of anger and resentment for an offence, flaw, or mistake.

To be able to say "I'm sorry I hurt you" (contrition and atonement), and to hear in return, "thank you for understanding, I know I hurt you, too, and I'm sorry" (contrition and forgiveness), makes a much better, stronger repair than the begrudging, "I'm sorry you feel that way," or, what is even more common, pretending the breach never happened and trying to behave as though everything is fine.[2] Yet, the value of expressing contrition and forgiveness is often overlooked. Many people, men and women both, feel quite humiliated about expressing contrition and will avoid it at all costs (McWilliams & Lependorf, 1990). In working with couples, I eventually try to learn all about each person's family history of repair processes, which typically has been troubled in various ways, if existent. Unfortunately, the cost for a couple who repeat dysfunctional patterns around the repair process can be intractable bitterness. Obviously, children pay a high price as well in families where parents live in chronic complementarity, where there is always a power struggle but no real winner. In fact, many patients who seek couples counseling are children of divorce, and quite often, one of those parents, or both, will be described as narcissistic.

The intersubjective process in couples, including the capacity for contrition and forgiveness, cannot function reciprocally in the presence of traumatizing narcissism. Contrition is impossible for the traumatizing narcissist because it entails the recognition of the validity of the other's version of the experience. This includes the recognition and acceptance of one's own capacity for dissociation. In other words, I need to be able to acknowledge that you may correctly perceive a flaw in me that I find shameful and do not want to perceive. For the traumatizing narcissist, it is extremely important to avoid acknowledging incomplete self-awareness, which in itself would be tantamount to an admission of shameful insufficiency. Shame and insufficiency are too humiliating to be owned and borne by the traumatizing narcissist, and must therefore be projected onto others. Those closest to the traumatizing narcissist, who are dependent on him in any way, will be the most likely to identify with the projections, since that is what will be required of them in order to maintain the attachment.

Growth and Change

Lorraine

Although my work with Lorraine began at the unhappy crisis point of her divorce proceedings, Lorraine's progress in therapy exemplifies some of the possibilities for growth and change that can occur after being in a relationship with the traumatizing narcissist. In the several years I have worked with Lorraine, I have been moved and impressed with the persistence of her efforts to break free of her tendency to self-objectify, and automatically assume the "Mary" role in relationships. I will conclude this chapter with her hopeful story.

Alan was the man Lorraine fell in love with in college, the first man she had sexual relations with, and a man who never lost his sexual attraction for her, even after the divorce. The problem was that Alan was controlling and demanding, intimidating and belittling. Although Alan was dismissive, belittling, and resentful of Lorraine's career aspirations, she nevertheless went on to become an accomplished author and professor during the years she was married to Alan and raising their two children. Lorraine grew up in a fairly conservative family, in which her younger and older brothers had been free to join their father in his authoritarian ways, while Lorraine was raised in the old-fashioned way—to be a good assistant homemaker to her mother, and to stand by her man, no matter what.

Alan was a big man on campus when they started going out in college, and Lorraine was thrilled to be the one he chose. Alan started getting good jobs in his field right out of college, while Lorraine pursued graduate work that eventually led to a full professorship and an offer to write a textbook in her field that became a great success. Not long after the birth of their second child, Lorraine discovered Alan was having an affair—because she discovered she had gotten a sexually transmitted disease from him. Alan confessed, he was contrite, they went to counseling, and eventually Lorraine believed that she had forgiven him. What she only came to realize much later was that from the point of her husband's affair on, she finally felt she had something she could hold over him. This realization came to Lorraine months and months after the divorce, but it marked a point for Lorraine where her identification as simply a victim of Alan's became more complex.

As devastated as she was by Alan's unilateral decision to divorce, Lorraine was also relieved not to have to go on feeling so unseen by Alan, so careful to try not to anger him, so pressured to submit to him. By the time the divorce was final, almost two years later, she had sold the old house, bought a new one at a good price in an excellent location with a mother-in-law apartment she could rent out, found excellent, helpful contractors for the needed repairs who were willing to work in her price range, had gotten a contract for a second book, had been offered a tenured position at her new job, and was well into some adventurous dating.

On the other hand, Lorraine often missed Alan, even after she fell in love with a new man, Tom, who passionately loved and respected her in return. She often felt alone, helpless, overwhelmed, not wanting to get out of bed, not wanting to have to do for herself the things that Alan had once done. We eventually came to understand that feeling disconnected was natural to her, so much a part of her upbringing and of her now defunct marriage. She could all too easily attend selectively to whatever it was that brought up feelings of aloneness, while dissociatively not being able to fully make real her experiences of being loved, respected, and admired—for her competence, her intelligence, her humor—for herself.

In spite of Lorraine's certainty for some time after the divorce that she would never find someone else, she found Tom, and they began to negotiate the terms of what for both of them was the first important relationship since their respective divorces. As for conflict and disagreement, Lorraine had never in her life managed either satisfactorily. If she wasn't submitting, either willingly or begrudgingly, clamming up and getting passive aggressive, and/or dissociating to the point of not knowing what she felt, she'd end up feeling out of control and blurting out explosive things she felt horrible for saying. So on several occasions, we play-acted conversations in which she acted the part of Tom, and I played her. She showed me what it was that Tom did or said that made her shut down, we explored why (he could react with disapproval just like her father), and I acted out how I would be if I were Lorraine—or a version of Lorraine that didn't freeze like a deer in the headlights when she got scared about the possibility of the whole relationship going up in flames.

In time, Lorraine was able to have different kinds of conversations with Tom, even including expressing different forms of anger (irritation, annoyance, resentment, hurt), that actually resulted in deepening their connection in ways she hadn't imagined possible. It turned out that even though her new partner could be stubborn, opinionated, and quicker with a reaction or a comeback than she, he was also someone who could be open and vulnerable, and who could let her know that he recognized her as her, and loved her as her.

While Tom was more loving than any man Lorraine had ever been with, she eventually could not ignore the extent to which Tom was dictating the terms of their relationship, and the extent to which she was going along with him whether she liked it or not. Stubborn, rigid habits of his that she had tried to overlook became more pronounced, and more and more she felt unheard and dismissed by him. She also noticed how she positioned herself to feel less than Tom, while another part of her became preoccupied with the things about him that made her feel superior to him. For the first time in her life, she realized how much her family of origin, and her relationship to her ex-husband existed on the binary seesaw (Aron, 2006; Benjamin, 1999) of complementarity, the superiority/inferiority matrix. I encouraged her to try to recognize when she experienced herself as the object of Tom, and when she was more centered on her subjectivity. She became a keen observer of her state shifts and the interplay of her different self-orientations. She began to realize that Tom was in many ways a more loving person than Alan had been, but that his unacknowledged ambivalence about intimacy, and his disavowed need to keep their relationship completely on his terms, was more depriving and required more submission than she was willing to tolerate.

Lorraine was afraid to fully speak her anger to Tom, because she couldn't imagine doing so without him ending the relationship. I encouraged her in one session to try to deeply feel what it was that frightened her so much about the idea of letting him go. She said she could feel terror about how unworthy and bad she really was. Are these like childhood feelings, I asked? She was crying.

I said that she must be touching an early, traumatized part of herself—when parental reproaches made her feel deeply ashamed, and fearful of banishment.

Lorraine spoke at length then about the different sides of her parents, their loving side, but also about her father's strict, rigid, contemptuous attitudes, and her mother's deflating, limiting ideas about what a woman was capable of achieving. As we worked more in these areas, Lorraine began to recognize more fully a subjectivity that belonged to her, that offered freedom that was otherwise unattainable so long as she remained in the subjugation of her orientation to herself as the object of others. She began to notice the kinds of thoughts she often had that sounded like her parents' way of being casually discouraging and deflating. She readily understood the idea of a "protector/persecutor" self, and she became able to make her conflict conscious—the conflict between wanting to express the excellence she felt capable of, and feeling stupid and underserving (the harsh version of her parents' evaluation of her). As we sorted all this out, she became able to mobilize a self-state she could identify as carrying her confidence and her worthiness, and have that part of herself soothe and comfort the protector/persecutor part, which she had come to see as operating out of fears that belonged to her parents, that she didn't need to identify with. She worked on paying attention to her needs and feelings, with much less of the hopeless kind of self-pity she had often felt, but rather with a sense of purpose: she was determined to stop her own automatic self-denigration and objectification.

All it took to end the relationship with Tom was for Lorraine to try to bring her concerns to him in a clear way. She was able to do so because she was able to feel that she would be okay if they had to break up. As she described their conversation to me, she certainly sounded like she had been loving, and hopeful that they could resolve their differences; but Tom would have none of it. Lorraine was ready to move on. As she re-entered the dating scene, she felt much more confident that she would not lose herself. She knew it would be hard for her to resist a man who appeared to be eager to become sexual, that she would have to focus carefully on her own desire, her own feelings, which in the past had often become imperceptible when a man made his desire for her obvious. She was able to stop herself from getting involved with men who pursued her that she didn't really have feelings for. She worked toward being able to discern if she was with someone who wanted to be with a whole person, or who just wanted someone who was willing to do all the accommodating. Lorraine was ready for mutuality, and not willing to settle for less.

Notes

1 As quoted in the documentary film *George Harrison: Living in the Material World* (Scorsese, 2011).

2 In what for me was the climactic moment of the film *The Fighter* (Russell, 2010), the younger brother, played by Mark Wahlberg, confronts his mother and releases a torrent of anger and hurt feelings about her lack of attention to him and her infinite focus instead on his troubled older brother. As she listens in shock, her face reflects her astonishment, and her dawning recognition. When she says, almost wails, "I'm sorry!," her contrition is palpable. I think that actress Melissa Leo's reading of just that line alone would have warranted the Academy Award she won for her performance.

Chapter 6

"But What Do I Do?"

Finding the Path to Freedom

In many cases of analyses where there has been extensive illumination of the patient's internal world, and the analytic couple are experiencing what they perceive as deeply meaningful insights, there comes a kind of impasse. This impasse comes not at a point of breakdown of the analytic bond, as is the case with the inevitable enactments, and disruption and repair episodes, that are an essential part of most analyses (see, e.g., Chapter 2). This kind of impasse comes *at a point of breakthrough*. "I see exactly how I've been living now," one patient said, after years of work and a series of particularly revelatory sessions. "It's been all about how I placate everyone, make everyone happy, and end up resentful, empty, and alone. But I have no idea who I am or how I am if I'm not him—the traumatized one, my mother's loyal little man, grown up to be the life of the party for a few hours, and then the lonely angry drunk at home by himself at night. That's all I know. Who am I supposed to be if not he?"

Particularly for the adult children of traumatizing narcissist parents, it is extraordinarily difficult to differentiate one's self—to construct a "me" from out of the "you" that the elders, sometimes generations of them, have defined. When the patient cries "but what do I do?"—as patients often do when dissociation dispels, and parts of the self that had been disavowed and/or dissociated come into focus—they are not really asking for instructions, though they may believe that is their aim. In fact, most often they are trying to stave off feelings of impotence, confusion, and hopeless despair about the possibility of change. They are trying to address the matter at the level of the intellect, because the feelings are unnerving. As the frozen traumatic past within first begins to thaw, the concept of living unhaunted and unimpeded by bad objects, both internal and external, feels inconceivable. Instead of a life of freedom and new possibility coming into view, what appears is an emptiness, a blank nullity. Dissociation has not worked; being stuck in hatred, toward the abusers and toward the self, is not working; feigning indifference fails as well. What is the path to freedom? I will discuss in this chapter how some I have worked with have struggled to find their way.

Seeking a self of one's own out of a life that has been overtaken by a traumatizing narcissist parent is a lot like being the son of the Manchurian Candidate. I confess to having seen only the superb 1962 film directed by John Frankenheimer;

I have not read the book. In that film, the mother of all maternal traumatizing narcissists, played memorably by Angela Lansbury, and her husband, a U.S. Senator, appear to be ferocious, McCarthy-like red-baiters—but she is actually spearheading a plot to take over the U.S. on behalf of Red China. The success of the plan hinges on triggering her adult son, who was brainwashed in a Chinese prison camp during the Korean War, to assassinate his father's running mate, who is certain to be nominated to run for president, at the electoral convention. This will then pave the way for her husband, running for vice-president on the same ticket, to step in as the presidential candidate. When he wins the election, they will have succeeded in placing the presidency in the hands of the Chinese Communists.

The brainwashed son, played equally memorably by Laurence Harvey, tries desperately throughout the story to be himself, and not the son his mother has had him brainwashed to be. In the extraordinary climactic scene, still stunning 40 years after it was first shown, with the convention night approaching, his mother tries to quell her son's doubts and make sure he behaves according to her plan. She seduces and bullies, he grows more and more docile, and finally she kisses him tenderly on the mouth, her kiss lingering for more than a few moments. She thus assures herself that she has sealed the deal, and that her son will now do exactly as he is told.

In the following scenes, the Laurence Harvey character, the son, conceals his weapon as he enters the electoral convention, disguised. We, the audience, assume he is fully hypnotized, ready to do his mother's bidding and shoot the presidential candidate dead. If you don't know what happens next, I apologize for spoiling it for you: at the last moment, the son turns the long range weapon away from the candidate, and turns it instead on his mother and father, shooting them dead. Even if he cannot tear them out of his heart and his mind, he can at least wipe them off the face of the earth.

This is the problem for my patient Tom—he reaches a fully alive understanding of his attachment narrative and the relational traumas of his developmental years, he can clearly recognize the narcissism of his parents and the oppressive aspects of their influence: but murder is out of the question. He cannot get there even in Loewald's sense (1979), where parricide is figurative and stands for that which allows the child to become an adult subject. Tom and I made it through the impasses of breakdown, when our working relationship was threatened. At this point, however, we are starting and stopping at the impasses of breakthrough.

Tom

Tom begins a session by mentioning that he picked up a book his wife happened to have around, something about "The Narcissist and You," or something like that. He laughs and says he thinks his wife was interested in it because she was pretty sure his parents were narcissists. I find this somewhat jarring, given that I thought we had been establishing pretty vividly for some time now just how unusually narcissistic his parents could be; and yet I read his laughter as suggesting that he finds it an odd and somewhat fanciful notion. He tells me a bit about what he has been reading, and wonders, is he a narcissist? The self-depreciation he read about sounds right; and he acknowledges some exhibitionist tendencies—but he found the information confusing.

As our session proceeds, we go over some of what we've discussed as we've worked together, about how he grew up feeling that he could never trust his version of his own experience—that in his family, only the mother's version was valid, and if his or anyone else's differed from hers, his mother found him guilty of highly offensive misconduct. His father would be upset with him for upsetting her. The kinds of abuse and the neglect that took place throughout his childhood would be sharply and clearly remembered in one session, seemingly forgotten the next. One of his concerns that we had often spoken of was how painful and difficult it felt for him, married now, with two children and almost 40 years old, to become aware of his own opinion, his own desire, his own feelings. His narrations of events that he had been a part of, past or present, were mostly told from the point of view of the other party—his mother's, wife's, or father's perceptions of what was happening—not his own. I often asked him: "Yes, but what was that like for *you*? What was *your* experience?" I hoped Tom could at least become curious about why he didn't know.

Now I ask, "Tom, I know that sometimes this seems clear, and at other times it seems anything but. Can you see a connection as we're speaking now between your mother's way of invalidating you, your subjectivity, and your present trouble with knowing your desire, your will, your need—with feeling that your point of view is valid at all?"

He is moved, I can see, as he says, "Yes, of course." Then he stammers a bit, and says, "But. . . . But what do I do?"

Tom loves his parents and has been dependent on them in many ways. He feels so guilty about his anger toward them that he almost manages not to feel it. Managing not to feel has become his dysfunctional way of life. How can he experience himself as a subject with agency, knowing what he wants and what he does not want, and feeling what he feels, if throughout his development he was primarily recognized as the object of his parents' projections, expectations, and needs—while as his separate subjective self, he elicited neither their interest nor their enthusiasm?

Tom told me of a particularly poignant fantasy of his, which he often had as a child, and has even still, when he goes to the bathroom. He would lock himself in there, and imagine that he could live there for the rest of his life, completely self-sufficiently, compressing all his possessions to fit in that tiny space, so that he would never have to leave. The paradoxical implications of how the most meager existence possible became so alluring a fantasy are not lost on either of us. Since we have been working together, Tom has been attempting in various ways to assert himself—both with his wife and with his parents, who live nearby and want constantly to be "in his business." However, asserting makes him terribly anxious;

he struggles with guilt, and he isn't quite sure who he is when he is asserting. What he *really* wants, he says, is to concede and to not really care. I empathize with and speak of his anxiety, his sense of only having choices that amount to lesser evils, or of being between a rock and a hard place. I admire the tenacity he demonstrates in his fantasy, even while expressing sadness about what he imagines it would take for him to be at peace, to feel safe. I tell him that I hope he will eventually come to be able to feel more real, more alive, and more like a self—like *him*self, as he defines himself, without having to live alone and locked up in a bathroom; and that I want to do my best to help him get there.

Tom's struggles with his parents and his wife are daunting. It has been too easy for him simply to appease and disappear; and this is what he and I will need to deal with in our relationship. Like many in the same situation, Tom wonders if he should talk to his parents about what he has understood. His impulse is to confront, discuss, and reconcile, to make everything right between them. However, Tom has experienced again and again that trying to make his point with them leads him to a place of unbearable guilt. His father, he says, will look at him like he's cruel and insane for suggesting that something in his father's behavior has been hurtful. In the end, Tom always feels that it is he, not father, who is the hurtful one, and that it is he that needs to make amends.

I will return to Tom and his progress in therapy later in this chapter. At the point where I leave off, we are at the impasses that accompany breakthroughs: will Tom continue to live as dissociatively as possible, or can he find a way to live with a switched on inner life? What will that mean for him, especially in terms of his relationships, with his wife, his children, and his parents?

Tom would like to be able to imagine that ruptures with his parents could be repaired without his having to take on all the responsibility. The traumatizing narcissist, as I have defined in previous chapters, however, is unwilling to acknowledge insufficiency of any kind, unwilling to be accountable or contrite, unwilling to atone, and sees no reason to ask for any kind of forgiveness. If the process of repairing ruptures and surviving destructiveness involves accountability, contrition, atonement, and forgiveness (see Chapter 3), how does the patient who has suffered at the hands of the traumatizing narcissist engage in a repair process with the traumatizers? The traumatizing narcissist has no interest in intersubjectivity—for him, the subjectivity of the other is a threat to his sense of superiority. The other's subjectivity is there to suppress, take over, and control. When Tom and other patients ask "So what do I do?" part of what they are saying is that with no conceivable way of being recognized by the parents, or of rewriting their histories, they can conceive of no way to change themselves. Hopeless, they fear that they will have to remain stuck where they are, ferrying back and forth between both sides of their ambivalence, loving then hating; other-blaming then self-blaming; needing connection then needing aloneness; loving aloneness, then hating aloneness, and often just trying to find a way to be numb. Adult children of traumatizing narcissists may spend much of their lives stuck in two ways: stuck in hating the parent, and stuck in hating the self.

I am sure many analysts, like myself, have worked with patients whose mental and emotional life remained so absorbed in hating their traumatizing parents, and who endlessly agonized over not having been loved, that at some point, their suffering seemed to be a means of remaining frozen in time like a helpless ant trapped in inexorable amber. We may have no doubts about the craziness or the cruelty of the parents, but I think most analysts, after years of witnessing a patient's pain about being unloved, would like to believe that at some point that patient could enter a mourning stage, leading ultimately to a hopeful, aspirational focus on the present and the future, with less rumination on the past. But helping our patients get to this place is rarely easy: it often takes much longer than feels comfortable for both analyst and patient; and it is not always possible.

Certain strategies for trying to move forward that are commonly attempted by relationally traumatized patients often yield temporary relief at best, the most typical among those being forgiving, hating, and indifference.

Forgiving

The adult child of a traumatizing narcissist parent, struggling to find a way of "letting go," or "moving on," often ends up dissociating large chunks of history and sacrificing internal coherence in a misguided effort at manic reparation: misguided in that it often ends in retraumatization, depression, the assumption of all of the responsibility for the badness, and the feeling of failing all over again. Suchet (in press) has written movingly of her concern for a patient, sexually abused by her grandfather and unwitnessed by her family, whose unrelenting hatred limits and suppresses the patient's ability to experience any kind of joy or satisfaction. Suchet wonders if forgiveness could be a way for this patient to free herself from the endless misery of unending victimization. Suchet and her patient make progress in diminishing the patient's self-loathing and self-blame; but forgiving the abuser seems out of the question for this patient, and Suchet worries. In the process, Suchet, a white South African woman now living in the U.S., wonders if wanting her patient to forgive might touch upon her own need to be forgiven—a personal and cultural need of many white South Africans to be forgiven for the horrors of apartheid, which they may not have approved of in any way, but in which they were implicated simply by living in a privileged position there. Suchet observes that true forgiveness has historically been most meaningful in terms of real progress, for example in South Africa between oppressor and oppressed, when it is experienced relationally. If Suchet's patient forgives her grandfather, but does so entirely intrapsychically, is that enough to set her free?

Unfortunately, I observe that forgiveness-in-theory, which is how I see this kind of one-sided forgiving, is usually ephemeral, ending up redounding either to self-blame or dissociation. Forgiveness in these cases is unilateral, not intersubjectively negotiated. As such, can it really be considered true forgiveness? What is often presented as forgiveness toward an abuser seems more like what Grand (2000) has called "retrospective falsification," i.e., a dissociation that minimizes or even disappears the abuse, and selectively attends only to what had seemed positive. When this is the case, the hate and desolation instilled by the abuser is not sufficiently expelled; it continues to be experienced as the bedrock of the self.

Hating

When Roger was ten years old, his father divorced his mother, and then faded out of his life, leaving Roger with a younger brother and an extremely needy, narcissistic mother. After a number of years working together, Roger decided he had taken enough of being infuriated by his helpless, incessantly draining mother, and he wrote her a long letter, stating in very clear and precise prose his numerous complaints, which seemed perfectly valid to both of us. His letter concluded with his assertion that he would no longer have anything to do with her. He was flying high as he showed the letter to me, but I had not been aware that he was writing it nor that he had already sent it. He must have seen the misgivings in my expression, though I was trying not to be obvious about what I was feeling, and he became quite angry with me. "How could you not support me? You know what she's put me through," he demanded. I did know, very well, and yet I could not help but feel that Roger's excitement and sense of freedom would be short-lived, and that his guiltiness and his self-pity would both come roaring back once the high wore off. Additionally, his mother possessed a substantial inheritance from her father's side of the family, where there had once been great wealth, and I was all too well aware of how precariously Roger was able to support himself. I expressed my concerns, but Roger just laughed them off. He knew what he was doing, and he was going to love the freedom he was finally creating for himself.

When Roger's brother contacted him to say that their mother was dying in the hospital, Roger refused to see her. He and his brother fought, and Roger decided to cut off his brother as well. Roger felt so empowered . . . for a little while. Unfortunately, my fears were not unfounded, and Roger's solution proved to be only temporary. His mother died, and while he undeniably had a taste of freedom for a short time, he was soon stuck again, panicked, dissociated, unable to move forward in his work, his relationships, his mood—back to square one. Just as had been the case before his mother's death, each period of confidence and growth he experienced would seem more and more hopeful, and then some setback, a hurt or disappointment that seemed small to me, would become the pivot; Roger would quickly plummet back to hopeless, unbearable despair. Hating his mother could shift his sense of impotence to a hypomanic state of strength and confidence, but only for a while.

This way of returning again and again to self-loathing, especially after any attempt to feel more free and strong, has been described in the trauma literature as belonging to "the self-care system" (Howell, 2005; Kalsched, 1996), which involves a part of the self set up to be the "protector," which ultimately acts like a "persecutor." Roger and I were able at times to identify the protector self, which had been with him since he was very young. It was self-protection and self-care that led him as a child to play quietly by himself in his room; and later to use opportunities when his parents were away on weekends at their country home to stay back in the city apartment, gorging himself on ice cream and cookies, and later, masturbating compulsively. This part of him, luring him to stay safe by keeping to himself, became the persecutor that made him feel that he was disgusting, undesirable, and unlovable.

Not unexpectedly, shortly after Roger's mother died, he learned by a letter sent by an attorney that he was indeed disinherited. His depression deepened. In the end, his hatred was impossible to sustain without his turning it on himself.

Indifference

There are some who are good at convincing themselves that they've been angry long enough, they've cried and grieved long enough, and now they are done and they don't care any more. Perhaps they have become so busy and successful that they really do believe they have moved on. Former U.S. President Clinton was a master compartmentalizer, his mother having taught him to create fantasy worlds for himself, which she was also good at, as the enabling wife of an abusive alcoholic (Jacobs, 1999). Clinton's ability to hold it all together, and be the man that his step-father was not, was belied when he became the target of political enemies, who were able to expose the reckless, out of control part of him—a part that came out mostly at night when his watchers were asleep.

Clinton's manic denial of his developmental trauma served him well as far as supporting his driving ambition. He learned to excel in every way, expertly hiding in his social and academic worlds, and later in professional life, the impact of the squalor and brutality he regularly witnessed in his home as he grew up, where he often had to intervene to protect his mother and brother from the battering of his step-father. It is plausible to suggest, I think, that Clinton took refuge from the depressive, fatherless part of himself by identifying as fully as possible with his own manic aspect, becoming someone who believed he could control his own destiny. However, omnipotence, as we all know and can tend to forget, given the chance, is always a double-edged sword. Hubris, and a very determined intern, led to the exposure of Clinton's self-destructiveness, and with it, the return of the dissociated: by which I mean that the world was then forced to watch Clinton take a humiliating beating in the "news" media day in and day out, month after month. The disavowed traumatic destructiveness of his childhood, the violence, and his deeply conflicted love and hate for his step-father, had to come out somehow, somewhere; the step-son that had dared to defy the father and stop him from beating his mother, became the man who was forced to endure the relentless beatings of his political rivals. Only after the media frenzy about the Lewinsky scandal had died down did Clinton return to, attempt to understand more deeply, and eventually speak publicly of the impact on him of his exposure to alcoholism and domestic violence as a child (Clinton, 2004).

The Sacrifice Solution

> Let all bitterness and wrath and anger and clamor and slander be put away from you, along with all malice. Be kind to one another, tenderhearted, forgiving one another, as God in Christ forgave you.
>
> Ephesians 4:31–32

Before moving on to consider what might be more enduring ways of recovering from narcissistic traumatization, I want to briefly discuss a solution encountered more rarely in the secular clinical setting: the path of devout religious devotion and self-sacrifice. Grand (in press) has written of her work with a man whose solution to living a good life in the aftermath of gross abuse challenges the very notion of the psychoanalytic subject. Her patient, born an unwanted twin among migrant farm worker parents, suffered neglect, cruelty, poverty, and hard labor at the hands of extreme fundamentalist Christian parents who fervently believed that to spare the rod was to spoil the child. Yet somehow he had survived the starvation and the cruelty, become a doctor, and raised a family. Grand soon learns, though, that her patient has determined to deal with his painful history by living a life of extreme sacrifice, offering himself charitably to the point of exhausting himself, with what appears to be suicidal determination. Grand urgently tries to understand, and to persuade him to keep himself alive; yet she recognizes that the commitments her patient makes to the relief of suffering, to social justice, and to the rewards and virtues of extreme self-sacrifice will require her to formulate a new psychoanalytic subject: a transcendent subject for whom suffering and sacrifice—on behalf of the "collectivized abjection" of those whose suffering is unrecognized—are legitimate means to redemption.

As I read Grand, it seems as though she had no choice but to recognize the rightness, for this particular patient, of this answer to the question of "what do I do?" Trying at first to persuade him that his chosen path was self-destructive and masochistic, she eventually recognized that her "diagnosis" was a misrecognition, a negation of who he truly wished to be. For her patient, redemption through sacrifice was a cherished path to a sacred place of rest; and it proved to be, in fact, the means of his premature death.

Whatever one may think of those saints and mystics whose divine love was so intense that they wanted nothing but to shuffle off the mortal coil and join their God sooner rather than later, intense devotion and self-sacrifice have long been deemed a means toward either 1) redemption and salvation (Judaism, Christianity, Islam), or 2) liberation from embodiment, karma, the wheel of birth and death, or reincarnation, etc. (Hinduism, Buddhism). Meeting a patient who has placed herself within the "sacrifice/redemption/liberation-from-embodiment" narrative challenges everything secular psychoanalysts believe about recovery from trauma. The fact is, however, curing the negation of self, by transmuting the negated self to a selfless self, may be a successful path to recovery from trauma for some. It is clear from Grand's account that her encounter with this patient was both deeply inspiring and tragically heart-breaking. Grand's patient was fortunate in that Grand was ultimately able to set aside her disapproval and the impulse to persuade her patient to cease sacrificing; coming instead to accept and honor her patient's right to his choices, and the rightness of his choices for him.[1]

Bearing the Pain

In the absence of the religious solution, and when forgiving, hating, or indifference do not bring relief, then what does? Understanding what it means to *bear* loss and its accompanying pain is potentially the way forward. It was Mitchell (2000b) who first drew my attention to the verb "to bear" in the psychoanalytic context. Mitchell spoke specifically of the sense of pathos for one's own suffering, and the sense of guilt for one's mistakes and wrong-doings, as crucially important for psychological growth. To be able to bear such feelings does not mean either erasing them, or assuming a pose of indifference, on the one hand, nor remaining hatefully, obsessively stuck in them, on the other—whether the hate is directed to the abuser, or directed to the self as guilt and self-loathing. Mitchell identified "guiltiness" and "self-pity" as static, degraded forms of true guilt and true pathos. The guilty self, stuck in guiltiness, is self-punished in perpetuity—demanding and then rejecting sympathy from others; and the self-pitying, victimized self is like a personified reproach with an insatiable need to condemn and punish the other. The sense of genuine pathos and guilt, on the other hand, are emotions that Mitchell viewed as making psychological growth and personal freedom possible. He wrote:

> If genuine self-pity is hard to bear because it entails an acceptance of the limited control we have over our worlds, genuine guilt is hard to bear because it entails an acceptance of the limited control we have over ourselves. We hurt those we love, and the damage of the past, like time itself, is irreversible.
>
> (2000b, p. 731)

In other words, if one's narcissistic illusions are not blinding and rigid, if we are not clinging to illusions of perfection and omnipotence we either imagine ourselves to possess or think we should possess, then we can have the humility to bear the knowledge of the pain we have caused, and the strength to bear the knowledge of the pain we have suffered. Psychological growth involves the tempering of one's narcissism—the fantasies of omnipotent control we can never actually fulfill—toward a balanced, realistic sense of self, such that one can continue living creatively and productively, bearing well enough one's own history, what has been, and bearing well enough life's vicissitudes, what is to come. What is to come ultimately, of course, is mortality. When true pathos is felt, the grievous knowledge of death, one's own and one's loved ones, can be borne. This is the work for the adult child of the traumatizing narcissist: learning to bear the knowledge of life's traumas and life's finitude, while continuing to seek vitality, pleasure, meaning, and connection in the present.

Loosening the Grip of the Narcissist and Finding Intersubjectivity

As it happens, acceptance of limited control is exactly what the traumatizing narcissist cannot come to grips with. Blind to the suffering he has caused others, he claims rights to victim status when his delusion of perfect innocence is challenged. He refuses guilt, but makes sure those around him feel it keenly, especially if they resist submission to him. As for pity, there is none for others; pity is reserved for himself alone. It is particularly hard, then, for the adult child of the traumatizing narcissist to experience genuine self-pity (pathos), *or* genuine guilt. The sense of badness (unworthiness of love) and guilt inculcated by the abuser has left her subjectivity severely weakened. Even for those keenly aware of having been abused, it is very difficult to realize that they suffer in large measure from living as though from the perspective of the abuser, as the abuser's object; and that the abuser's objectification of them is constantly present as a brake to their own subjectivity.

As the object of the traumatizing parent, one's psychic core is all about one's reactions to the traumatizer. Reactions that were entirely appropriate as a child—helplessness, despair, rage—curdle into self-pity, blame, and self-loathing when they persist in adult behavior. The adult child can live with some measure of freedom and peace when she becomes aware of her objectification, and her ongoing self-objectification, and finds the true pathos behind the loss of her own subjectivity. With this kind of self-awareness and self-understanding, she can begin to believe in and trust herself as subject.

One thing this means is that Benjamin's theory of intersubjectivity, in which the infant gradually comes to recognize the mother less as object and more as a separate subject, is in this case turned on its head: trained early in life to experience herself as the object of the narcissist parent, the developmental achievement for the adult child of this parent is to shift out of her objectified position, and into recognition of her own subjectivity—in spite of the lack of such recognition from the narcissist parent.

For these patients, true mourning—the alleviation of the pain of loss, or consolation, and the renewal of the desire to live, creatively and with engagement—cannot proceed to its natural course as long as the adult child remains obsessively stuck in the hatred and/or the self-hatred of being the object/victim. As object, the adult child of the traumatizing narcissist is trapped in repetitive re-enactments of old victimizations; but as subject, the abuser is out there. There is separation. The subject is not hosting the abuser internally at the expense of his own subjectivity.

With the development of this de-objectified subjectivity comes the possibility of intersubjective relatedness—i.e., relating to others without assuming the object position and without the need to objectify the other.

Toward an Answer

How does it become possible to bear what can be a lifetime of hurt and loss that the traumatizing narcissist—parent, sibling, partner, teacher, therapist, guru—has inflicted? What can be done to live a meaningful, creative, fulfilling life, even while bearing such pain? How does the analyst support these goals?

I was moved and amazed to find these questions at the center of the extraordinary Patrick Melrose novels by Edward St. Aubyn: *Never Mind*, *Bad News*, *Some Hope*, *Mother's Milk*, and *At Last* (2011, 2012). These are five short novels, chronologically sequential, that comprise the closely autobiographical but fictionalized account of St. Aubyn's tortured, traumatic life. Most importantly, the novels mark the path he was able to find out of victimization and nihilism, toward a full, meaningful life. I will quote several passages from these novels in which the author's stand-in, Patrick Melrose, works out, in conversation with others and with himself, how he can finally feel that he is able to bear all that he has experienced. By the end of this series, Patrick is not stuck in guiltiness, self-loathing, or self-pity. He is able to see himself and his abusive family of origin clearly, and see it all from a perspective informed not by self-pity, nor by self-negation, but by true pathos.

As a child, at the age of five in the first novel, Patrick is ignored by his masochistic, heavily medicated, alcoholic mother, and is sexually abused for the first of many times by his sadistic father, as was the author himself. His father's sexual abuse continued until, at the age of nine, Patrick firmly refused to comply with his father, who then took sick, blaming Patrick. His father remained a bitter, needy invalid until he died, when Patrick was in his twenties. As a young adult, Patrick—like the author, an exceptionally intelligent young man, of noble birth and ancient aristocratic lineage on his father's side, and of once-great industrial wealth on his mother's side—becomes a full-blown, suicide-bent heroin/cocaine addict for many years. Having kicked narcotics, Patrick marries a very loving woman, who herself experienced a great deal of neglect as a child. She becomes a wonderful mother to their two boys, but Patrick remains restless and lonely. He turns increasingly to alcohol, and eventually he and his wife divorce.

Only fully sober by his late thirties, he is middle aged by the time he comes to terms with the profound neglect and abuse he experienced as a child. Interviewed in *The New York Times* upon the publication of the fifth and reportedly last novel in the series, St. Aubyn (whose story, again, is almost indistinguishable from his fictional protagonist's, Patrick) spoke to the interviewer about his late parents, and I find what he says to be extraordinary. Here is an excerpt from the article:

> By the end of "At Last" there is a resolution of sorts, as Patrick finds a new compassion toward himself and those who wronged him. Mr. St. Aubyn has made his own peace, too, not by forgiving his parents, exactly—"there is something morally condescending about forgiveness," he said—but by being able to see them clearly. "Detachment is what interests me, seeing how people couldn't have been any other way, how they were the product of forces that they had no control over," he said. "I was in the downstream of my father's unhappiness, but it must have been hell to be him."
>
> (Lyall, 2012)

"But it must have been hell to be him" is a sobering, clear-eyed way for St. Aubyn (Patrick in the novels) to speak of his grotesquely sadistic father. How did he find clarity, and however ambiguously, compassion? And what does he mean by detachment?

To speak to the latter question first: his detachment is not indifference, and not "closure," which all too often amounts to a willful suspension of feeling—a forced dissociative numbness. I do not think this is what St. Aubyn means by detachment—he is not talking of the magical production of a *tabula rasa*. Magical closure is what I often suspect when patients tell me about their extraordinary epiphanies at their large group awareness trainings (LGATs, as they are known in the cultic studies community), or their intensive retreats. They describe how they wept, screamed, laughed, sang, and climactically phoned their various friends and relatives and "completed" what was unfinished, and got "clear." A few weeks go by, the euphoria has completely leaked out of the breakthrough balloon, and the patient who opened up their hope and vulnerability to the abuser reports that the abuser has once again cut them to the quick, in the same old way. My analytic work with these patients has revealed, in every case, that unhealed, unresolved, or unconscious stuckness can be as deeply embedded in the graduates of these "breakthrough" seminars as may be found in the seminar-free population.

In St. Aubyn's story of Patrick Melrose, the path to breakthrough and healing from trauma is given its due. It is often a long, slow, winding path, with many slips and false leads along the way. At the point where I will be citing some of the dialogue he speaks, Patrick has reached a stage in which he has gotten freer from loathing and self-loathing, but he knows that he is not yet where he wants to be. Attempting to work out not just how to heal, but why it might be worthwhile to even go on living, he rules out religion right off the bat. He pointedly notes that *The Greatest Story Ever Told* (Oursler, 1949), as the life of Jesus Christ was referred to in the book and the film of that name, leads humans to believe that they too can turn the other cheek in the face of torture. He finds the idea of emulating Christ's perfect forgiveness, and "forgiving" his now deceased father, not only impossible, but unrealistic and even grandiose. We are, after all, only human, we are not gods. As Grand (2000) has said, referring to attempts to grant forgiveness unilaterally to unrepentant perpetrators,

> the implied neutral acceptance of the unrepentant is a solipsistic process . . . Forgiveness/acceptance of the unrepentant is a monologue, in which the monologue of forgiveness mirrors the perpetrator's monologue of torture: it is another collapse of intersubjectivity.
>
> (p. 157)

Forgiving his sadistic, sodomizing late father will not work for Patrick as a way toward freedom—which I define at least in part as emancipation from objectification, with emerging clarity about one's subjectivity, and with the evolving capacity for intersubjective relatedness.

In the third Patrick Melrose novel, *Some Hope*, St. Aubyn begins to explicitly describe Patrick's struggle to free himself from guiltiness and self-pity. At this point, Patrick's father has passed away. His mother, who was conveniently drunk and heavily sedated for the four years, age five to nine, when Patrick was being regularly sodomized by his father, is now doing charity work in Africa for—yes—the Save the Children organization. Patrick, now in his thirties, has kicked his drug habit, as has his best friend, Johnny, and Johnny has become a psychoanalyst. Patrick and Johnny are having dinner before attending a large party where many friends of Patrick's parents will be in attendance. Patrick has decided to tell one person about his childhood sexual abuse, and he knows that Johnny is that person. Feeling that he has wasted too much time in self-pity, hatred, and desire for revenge, and rejecting the idea of forgiveness, Patrick struggles to find what he needs to feel some measure of peace. I quote at some length their conversation, which begins here after Patrick has revealed his abuse. While witty banter is *de rigeur* in Patrick's social circles, the intense seriousness of Patrick's process is really a matter of life and death, and no joke. He says:

> 'neither revenge nor forgiveness change what happened. They're sideshows, of which forgiveness is the less attractive because it represents a collaboration with one's persecutors. I don't suppose that forgiveness was uppermost in the minds of people who were being nailed to a cross until Jesus, if not the first man with a Christ complex still the most successful, wafted onto the scene. Presumably those who enjoyed inflicting cruelty could hardly believe their luck and set about popularizing the superstition that their victims could only achieve peace of mind by forgiving them.'
>
> 'You don't think it might be a profound spiritual truth?' asked Johnny.
>
> Patrick puffed out his cheeks. 'I suppose it might be, but as far as I'm concerned, what is meant to show the spiritual advantages of forgiveness in fact shows the psychological advantages of thinking you're the son of God.'
>
> 'So how do you get free?' asked Johnny.
>
> 'Search me,' said Patrick. 'Obviously, or I wouldn't have told you, I think it has something to do with telling the truth. I'm only at the beginning, but presumably there comes a point when you grow bored of telling it, and that point coincides with your "freedom".'
>
> 'So rather than forgive you're going to try and talk it out.'
>
> 'Yes, narrative fatigue is what I'm going for. If the talk cure is our modern religion then narrative fatigue must be its apotheosis,' said Patrick suavely.
>
> 'But the truth includes an understanding of your father.'
>
> 'I couldn't understand my father better and I still don't like what he did.'
>
> 'Of course you don't. Perhaps there is nothing to say except, "What a bastard." I was only groping for an alternative because you said you were exhausted by hatred.'
>
> 'I am, but at the moment I can't imagine any kind of liberation except eventual indifference.'

> 'Or detachment,' said Johnny. 'I don't suppose you'll ever be indifferent.'
>
> 'Yes, detachment,' said Patrick, who didn't mind having his vocabulary corrected on this occasion. 'Indifference just sounded cooler.' The two men drank their coffee.
>
> (St. Aubyn, 2012, pp. 374, 375)

Patrick establishes here that his goal is freedom, liberation; and that so far, he sees telling the truth, and being able to detach, as the likeliest means to his goal. Forgiving, however, is out of the question.

Later in the evening, Patrick is speaking with Anne, an old friend of his mother's. Anne is the only contemporary of his parents that Patrick remembers as having shown him any kindness as a child. She has asked him how he is feeling about his father. He is thinking now about how his detachment, if he is going to be free, might need to go hand in hand with some form of compassion, or "mercy." He says to Anne:

> 'Well,' said Patrick, 'over dinner I was rather against forgiveness, and I still think that it's detachment rather than appeasement that will set me free, but if I could imagine a mercy that was purely human, and not one that rested on the *Greatest Story Ever Told*, I might extend it to my father for being so unhappy. I just can't do it out of piety. I've had enough near-death experiences to last me a lifetime, and not once was I greeted by a white-robed figure at the end of a tunnel—or only once and he turned out to be an exhausted junior doctor in the emergency ward of the Charing Cross Hospital. There may be something to this idea that you have to be broken in order to be renewed, but renewal doesn't have to consist of a lot of phoney reconciliations!'
>
> 'What about some genuine ones?' said Anne.
>
> 'What impresses me more than the repulsive superstition that I should turn the other cheek, is the intense unhappiness my father lived with. I ran across a diary his mother wrote during the First World War. After pages of gossip and a long passage about how marvellously they'd managed to keep up the standards at some large country house, defying the Kaiser with the perfection of their cucumber sandwiches, there are two short sentences: "Geoffrey wounded again", about her husband in the trenches, and "David has rickets", about her son at his prep school. Presumably he was not just suffering from malnutrition, but being assaulted by paedophiliac schoolmasters and beaten by older boys. This very traditional combination of maternal coldness and official perversion helped to make him the splendid man he turned into but, to forgive someone, one would have to be convinced that they'd made some effort to change the disastrous course that genetics, class, or upbringing proposed for them.'
>
> 'If he'd changed the course he wouldn't need forgiving,' said Anne. 'That's the whole deal with forgiving. Anyhow, I don't say you're wrong not to forgive him, but you can't stay stuck with this hatred.'

> 'There's no point in staying stuck,' Patrick agreed. 'But there's even less point in pretending to be free. I feel on the verge of a great transformation, which may be as simple as becoming interested in other things . . . As to my "father-bashing", . . . I thought of him this evening without thinking about his influence on me, just as a tired old man who'd fucked up his life, wheezing away his last years in that faded blue shirt he wore in the summer. I pictured him sitting in the courtyard of that horrible house, doing *The Times*' crossword, and he struck me as more pathetic and more ordinary, and in the end less worthy of attention.'
>
> (St. Aubyn, 2012, pp. 428–430)

Patrick is here in the process of identifying multiple self states that engage diverse affects connected to different ways of being with his father and of seeing his father—including seeing his father as a traumatized child victim of neglect and cruelty. Patrick is also beginning to envision himself as a person in his own right, whose emotional life does not constantly revolve around his various traumatic affect states. "I feel on the verge of a great transformation," he says, "which may be as simple as becoming interested in other things." As his subjectivity emerges and his objectification recedes, he can imagine his interest (desire, vitality) expanding and growing beyond the limits of his trauma. As the idea of living his own life becomes more desirable, he wants to find a way to be less involved, less obsessed with his trauma. He thinks of this potential state as detachment but not indifference.

I believe that what St. Aubyn means by detachment here is very much like what I mean by the shift in the sense of self-as-object to a firmer, more clear sense of self-as-subject. Releasing one's self from the hegemony of the traumatizing narcissist's subjectivity; rejecting objectification; searching for and growing one's subjectivity—these are ways that one detaches from the objectifying, traumatizing narcissist. Analyst and patient together must now try to envision how the patient can experience agency and desire in the process of self-redefinition, how she can come into being as a subject, able to experience ownership of a subjective point of view that is not unconsciously shaped by the traumatizer.

This does not happen only by co-constructing narratives that generate insight: insight without affect will not be enough to bring about lasting change. It is up to the analyst to recognize when a patient has taught himself not to feel, while looking like he is feeling; if this goes undetected, insight will not penetrate to the depths. Then, even when insight is linked to deep levels of affect, it will take many more experiences of forgetting, or not seeing, and then remembering and seeing, before the shift, the detachment from objectification and the emergence of subjectivity, will consolidate sufficiently to be the new baseline. When I think of the patients I have known who have successfully made this shift, an affectively alive shift from object to subject, I believe it was by means of a bootstrapping process, a process I encouraged, yes, but a process they themselves chose and pursued, because they came to believe they had a right to their own emancipation and they were not willing to give up.

Emancipation

What is meant in the psychoanalytic context by the word emancipation? It is not a word we encounter very frequently in the psychoanalytic literature, but it is a familiar and central term in critical theory:

> "Critical Theory" in the narrow sense designates several generations of German philosophers and social theorists in the Western European Marxist tradition known as the Frankfurt School. According to these theorists, a "critical" theory may be distinguished from a "traditional" theory according to a specific practical purpose: a theory is critical to the extent that it seeks human emancipation, "to liberate human beings from the circumstances that enslave them" (Horkheimer 1982, p. 244).
>
> (Bohman, 2005)

Among psychoanalysts, it was Erich Fromm (1961), a member of the original Frankfurt School, who put the most emphasis on emancipation, in line with his understanding of Marx's concept of alienation. For Fromm, man is alienated from himself and from others because he lives in submission to his idols—which may be a godlike figure, the state, the church, a person, possessions. "Idolatry," says Fromm, "is always the worship of something into which man has put his own creative powers, and to which he now submits, instead of experiencing himself in his creative act" (1961, Chapter 5).

For the child of a traumatizing narcissist parent, it is the parent who is the idol, applying Fromm's language. The traumatizing narcissist parent, cloaked in the righteousness of delusional perfection, which I call the "complementary moral defense" (see Chapter 2), presents himself as an idol for the child to worship—or else. The child's attempt at a creative act is the giving of love to the parent. Suttie (1935/1999) put it memorably: "The mother gives the breast, certainly, but the infant gives the mouth, which is equally necessary to the transaction of sucking" (p. 38). However, the traumatizing narcissist wants only what she gives to have value, and will not recognize value in what the child gives. As Fairbairn (1952) noted, "frustration of [the child's] desire to be loved as a person *and to have his love accepted* is the greatest trauma that a child can experience" (pp. 39–40, italics mine). The child traumatized in this way now strives to be the right kind of object for the narcissist, because his separate subjectivity has been deemed of no value. The idol parent is the only one who has something of value to give, and the adult child can either kneel at the throne, or be banished, disinherited.

One reason I find St. Aubyn's novels so powerful is that I have worked with several people much like Patrick Melrose over the years, and I have come to know quite well the particular ways their suffering takes form. Alan is one such patient.

Alan

Alan's many years of work entailed remembering countless abuses at the hands of his mother. He reported a dream in our eighth year of treatment that captured this theme evocatively:

> I was in a dimly lit cave, but in the distance, through what seemed like layers and layers of gauzy sheets, like a loosely built tent, I could see a glow. I began to walk toward it, and I realized it was my mother—the glow was coming from within her, and it was getting more and more bright and beautiful. I just wanted to get there, to lift off every layer until I could find her, and be embraced by her. It was like I was in an ecstasy of hope and longing. And then as I was about to enter her presence, I came back to myself, I remembered who she really was, and I turned around and ran. I was sobbing, devastated.

I have heard this type of dream, of the abuser parent appearing as a magical iconic god/goddess, seemingly offering the promise of a sublime reconciliation, from a number of patients. The dream never comes true, because the traumatizing narcissist and her child cannot both be good at the same time. The narcissist's adoption of the complementary moral defense means that the child can only be defined as bad. As Alan and I discussed his dream, I told him that I thought his longing and wish to love and connect was the part of him that believed he had good love to give—and that it was still a part of him, or he wouldn't have dreamt about it. I said I believed that his mother not recognizing the value of his love was entirely her shortcoming, not his. We returned to this theme many times before Alan felt fully able to value the love he had to give. In terms Fromm might use, Alan was emancipated when he ceased to worship his mother as an idol. In my language, Alan ceased to objectify himself or allow himself to be objectified, feeling instead entitled to be loved as himself, according to his own self-definition. He did not have to give himself up and make himself the perfect object for the other's use.

With the women he dated, Alan had always subtly and automatically positioned himself to be for them what they seemed to need of him. In spite of Alan's status as a highly desirable bachelor, with outstanding looks, intelligence, humor, athleticism, and business success, relationships that got off the ground at all could only last a year or two at most. Alan soon came to feel used and trapped, staying only because he didn't want to hurt the other, but actually strongly resenting her. (We had already enacted this scenario between ourselves as analyst and patient.) It took Alan a number of years before he could actually take the risk to feel his own desire for the other, and pursue a woman because he truly wanted her. He took up the task, with determination, of trying to connect to his own inner world, but for a long time he felt terribly self-conscious about trying to stay connected to his own subjectivity. Sometimes he would have to stop himself in mid-sentence, noticing himself slipping into object mode (focused on trying to read the subjectivity of the other and mold himself to her needs); he would stop, breathe, and try to figure out what he was feeling. He felt like an idiot, he said, laughing ruefully. Alan was eventually able to make knowing what he was feeling a more natural, less forced way of being.

Though Fromm was the analyst who made the concept of emancipation most central in his thinking, Loewald (1979) also spoke of it, from the childhood idealization of and compliance with parents, as the natural goal of healthy development toward, as he put it, "the assumption of responsibility for one's own life and its conduct" (p. 757).[2] Brandchaft et al. (2010) also view psychoanalysis as emancipatory. By focusing on how certain patients—who have learned to "pathologically accommodate" to non-recognizing caregivers—continue to subtly accommodate to the analyst, Brandchaft et al. seek to emancipate the analytic couple: the analyst from his doctrinal commitments that support presumptive knowledge rather than direct experience, and the patient from his accommodating tendencies that have obscured his authentic self experience.

What I mean by emancipation as a goal of psychoanalytic work, especially with patients whose development of their subjectivity has been co-opted by narcissist parents, is illustrated in the process that St. Aubyn shares with the reader as he traces Patrick's journey: the healing process of identifying and understanding toxic, enslaving, externally imposed self-perceptions; developing and consolidating conviction about the significance and validity of one's own subjective experience and perspective; and becoming aware of and reflective about the interplay of the two perspectives—how and when and why we experience ourselves as we were historically defined by parents, and how we choose to define ourselves as subjects in our own right.

Finally, emancipation as I am conceptualizing it would lead to a more or less stable detachment from toxic internal objects, and, if still present, from living traumatizers. This kind of emancipation would involve detachment, self-deobjectification, and self-subjectification, as well as understanding, and some measure of compassion for all the parts of the self, for the harm one has done, the harm one has suffered, and even for those who have inflicted harm.

Of course there can be no absolute distinctions made about how free we are of unconscious identifications. A person with absolutely no residue of parental projections, identifications, accommodations, shared DNA, and so on, does not exist in nature. With trauma, the sense of time is so often warped (Reis, 1995), and what was in the past is chronically experienced both as present and future. Emancipation would mean that past and present both exist, distinguished from one another, and the future can be imagined without the dreadful anticipation, conscious or unconscious, of retraumatization (Ornstein, 1974).

The sense of what I want to say here has been expressed memorably by Bromberg (1993):

> Health is the ability to stand in the spaces between realities without losing any of them. This is what I believe self-acceptance means and what creativity is really all about—the capacity to feel like one self while being many.
>
> (p. 166)

I think this way of understanding self-acceptance has especially poignant meaning for those whose trauma has led to extreme dissociation. To be able to recognize and accept the various self states generated by cumulative trauma, with true pathos rather than shame and repudiation, is an extraordinary feat. It may not happen completely, and certainly not all at once. For Tom, whom I spoke of earlier, it remains a work in progress.

Back to Tom

The session with Tom I present here took place in our third year together. Tom, who works at a demanding and important job in his father's company, was about to embark on an important business trip, and we had been working in prior sessions on why he found himself feeling so overburdened and intimidated, when he might instead be excited and proud to have been given such an important assignment. Tom had been at an emotional standoff about his job for a long time, highly ambivalent, even while being quite successful. In our conversations leading up to the session I present here, Tom had come to acknowledge more clearly than ever before that he found his work gratifying, and that he saw for himself a realistic and desirable possibility of continuing to advance with great success.

In our meeting before he leaves for his trip overseas, Tom speaks of his efforts to better manage his habitual feelings of being overwhelmed and stressed.

Tom: I'm trying to focus on getting ready for the trip to Asia; Angie and I had a good talk in couples therapy, we are really going to try to stay in communication. Angie has a lot of work [in her own business she runs from home] on top of dealing with the kids—and we're trying to focus on communicating. I'm trying to create boundaries at work, and get more help. My body doesn't respond well to stress, I start somatizing—exhaustion, foggy dazy feeling, heart palpitations, a little bit of anxiety, I'll just be out of it. It's like my mind wants to check out, so my body feels everything. It's hard to keep up, and I'm trying. It's been better the last few days, and I'm trying to get more help. It's positive stuff, the responsibilities I have are because I've been something of a leader at work, I've pioneered some things, and I'm proud of that. So I've done stuff to be awarded this opportunity. We spoke about it here last week, it's sort of a take charge moment. So I'm trying to approach it like that, because I really do want to take it seriously, and perform well. I do want it, I may be a little bit scared of it, but I do want it.

DS: Scared? How? (I want to help Tom be more specific, more connected, to what he says he fears. He habitually uses minimizing qualifiers: "a little," "sort of," "maybe," etc.; and not "I am," but "I think I am.")

Tom: Well, will I be pigeonholing myself in a certain spot?—I'll define myself as that, and is that me? I feel worried about that.

DS: It's not you compared to what? If you're pigeonholed as not you, who *is* you?

Tom: A good question. I don't know. I think the lack of knowledge about that is frustrating.

DS: Maybe it's just being pigeonholed, period, is the fear? Limited, controlled, not having freedom? (I am thinking of how overbearing and insistent his father is with him, but he's getting at something else.)

Tom: Yah, I think so. There's a little bit of ego in there, I thought . . . I don't know.

DS: You thought what?

Tom: I thought a path would shine its light for me, to be more creative, artistic, more celebrated. Stuck in ego I think.

DS: Ego? . . . Or dreams; fantasies; aspirations. . . . Longings? For what? (I know of these interests of his, some of which he has pursued with pleasure at times. I am taken aback to hear him denigrating these interests as part of what he thinks is his egotism.)

Tom: I don't know, for what?

DS: Longings for what? Dreams of what? Longings and dreams are inspiring, exciting words. The way you are using ego, you make it a mean word; as in "stupid dumb ego." But what if it's not stupid?

Tom: I don't think it's stupid. The part of me that wants to have a more creative outlet, I don't think that's stupid. But there is a part of me that wants acknowledgment, and to be viewed, maybe in an exhibitionist way, it might link up with that part of my personality.

DS: Do you imagine that most people don't want acknowledgment and to be recognized for their achievements?

Tom: I think most people do—everybody wants that, sure. Ok.

DS: But for some reason, that ends up smelling like "ego" for you?

Tom: I don't know. The discomfort and frustration and fear is from unknowing—is this really what I'm doing? Yeah, I could have a dream, that I'm an actor, or a pro baseball player; but in fact I always thought growing up that I would end up in the family business. The fact that it turned out just that way, I feel a little weird about that.

DS: You recall thinking you'd be in the business . . . was that your desire? (This is news to me.)

Tom: I don't know what it was, it seemed like . . . I don't know . . . there were times when I thought of it in a romantic way, like how generations of families transfer ownership—kind of grandiose, I guess.

DS: What's grandiose about that? (My tone, I think, is not oppositional—rather, I really want to know how Tom finds these fantasies grandiose.)

Tom: I don't know. The point I'm trying to make is that at a young age I romanticized it somehow, instead of really trying to think, is it what I want? I don't know if I really thought about it. I guess part of me feels a little ashamed that it worked out that way, that I didn't figure out something on my own. I don't know, do I need to feel guilty or negative about that?

DS: That's what I'm wondering. You're talking about dreams, aspirations, desires, ways that you would enjoy being seen, recognized, appreciated—ways you could feel proud of something that's in your family—and you put it all in the shame pile. Why does it have to go there?

Tom: It was handed to me on a silver platter . . . I hate that people think that, which they do, and it's not the case. In fact, it's motivated me to try to be a trailblazer at work . . . I'm trying to let myself be proud of that . . . I don't need to feel ashamed. *There's just a big push pull.*

DS: Yes, and it is so good that you are really in touch with that, trying to make sense of it.

Tom: You know my relationship with my father. I respect him highly. But he's so intrusive in his views. We had a political conversation on the way home, he's difficult because he's ultra left wing, he hates Republicans—it bothers me, the way he gets caught up in it, and it makes me want to be oppositional, in a ridiculous fashion. He rattles me, and I react against him, and then I don't even know, would I actually vote for Romney? I'm not a Republican, I'm an Independent. We're having this huge argument, and afterwards, I'm thinking, do I even believe what I'm saying, or am I just fighting him?

DS: What are you fighting for? It's important to understand what you are fighting for.

Tom: Just to be left alone, and to be able to make a comment without being slammed with 15 additional comments, that's all. Just a little bit of peace and quiet with a thought that I have, that's all I'm looking for, and I can't get it with him. And it blends into the work environment. Do I want to be here, do I not? It's very confusing.

DS: Maybe you could actually figure that out. If you put your mind to it. Your father is so certain and so all over it and all over you that it doesn't give you a chance to sort out your own real feelings and thoughts.

Tom: No, I have to react quickly and take a stand, or the other way is to just not say anything and just agree. The other path is unfounded reaction, I'm dancing trying to find my place. He's very intelligent, so sure of himself. It takes so much effort. Sometimes I just don't want to do it!

DS: Have you ever told him that?

Tom: Not really. The way I end conversations is I just stop talking.

DS: What makes it feel like you can't tell him?

Tom: That's Mt. Everest—being able to draw clear boundaries . . . It gets so uncomfortable.

DS: Uncomfortable in what way?

Tom: I just fumble around, seeing his reaction. He has this face, like he's hurt and astonished, like "You're persecuting me? Me?? Unselfish, generous, loving *Me?*" You can see it on his face—it's very disconcerting. I automatically go to a guilty place, and fumble around.

DS: He's saying you have no validity—and you buy into it. He's saying your point has no validity, and you are deeply wounding him to boot, and you're buying that.

Tom: I'm buying it big time. It's ancient. Ancient way for me to feel, I remember since I can remember. His disbelief in what I would say or do, his disappointment—sort of subtle, but I'm always taken aback.

DS: Doesn't sound sort of subtle to me, at all. He's figured out how to stop you in your tracks—how to get you not to be able to make your point—I'm not saying that's his conscious motivation. But it's there, and it's very effective—like the Wizard of Oz's huge booming voice and all the smoke and mirrors, it's effective.

Tom: I keep coming back to the political thing, he's so impassioned about it, so I create this alternate persona that agrees with Mitt Romney! I make up this persona, just to be the opposite of my father. He gets so pissed, and then he starts saying if Romney gets elected, he will move himself and all his money to Canada. He makes it clear that it will affect me, disagreeing with him. It's so crazy. It makes me want to vote for Romney more. And then I was laughing on the way home to myself. Fuck it, I'll just vote libertarian, that'll be a vote of none of the above.

DS: So he's succeeded in controlling you by forcing you into being this oppositional . . . (I manage to restrain myself from telling him for whom to vote.)

Tom: I know, he's controlling who I'm going to vote for! I don't even know where I begin or start or stop. It was all just to get his goat and try to level the playing field with him.

DS: Tom, this is serious, this is at the core. He has the effect of confusing you so you can't figure out who you are, and you have to grasp at something, anything, to keep you from feeling like you're disappearing.

Tom: Yeah, that is completely, completely it.

DS: I think he's convinced you that you should stop short—that you cannot be there as your whole self. I don't think you know what happens when you stay there with him as you. What happens when you do that? He's managed never to let you get that far.

Tom: (after a pause) That's really interesting.

DS: What does it bring up for you?

Tom: It clarifies that situation for me, and what I want out of it when I'm in it. It's a little bit . . . It's sad, he's comfortable in his own skin with me; but he's not so comfortable if I'm divergent from him, in almost any way. He certainly has difficulty if I'm in opposition to him, he can't deal with it.

DS: Right, but this is your secret weapon, it's your way of claiming some kind of victory. You didn't disappear! You may become somebody you might not even be, but at least your outlines are distinct.

Tom: Yeah, it's weird, I can see the positive in that. I do that so often, for example with the people at work. Like I was born like the guy from Silver Spoons—a couple of girls like to tease me that I'm always on vacation—and it's so preposterous to me, that I end up validating what they say by saying ridiculous things, and play this arrogant persona and ten times more. I keep them off guard. I don't think it's good for me, particularly.

DS: Well, when and where is the coast clear? When can you can be entirely you?

Tom: Shit, when I'm home alone? I don't know.

DS: This is like the marriage, I think—maybe there are ways your wife is like your father, and she doesn't want you to deviate . . .

Tom: Honestly, at home I do try to be me, or I'll get caught trying to be me, sort of—and I'm not sure Angie likes it so much, or that she likes that me. In her mind, that person does not pay a lot of attention to her.

DS: That's the problem—there's only room for one "me" at a time. Your father has to be the only one in the space—if you're there, you have to be his clone, his object, and if not those things, then his opponent. But you—the whole you—can't be there. That model of being with somebody was imposed and impressed so deeply . . . but that's not how it's supposed to be. We should both be able to be here. Wouldn't that be better?

Tom: It sounds glorious. Utopian!

DS: Yeah, in your family culture, it's utopian, but in life, it might not be so rare as you think.

Tom: That might be really important for my marriage . . .

DS: Yeah, you might have a chance with Angie; with your dad, maybe you might just have to learn how to better manage him—and yourself with him.

We are at the end of the session. I can see and hear and feel how much Tom is changing from when we first began our work. We have reached some important understandings. Tom knows he plays different roles, working out how to appease others, ending up hidden, alone, and hopeless about being able to be in relationships. He is frightened at the moment, ostensibly about an important overseas business trip; but the fear is deeper, and about something much more crucial: Can he bring himself out to others as subject? Can he trust himself as subject? Repelled by the domineering grandiosity of his father, he cannot mobilize his own subjectivity without attacking himself with charges of egotism, and then feeling guilt, self-doubt. If he is not the other's gratifier or the other's victim, and if he is not invisible, and not an egomaniac, can he be anything? Anyone?

As our work continues, I try to help him begin to imagine a place beyond what is between the invisible-victim rock and the ridiculous-grandiose hard place; a place where it is possible to take pride and pleasure in his successes, his trailblazing, his stewardship of the family company; a place also where he can be with his wife not as victim or victimizer, but as himself, giving love and taking love. I hope that if he and I can co-construct sustainable experiences of intersubjective relatedness in the analytic relationship, then he can find the desire and the agency to do that in the rest of his life. It's a tender beginning, but we can both see that potential as real now, and we have reached a turning point, where it isn't just me that wants that for him—that desire has become very real and alive for Tom as well.

And Then What?

For Tom, and in general for adult children struggling with the search for a self of one's own, recognizing how one has been subjugated and objectified in the traumatizing narcissist's relational system is a beginning on the way toward emancipation. The clinical work from this point involves supporting the patient to diminish the dissociation that leads to repetition of the system. This means tracking, with the patient, in his reported experiences and especially in the analytic dyad, how dissociation creeps in, especially after a breakthrough—as minimization, lack of clarity, amnesia for insights as though they never happened, self-denigration, and so on. Dissociation creeps in as well when these patients automatically assume a subjugated position in a relationship and don't even know they are doing it. We, as the analysts, must seek to free ourselves from dissociation with our dissociative patients, and help them learn to become experts in detecting their own dissociative tendencies.

This is the working through. Speaking strictly clinically, this means working to reduce dissociation and moving toward the experience of standing in the spaces, toward being able to know and accept the whole self, toward lessening the grip of shameful not-me self states, toward calming and taking charge of the internal "self-care system" (Howell, 2005) that says "don't even try, you'll only fail." The patient feels stronger because he is less divided; he has become skilled at recognizing objectification and self-objectification; at strengthening subjectivity, and expanding intersubjective relatedness.

The "Grandiose Fantasy"

With most of the patients with this kind of developmental trauma that I have worked with, we eventually reach a point in which the patient spontaneously recalls a particular fantasy—Kohut (1966, 1968) called it the "grandiose fantasy." For example, in the session with Tom referred to previously, he spoke of his romantic view of stewardship of the family company, and his dreams of baseball and theatrical fame. Tom had labeled these longings grandiose, and was ashamed of himself for dreaming. The hidden longings and the potentials that fed the longings were barely allowed expression; when he put everything into being a trailblazer at work, it was extremely difficult not to negate himself. Instead of taking pleasure and pride, he took the taunts of his co-workers, who claimed his status at the company was due only to nepotism.

Another patient, Alan, whose mother was extremely overbearing, attention-seeking, and seductively fascinating, had this fantasy, which he both spoke of and experienced in session. He would begin to experience a kind of derealization, and would feel himself expanding, like a balloon, to fill up the entire space of the room he was in. These fantasies occurred often, throughout his childhood, at times when he was alone. They seemed readily understandable to us. On the one hand, he became so big that he became everything, and there would be no room for mother to take up all the space. On the other hand, the fantasy could feel dangerously out of control, and it always ended with deflation. Mother had taken over Alan's self-esteem regulation, and he grew to have little or no control over the levels of inflation and deflation he typically experienced.

The discovery of this kind of grandiose fantasy for the adult child of the traumatizing narcissist is an important moment in the therapeutic process. The fantasy expresses both the pain of unrecognition, and a magical escape from that pain. Kohut observed that when there was developmental trauma (not his words, but certainly the same meaning) to the child's self-esteem and secure attachment, the "grandiose fantasy" would have to be "repressed," and therefore could not contribute to the formation of a healthy sense of self (1966, p. 253). I would say in more contemporary language that this fantasy becomes a shameful secret, a source of some hope and joy up to a point—and then a focal point for hopelessness and disappointment. It can be understood as an expression of the "protector/ persecutor" part of the self—an escape fantasy, that ends with the rude awakening of feeling permanently trapped.

Encountering the grandiose fantasy with these patients can happen at any point in the course of a treatment. In the "getting closer" stages, however, where much has been understood and is being worked through, the grandiose fantasy takes on greater poignancy. The hopefulness, the possibility of freedom expressed in these fantasies, is potentially on the table again. Instead of the fantasy feeling humiliating, parts of it can be recovered and reconstructed. The analyst can offer the patient encouragement and validation simply by reflecting back the creativity and hope the fantasy contains. If that fantasy had stood a chance—if a narcissistic caregiver hadn't failed to provide the necessary nurture—it would have evolved with less grandiosity and more maturity; the fantasy could have been integrated as an active, conscious part of the self. In Alan's case, he could enjoy himself more—his ability to "work a room," and be the life of the party—without then plummeting back to shame and isolation.

These grandiose fantasy moments I have experienced with patients have often marked a turning point in the treatment—a way toward an ending. The fantasy stops being shameful; some of the potentials that were abandoned because they seemed ridiculously grandiose can be salvaged and put to constructive, creative use. It becomes possible for the patient to take pride and pleasure in what she has achieved, and to feel renewed enthusiasm for what lies ahead. As these patients end therapy, they usually feel some wariness, trying to hold on to faith in themselves, hoping they can keep growing without slipping backward too much, for too long. They expect ups and downs, but better handled ones. The coalescing of their inner world is usually accompanied by outer changes—changing jobs, deciding to have children or to adopt, deciding to divorce, moving to a new home or city. Often, I hear from them years later, sometimes with pictures of the partner they had found at last, or the babies, publications, awards, shows. We take joy and pride in their accomplishments, together.

Conclusion

I end this chapter with the words of Edward St. Aubyn, speaking in the voice of Patrick Melrose, writing of his experience of healing in the last pages of the

Patrick Melrose novels. Patrick grew up rich with beautiful parents who were both narcissistic in the extreme; he lived in a hell of self-destructiveness for much of his youth and twenties; he recovered from addiction; he survived his divorce and sought to atone for his destructiveness toward others. He broke through his shame and spoke to others of his abuse. He sought to make sense of it all and to free himself of dissociation and self-destructiveness. At last, alone after getting through his mother's funeral, as the books he has narrated come to an end, he experiences the deepest healing. Feeling something huge welling up inside of him,

> he opened himself up to the feeling of utter helplessness and incoherence that he supposed he had spent his life trying to avoid, and waited for it to dismember him. What happened was not what he had expected. Instead of feeling the helplessness, he felt the helplessness and compassion for the helplessness at the same time. One followed the other swiftly, just as a hand reaches out instinctively to rub a hit shin, or relieve an aching shoulder. He was after all not an infant, but a man experiencing the chaos of infancy welling up in his conscious mind. As the compassion expanded he saw himself on equal terms with his supposed persecutors, saw his parents, who appeared to be the cause of his suffering, as unhappy children with parents who appeared to be the cause of their suffering: there was no one to blame and everyone to help, and those who appeared to deserve the most blame needed the most help. For a while he stayed level with the pure inevitability of things being as they were, the ground zero of events on which skyscrapers of psychological experience were built, and as he imagined not taking his life so personally, the heavy impenetrable darkness of the inarticulacy turned into a silence that was perfectly transparent, and he saw that there was a margin of freedom, a suspension of reaction, in that clarity. Patrick slid back down in his chair and sprawled in front of the view. He noticed how his tears cooled as they ran down his cheeks. Washed eyes and a tired and empty feeling. Was that what people meant by peaceful? There must be more to it than that, but he didn't claim to be an expert. He suddenly wanted to see his children, real children, not the ghosts of their ancestors' childhoods, real children with a reasonable chance of enjoying their lives . . .
>
> (St. Aubyn, 2011, Kindle pp. 2633–2634)

Patrick Melrose spent his first 40 years or so living in reaction to the abuse, neglect, betrayal, and exploitation he suffered at the hands of his parents. By the end of the story, as he narrates in the passage above, he is no longer enslaved to the ghosts of his ancestors' childhoods, and he is determined that neither will his children be. He knows his love matters to his children and he wants to give it; just as he wants to accept and cherish the love they have for him. He hopes that his children can have a reasonable chance to enjoy their lives; the reader can infer that Patrick too may have that chance. His emotional life, his heart, has burst open; he is alive. Letting the pain he had run from for so long come fully out of him, he discovered that his pain was not unbearable, because along with it came compassion, and consolation.

There are many patients I have known whose lives were blighted by their exposure to traumatizing narcissist parents, siblings, spouses or ex-spouses, gurus, and so on. More than any other complaint they presented, what they had in common was that they were not enjoying their lives, and didn't see how they could. Learning to bear the pain of the past caused by the traumatizing narcissist is one of the therapeutic goals we can help our patients reach. Helping our patients differentiate a subjective self from the self as the object of the other is another. We can help the patient develop an internal dialogue between his "protector/persecutor" self and the self that wants to live, with creativity and freedom; then the protector self can cease to be afraid of being alive, and of loving and being loved. He can relax his vigilance and feel confident that the creative self will be okay. Most importantly, we can encourage the patient to feel fully, without holding back; and we can be with them with our hearts open. If we can support the patient in growing into this way of living, we can be confident that the patient has more than a reasonable chance of enjoying his life.

Notes

1 As noted in Chapter 3 and elsewhere throughout this book, religious or spiritual fervor may also serve as a vehicle and a cloak for the delusional omnipotence and self-righteousness associated with the traumatizing narcissist. Any role involving being a helper or a healer, a motivator and inspirer, can attract the traumatizing narcissist.

2 See Hewitt (2012) for a very interesting review of concepts in Loewald's work that intersect with the Critical Theory of the Frankfurt School.

Chapter 7

On the Therapeutic Action of Analytic Love[1]

If our patients who are adult children of traumatizing narcissists have struggled to the point of exhaustion with the pain of lovelessness, is there something that we as their analysts provide that addresses this? Is it love? These were the questions I began to ask myself when I first worked with Ari.

Ari was a patient who was not easy to love, at least not at first, and not for me.

Ari was 40 when he began to see me. His marriage was falling apart, and had been miserable for years. He felt close to becoming violent with his wife. He was burned out, always angry and always anxious, at home and at work. His daily marijuana smoking for 20 years, along with cigarettes, was literally making him feel sick.

Ari is physically imposing, athletic, muscled like a bull, with a military and soccer background. He wears an expensive watch, a diamond earring, and a leather jacket. He shaves his head close and rides a motorcycle, around town and across country. When I first met him, he spoke in a gruff voice, volubly, bitterly, loudly, and without pause for me, even if I did attempt to get a word in edgewise, which I often didn't. He was marvelously articulate about how enraged he felt about everyone and everything in his life. I noticed how often I felt anxious about what I was thinking of saying to him, and realized I feared he would explode with rage and possibly assault me if I said something he didn't like.

Ari spent most of a year splenetically venting, about his wife, his son, his partners, his employees, etc. Feeling shut out, I often found myself shuttling between resentment, detachment, and feeling intimidated. Eventually, I understood that I was withdrawing, withholding a necessary confrontation, in retaliation for the narcissistic injury I felt about my perceived lack of impact on him. This understanding helped me to reorganize and mobilize the assertiveness I needed in order to reach Ari. One day, I finally raised my voice and said, quite loudly, "You know, I would like to say some things to you, but I'm afraid if you don't like what you hear, you will bite my head off, possibly literally."

Ari looked up at me with his sharp, penetrating eyes, and I was scared. I was quite surprised and touched, though, to see Ari's eyes go moist, his face reddening. He said sadly, "I'm just like my father. Yes, this is what I do to everyone, my wife, my son, everyone, just like my father did."

I said, "It must be awfully lonely, with everyone afraid of you like that." He looked up at me, silently. I added, "You know that song 'Desperado?'"

"Yes, I know it," he said, still looking intently at me.

"You remind me of those lines, 'you better let somebody love you, before it's too late.'"

Ari looked down and began to weep. I was quite moved. Right then, my very mixed feelings about Ari melted into an unexpected warmth, respect, and tenderness, and I heard myself say to myself, "I really love this guy." I was able from then on to feel safer to confront, and try to help him contain, his obsessional anger. I was in a position to address the tender, wounded part of him, which he had wanted not only to hide, but also, with great trepidation, to show. This shift in me and between Ari and myself allowed Ari to enter a new phase in the treatment. He began to reveal the traumatic aspects of his history he felt so ashamed of and hurt by, a history he had been trying all his adult life to sweep under the rug.

Ari is one of many analysands I have come to love. Each analytic dyad I have been a part of has had its own unique history of how love did or did not develop, and how it was or was not expressed. What is this thing called "analytic love?" What do and don't we do with it? How does its presence or absence impact our analysands, and ourselves?

Psychoanalysis provides a ritualized setting for a process that encourages the development of the analysand's intimate awareness of himself. In the process, analyst and analysand inevitably and necessarily become intimately involved with each other, intellectually and emotionally. At the heart of this endeavor, I believe, for both analyst and analysand, is a search for love, for the sense of being lovable, for the remobilization of thwarted capacities to give love and to receive love. This may at first seem a more fitting description of the analysand than the analyst, but consider our choice of profession. Is it not likely to be the case that we have chosen our work, at least in part, because it affords us the means of realizing the aim of being especially important to, especially loved and valued by, our analysands? We have long been free to discuss hating our analysands (Winnicott, 1949) and more recently to discuss having sexual feelings for them, including disclosing such feelings (Davies, 1998).[2] It is less often that we discuss our feelings of tenderness and loving affection for our analysands, not with the kind of thoughtfulness and seriousness of many of our other discussions. Erotic or aggressive countertransferences are now widely conferred the status of therapeutic agents, and natural warmth, openness, and expressiveness are no longer considered antipsychoanalytic per se. Yet, case presentations where feelings of tenderness, affection, and love for an analysand are openly expressed are often greeted with the suspicion that the analyst has "acted out" his narcissistic need to cure by posing as an impossibly perfect parent to a perennially infantilized patient (Freud accused Ferenczi of *furor sanandi* on similar grounds). In my view, these suspicions against tenderness in our work have gone beyond their proper safeguarding function and have led instead to the inhibition of the growth and development of our thinking about analytic love.

This gap in our developmental and clinical theories was noted long ago by Ian Suttie (1935/1999), who asked if "[i]n our anxiety to avoid the intrusion of sentiment into our scientific formulations, have we not gone to the length of excluding it altogether from our field of observation?" (p. 1). Although Suttie's question is more than 60 years old, I observe nevertheless that it is still rare to find the role of analytic love referred to in any detail in the case histories of our recent literature.[3]

Even when analytic love is spoken of, it is often only touched upon, briefly and indirectly. Ghent (1992), for example, speaks of the needs our analysands often have as "genuine longings for human warmth, empathic responsiveness, trust, recognition, faith, playful creativity—all the ingredients we think of when we speak of love" (p. 142). He goes on, though, to caution that "I would want to make clear that I am by no means suggesting that all of the longings, as they appear in the adult, can be, or should be, directly responded to in the analytic setup" (p. 142). Ghent refers tantalizingly to analytic love here, offering a description of what our analysands have so often been deprived of, and so often seek in vain, that seems beautifully right; yet he omits, to the disappointment of at least this reader, a more detailed exploration of the analyst's response to these needs. While such precautionary considerations are not only valid but of undeniable import, it is nevertheless the case that disclaimers and precautions concerning analytic love are ubiquitously emphasized in the literature, while the therapeutic action of analytic love, its power and value, is comparatively under-theorized.[4]

In this regard, many psychoanalysts have for the last century taken their lead from Freud, shunning the concept of "cure through love" as anti-therapeutic. When Freud advises Eitington that "the secret of therapy is to cure through love" (quoted in Falzeder, 1994), he is referring to the therapeutic traction provided by the patient's transference love for the doctor. Freud had very little to say of the doctor's love for the patient, and was concerned with distancing himself from therapies (associated with Rank, Adler, Jung, and, finally, Ferenczi) that promoted sentimental, spiritual, and hypnotic types of cures, and especially from the aforementioned "cure through love."[5]

Freud erred in that he sought to innoculate psychoanalysis from the potentially dangerous effects of analytic love (pseudo-cure by dint of the analyst's influence; recruitment of the analysand into pathological accommodation (Brandchaft, 1994) to the analyst's need for power and control) by enjoining the analyst to suppress his love altogether. Of course, one might argue that seduction for the purpose of attaining control and domination over another might often happen in the name of love, but it is not actually what love is meant to be. On the other hand, professional neutrality, abstinence, and deliberate withholding of gratification can be equally manipulative means of maintaining domination over and controlling others. This is precisely what Ferenczi argued, and what some of the Interpersonalists and some of the Object Relationists who followed him sought to reform. At any rate, as is usually the case with strategies that depend on suppression, and as the ever-increasing influence of the relational tilt in psychoanalysis demonstrates, efforts to sterilize the analytic milieu have not been successful. The analyst's forbidden and suppressed (i.e., repressed) love returned, cleverly disguised and reversed as the once *de rigeur* practice of what amounted to the shaming of the analysand for the persistence of his so-called infantile longings, and requiring of the analysand that such longings be renounced and relinquished.

While analytic love is by no means exiled today, I think it is fair to say that it is not readily and universally embraced, either.[6] With the popularity today of concepts such as Winnicottian holding and Kohutian empathy, this statement may seem surprising; but what I wish to focus on in this paper is the analyst's love in a broader sense, not just specific components of love, such as holding, empathy, or recognition.

Themes similar to those I wish to address have been taken up in recent years by Irwin Hirsch (with Kessel, 1988; Hirsch, 1983, 1994). In a series of papers, Hirsch has carefully considered, from a variety of angles, the analyst's loving, sexual, and romantic feelings for analysands, and the ways in which these feelings may or may not enhance analytic work. While in his earlier work, Hirsch (Hirsch & Kessel, 1988) attempts to distinguish the analyst's mature, adult-to-adult love from countertransference love, and maintains a distinction between loving and sexual feelings, in his later work (Hirsch, 1994) he speaks of such feelings more broadly as enactments of sexual and romantic countertransference love. I am more in accord with Hirsch's earlier work.[7] I do not wish to focus here on the analyst's sexual countertransference feelings, because I believe they may be and often are something quite different from analytic love. Erotic countertransference and analytic love need not be mutually exclusive, but they are not the same thing. Further, I do not conceptualize analytic love as equivalent to countertransference love, nor do I see the experience of or exchange of loving feelings between analyst and analysand as always best understood under the umbrella of "enactment." Analytic love is not necessarily evoked by the analysand's transference, although it will undoubtedly be mixed in with the analyst's concordant and complementary countertransferences.

In this paper, I wish to attempt to articulate my view of what analytic love is, why it matters, and why I believe it is worth distinguishing from the analyst's experience of romantic, sexual, and countertransferential love. I wish to join those analysts who see love as central to analytic work, and identify a lineage of psychoanalytic forebears who place love at the center of their theories of development. Rather than seeking to explore the balance of pros and cons, and reiterating the well-known problems connected to analytic love, which Hirsch, Hoffman, and others have already done quite well, I will maintain an admittedly lopsided focus on the ways that analytic love might enhance and further the analytic process. Before presenting my attempt at a definition of analytic love, I will focus on a review of this theme in the work of Ferenczi, Suttie, Balint, Fairbairn, Loewald, and Kohut. I do not attempt here to provide a comprehensive literature review, a task again already well executed by Hirsch and Kessel.[8] Rather, I choose the theorists above, and omit others, because they are the analysts whose work has had the most influence on my thinking on this subject, and whose views most support those I wish to advance in this paper.

My central thesis is that given the specific ways in which many of our most important theorists have emphasized the crucial role of love in their theories of development, it should follow that our clinical theories call for and make use of the analyst's emotional responsiveness—in particular, the analyst's capacity to love authentically and use his love therapeutically. This has long been a controversial issue in psychoanalysis, as Friedman (1978) points out in his comparison of the 1936 Marienbad and 1961 Edinburgh Symposia. Both meetings were concerned with understanding what is curative in psychoanalysis, and both raised the question of how or if the psychoanalytic theory of mind corresponds to its theory of technique. The Marienbad participants readily considered, without controversy, how analysands introject aspects of the analyst and aspects of their relationship to the analyst, and how such processes can be therapeutic. Yet by 1961, when Gitelson (1962) cautiously introduced similar themes, his effort was greeted with almost universal rejection, his numerous discussants holding that interpretation alone was the only officially permissible route to psychoanalytic cure. A lone participant in Edinburgh joined Gitelson. Sasha Nacht (1962) summed up poignantly much of what I wish to expand on in this paper:

> I have had the experience, as we all have, of treating successfully patients who have been treated unsuccessfully by a colleague. And yet the former analyst had conducted the treatment correctly, and I have been led to ask myself: "What did I do more than he?" I have also had the experience of being unable to cure the patient, and asking myself what I did less for him than for others. For a long time this problem worried me, until I reached the conclusion that in one case or the other it was to my own deep underlying attitude towards the patient that I had to attribute the responsibility of success or failure. No one can cure another if he has not a genuine desire to help him; and no one can have the desire to help unless he loves, in the deepest sense of the word. (p. 210)

Was Nacht ahead of his time? Or was he attuned to something deeply rooted in psychoanalytic theory that his contemporaries, the members of the psychoanalytic establishment at the beginning of the 1960s, had lost sight of?[9] For in fact, the story of the acceptance or rejection of analytic love as a valid therapeutic agent begins early in the history of psychoanalysis, most notably with what Lothane (1998) has called "the feud between Freud and Ferenczi over love."

Sigmund Freud and Sándor Ferenczi

It was just at the critical juncture concerning the nature of the analyst/analysand relationship that Freud and Ferenczi, who had long been Freud's closest disciple, encountered irreconcilable differences between themselves (Aron & Harris, 1993; Lothane, 1998). Ferenczi eventually came to see the quality of love, specifically the mutual exchange of tenderness between parent and child, as crucial to development and central to the understanding of human motivation. He emphasized these themes in direct and deliberate contradiction to Freud's emphasis on sexual and aggressive drives as the foundation of the structure of the human psyche. Correspondingly, Ferenczi saw the ability to generate mutual tenderness between analyst and analysand, constituting mutative new relational experience (Fosshage, 1992), as essential to cure. Ferenczi saw transference, not primarily as an expression of infantile id pressures, which, through analysis, would be made conscious and renounced, but rather as a forum for the analysand to reenact and work through traumatic developmental experience within the parent/child matrix. Ferenczi believed this could be achieved optimally with an analyst who was more empathic, authentic, and emotionally alive than with one who was anonymous, neutral, and abstinent. Ferenczi's analysand, Clara Thompson (1943), summarized his views succinctly when she said that Ferenczi "believed that the patient is ill because he has not been loved" (p. [illegible]

> [illegible] on is a repetition through the trans- [illegible] same things must be important in [illegible] ved and accepted by the analyst . . .
>
> (Thompson, 1964, p. 77)[10]

[illegible] are often perceived as the worst case [illegible] ly came to recognize both the power [illegible] Diary (DuPont, Ed., 1988), he speaks [illegible] toward the patient than one really [illegible] (1933/1980), Ferenczi wrote:

> [illegible] especially that which comes from [illegible] fferent kind from that which they need, is forced upon the children in the stage of tenderness, it may lead to pathological consequences in the same ways as the frustration or withdrawal of love . . .
>
> (p. 164, italics in original)

The greatness of Ferenczi's contribution lies in his persistent effort to understand and make therapeutic use of his feelings about his analysands, at a time in analytic history when countertransference feelings were considered a sign only of the analyst's insufficiently eradicated neurosis.

Izette DeForest, an analysand, student, and friend of Ferenczi's, and later a friend and colleague of Erich Fromm's, points to the previous quote, and to her personal conversations with Ferenczi, as evidence that he was well aware of the difficulties involved in using his capacity for love as a therapeutic instrument. DeForest (1954) wrote:

> The offering of loving care cannot be given, either by parent or by psychotherapist, on demand or in answer to threat. It must be given freely and spontaneously as a genuinely felt emotional expression. And it must provide an

> environment of trust and confidence and hope, so that the neurotic sufferer can gradually unburden himself of his conscious and unconscious anxieties; of his shame and guilt; of his hostility and plans of vengeance; of his rejected longing to love; of all his deeply hidden secrets. It must provide the environment (no matter how absurd it may objectively appear) which is essential to growth, to the unfolding of individuality. In other words, the therapist must give to the patient a replica of the birthright of love which was denied him, as an infant or a growing child, but which, if granted, would have assured him full stature as an individual in his own right.
>
> (pp. 16–17)

For Ferenczi, it was not possible to facilitate the analysand's realization of his "full stature as an individual in his own right" without also helping him, via the analytic relationship, to recognize and claim his "birthright of love."

Ian Dishart Suttie

A close examination of the work of Ian Suttie would suggest that his contribution to the relational schools of psychoanalysis is nearly as seminal as that of Ferenczi's. In accord with Ferenczi, Suttie believed that what children want first and foremost is to exchange, both to receive and to give, loving tenderness with their parents and other caregivers. Suttie's relational alternative to drive theory focused on the importance of the bond between mother and child. In deliberate contrast to the work of Melanie Klein (Klein, 1932) (whom Suttie knew and argued theory with at the British Psychoanalytical Society in the 1920s), Suttie saw the wish for mutually exchanged love, and not instinctual forces of envy and aggression, as the organizing force in development.

As noted by Suttie's niece, Dorothy Heard, in her introduction to the 1999 edition of his book (Suttie, 1935/1999, p. xxii), Suttie greatly admired Ferenczi. Suttie's wife, Jane, also an analyst, was the English translator of many of Ferenczi's papers in *Further Contributions to the Theory and Technique of Psychoanalysis* (Ferenczi, 1926). Today's interest in Ferenczi can probably be traced from Winnicott to Ferenczi's disciple, Michael Balint, and from there to Ferenczi. Yet Suttie, in his highly popular discussion groups at the British Psychoanalytical Society, where he also read his papers from the mid-1920s until his untimely death in 1935, was an early champion of Ferenczi's. Long prior to Balint's arrival in England in 1939, Suttie had been promoting and elaborating Ferenczi's ideas, even as Ferenczi's former analysand, Melanie Klein, was taking many of Ferenczi's ideas, and taking many British analysts, in different directions. Both Fairbairn (in Guntrip, 1971, p. 24) and Winnicott (1967, p. 575) directly acknowledge Suttie's influence on their work, and Bacal (1987) notes that Suttie's ideas were seminal, significantly anticipating those of Fairbairn, Guntrip, Balint, Winnicott, Bowlby, Sullivan, and Kohut (see also the Foreword by Bowlby in Suttie, 1935/1999). A thoughtful and extensive review of Suttie's book, appearing in the *Psychoanalytic Review*, was written by William Alanson White (1937), the mentor to H.S. Sullivan, suggesting that Sullivan may also have known of Suttie's work.[11]

In perhaps his most cogent and enduringly relevant observation, Suttie found that "tenderness itself was tabooed in our culture and science—tabooed more intensely even than sex—and that even psychoanalytic investigation and treatment was sharply limited by this bias" (p. 5). Suttie sought to "put the conception of altruistic (non-appetitive) love on a scientific footing" (p. 3), and in so doing, to make a clear case for a fully interpersonal, as opposed to id-driven, model of development. Anticipating Fairbairn's claim that the infant is object-seeking, Suttie's alternative to drive theory was "the conception of an innate need-for-companionship which is the infant's only way of self-preservation" (p. 6).[12]

Suttie saw the need to give altruistically as innate and universal. He wrote:

> In the beginning of life none of the transactions between mother and infant could be distinguished . . . as "giving" or "getting" in the sense of "losing" or "gaining". The mother gives the breast, certainly but the infant gives the mouth, which is equally necessary to the transaction of sucking [p. 38] . . . I consider the child wakes up to life with the germ of parenthood, the impulse to "give" and to "respond" already in it. This impulse, with the need "to get" attention and recognition, etc., motivates the free "give and take" of fellowship.
>
> (p. 58)

Suttie's ideas here anticipate recent discoveries in the field of infant research (Stern, 1985) and in the literature on the "bidirectional model of influence" (e.g., Beebe et al., 1992).

Suttie, like Michael and Alice Balint after him, deplored the demand in Western culture that children, for the sake of impatient parents, prematurely relinquish their rights to be childish, i.e., dependent and in need of secure attachment. In contrast to Freud, he saw pathology as rooted less in Oedipal jealousy and fear of the father, but rather in the thwarted need for the mother, which "must produce the utmost extreme of terror and rage, since the loss of mother is, under natural conditions, but the precursor of death itself" (p. 16). Further, pathology arises for Suttie, not just when the mother fails to give adequately, but especially when the infant feels that its own gifts are rejected by the mother. Suttie anticipates Fairbairn's (1952, p. 25) later work when he says, "The rejection of the child's 'gifts', like any failure to make adequate response, leads to a sense of badness, unlovableness in the self, with melancholia as its culminating expression" (p. 50). As in Fairbairn's (1952) "moral defense," Suttie described how the child "exonerate[s] the mother by condemning the self" (p. 45), saying, in effect, "mother is good and kind; if she does not love me that is because I am bad" (p. 43). Anticipating Winnicott's (1960) concept of the false self, Suttie took note of the infant's "impulse to earn love by becoming what is wanted" (p. 45), as in the defensive strategy of identification with the aggressor (Ferenczi, 1933/1949).

For Suttie, "the 'overcoming of resistances' might almost be paraphrased as the development of a trust in the analyst-parent which will be capable of surviving the reproaches arising from repressed anxiety and rage" (p. 217). The analyst must encourage:

> the willingness of the patient and his emboldenment to relax his defenses against expressing his hate and so running a risk of being hated. This willingness or trust is a function of transference (positive) or love so that the original ambivalent attachment to mother is 'played off' upon the physician.
>
> (p. 213)

Suttie introduces here the theme of the developmental necessity for the parent/analyst to survive the child's/analysand's hate and destruction, which Winnicott (1969) would later elaborate as a cornerstone of his own theory.

Suttie saw the goal of psychoanalytic work as consisting of "the overcoming of the barriers to loving and feeling oneself loved, and not as the removal of fear-imposed inhibitions to the expression of innate, anti-social, egoistic and sensual desires" (pp. 53–54). While I share Suttie's emphasis on overcoming the barriers to love as a central analytic focus (as does Coen, 1994), it may be the case that his tendency to draw sharply polarized distinctions between his beliefs and those of both Freud and Melanie Klein has contributed to his relative obscurity now. Additionally, Suttie's efforts to develop his theories were sadly foreshortened by his untimely death. While his work remains largely unread by the psychoanalytic community, at least in the U.S., there is no question that many of his important ideas were inspirational to and were further developed and disseminated by Balint, Fairbairn, Winnicott, and Guntrip.

Michael Balint

Michael Balint, Ferenczi's chief disciple, fled Hungary in 1939 and settled in Great Britain, where he became identified with the British Middle School. Balint's and Suttie's views are remarkably similar, although there is no indication in their writings that they knew each other. It is my speculation that Suttie, through his and his wife's contact with Ferenczi, was familiar with the work of both Michael and Alice Balint (1933), and vice versa.

Balint introduced his concept of primary love (Balint, 1937) specifically to refute Freud's concept of primary narcissism. Balint believed, like Ferenczi and Suttie, that human beings are relationally oriented from the beginning. In the stage of primary love, mother and child ideally live interdependently, with boundaries blurred, in "an harmonious interpenetrating mix-up" (Balint, 1968). He saw the origin of psychopathology in disruptions and failures of this primary love experience. He observed that analysands, often after reaching more mature forms of relating to the analyst, would regress to the level of "the basic fault" (1968), the area of the personality formed by traumatic disruptions of the state of primary love. Analysands would then seek to use their analysis for the purpose of making a "new beginning." The new beginning helps the analysand to "free himself of complex, rigid, and oppressive forms of relationship to his objects of love and hate . . . and to start simpler, less oppressive forms" (Balint, 1968, p. 134). Balint spoke memorably of the analyst's stance at this stage:

> the analyst . . . must allow his patients to relate to, or exist with, him as if he were one of the primary substances. This means that he should be but like water carries the swimmer or the earth carries the walker . . . [H]e must be there, must always be there, and must be indestructible—as are water and earth.
>
> (1968, p. 167)

Some may see Balint as suggesting here that the analyst be constantly capable of an intrinsically false, utopian kind of bottomless empathy. In this interpretation, Balint is seen as endorsing a clinical technique promoting the analyst's masochistic self-effacement, leading undesirably to the infantilization of the analysand, and to the exaltation of the analyst as an impossibly perfect parent. I believe, rather, that Balint is poignantly describing a particular form of analytic love, evoked by analysands deeply in touch with traumatic developmental experience, in which the analyst attempts as much as possible to set his own needs and analytic agendas aside. The analyst provides the analysand a new beginning with his non-impinging, abiding presence, offered in the service of the analysand's efforts at reparative self-delineation. The idea here is similar to Winnicott's (1958) concept of the development of the capacity to be alone, to feel alive and real, in the presence of the other.

Balint's version of analytic love is intended to provide a new relational experience. For the analysand who has never felt he had the right or the safety to be real, the new beginning is the point at which, starting with his analyst, he can begin to build trust and hope in the possibility of being in connection with others, without inevitably and inexorably having to become lost, false, or deadened. In contrast to Balint, who saw the basic fault developing at the chronological stage of primary love, I conceptualize the basic fault as crystallizing within the whole course of childhood development, and comprising internalized elements of traumatic aspects of the relationships with both mother and father.

The basic fault, reconceptualized in this way, most often manifests clinically as a central organizing principle (Stolorow & Atwood, 1992) consisting of the analysand's profound dread or deadly conviction that he is hopelessly unlovable.

W.R.D. Fairbairn

Although Fairbairn says virtually nothing about the role of analytic love in therapeutic cure, he is explicit, more so than any other theorist, about the role of love in development and pathology. His placement of love squarely at the center of his theory of development is worthy of quoting at length.

> [T]he greatest need of a child is to obtain conclusive assurance (a) that he is genuinely loved as a person by his parents, and (b) that his parents genuinely

> accept his love. It is only in so far as such assurance is forthcoming in a form sufficiently convincing to enable him to depend safely upon his real objects that he is able gradually to renounce infantile dependence without misgiving . . . Frustration of his desire to be loved as a person and to have his love accepted is the greatest trauma that a child can experience
>
> (Fairbairn, 1952, pp. 39–40)

Fairbairn here describes the theoretical underpinning of his concept of the basic endopsychic situation. With love so central to Fairbairn's theory, it is puzzling that he did not seem to consider the role love might play in analytic treatment.[13] Whatever his reasons for this omission, Fairbairn's emphasis on love, from my perspective, leads logically to the idea that the analyst's love, and how that love is exchanged and regulated in the analytic dyad, will play a central role in the recovery of the analysand's capacity to love and be loved.

Hans Loewald

While Loewald was a passionate Freudian, his early work with Sullivan and Fromm-Reichmann (Mitchell & Black, 1995, p. 186) may have been an important conceptual link to the Ferenczian relational concepts that emerge in his work (see Mitchell, 2000a, for a full elaboration of the relational themes in Loewald's work). Although comparing the analyst's functions to those of parents is as old as psychoanalysis itself, I find Loewald's formulation of this analogy particularly significant because of the linkage he makes between love and respect (it is for this reason that the title of this chapter pays homage to Loewald). Loewald (1960) speaks of the parents' "love and respect for the individual and for individual development" (p. 229) and how, ideally, love and also respect inform the parent's attunement to the child's developmental process. In Loewald's formulation, the parent holds and mediates to the child a hopeful vision of the child's potential, a vision based in an empathic, loving, and respectful recognition of the child's emerging identity. Loewald (1979) wrote that "it is the bringing forth, nourishing, providing for, and protecting of the child by the parents that constitute their parenthood, authority (authorship), and render sacred the child's ties with the parents" (p. 387).

Thus, for Loewald, analytic work is optimally conducted as a medium in which the analyst's love and respect for the individual and for individual development serves to revive the analysand's derailed developmental processes—derailments caused by failures in the regulation of love and respect in the parent/child matrix. I will speak further of the crucial link between love and respect, as I understand Loewald's formulation, later in this paper.

Heinz Kohut

Kohut's views on analytic love are not explicit in his writing, although he defended self psychology more than once from charges that his theory offered little more than the despised "cure through love." Yet, as Teicholz (1999) points out in her study of the resonance between the work of Kohut and Loewald, Kohut's concept of the archaic selfobject can be linked with both Ferenczi's stage of tenderness between infant and mother, and with Balint's stage of primary love (p. 102). Teicholz notes that "Kohut's selfobject concept expressed an insistence on a lifelong, mutual interpenetration of selves, rather than on autonomy" (p. 34). This pro-relational view of health led Kohut to recommend that the analyst protect and accept the analysand's idealization, rather than attempt to interpret it away. Kohut believed that this would allow disrupted developmental processes, based on the unavailability of a sufficiently idealizable archaic selfobject, to have a second chance to resume and take on new, more mature forms with the analyst. Kohut's ideas about the acceptance of the analysand's idealization seem especially congruent as well with Fairbairn's position regarding the crucial importance for the developing child of a sense that his love is recognized, felt, and welcomed—i.e., that his love is good.

While originally concerned with empathy primarily as the optimal psychoanalytic tool with which to gather data (Kohut, 1959), Kohut eventually asserted (1984, p. 74) that the analyst's empathy was in and of itself a therapeutic agent. With his emphasis on the importance in both development and the clinical situation of the recognition of mirroring, idealizing, and twinship selfobject needs, and with the privileging of an empathic listening perspective (Fosshage, 1997), I believe that Kohut identified crucial ways in which love is provided and experienced, between parent and child and in the analytic dyad. Ironically, but not surprisingly, given the climate of his day, he did so without actually using the word love, and while strongly rejecting the concept of "cure through love." Nevertheless, Kohut, following Ferenczi, opened the door to love in the analytic relationship, whether he wanted to or not.[14]

Discussion

In my clinical work, I repeatedly observe in analysands the pain, suffering, and stunted potential that has resulted from their feelings of being unlovable; unworthy of loving; unable to love satisfactorily; afraid to take love from others; and unable to hold as valuable both their own love and the love of others.

In his discussion of the goals of contemporary relational psychoanalysis, Mitchell (1993) poses a series of questions:

> How does life come to feel real? significant? valuable? What are the processes through which one develops a sense of self as vital and authentic? How are these processes derailed, resulting in a sense of self as depleted, false, shallow? (p. 24)

In my attempt to facilitate the analytic exploration of these central questions, I maintain an ongoing focus on the analysand's experience of parental love, which

I see as crucially determining the analysand's sense of vitality and his sense of the purpose and meaning of life. In seeking to understand and know the person before me, I assume that experiences of loving and being loved are either figure or ground at any given point in the analytic process. I seek to learn how these experiences have shaped his central organizing principles. For many analysands, I have found that framing their relevant issues in these terms promotes access to dissociated affect and experience.

To give a brief example, Jane, an analysand in her mid-thirties, had described in the first months of treatment a history of painful, dissatisfying relationships, and had expressed agonized concerns about the impact of her mother's coldness, and her father's inappropriate sexual seductiveness during her childhood. Nevertheless, she had great difficulty justifying to herself that she needed therapy, and became intellectualized and ruminative in many sessions.

In the midst of this struggle, she said forlornly, "I just don't know what I'm doing here."

I replied,

"I think you're trying to figure out whether or not it might ever be possible for you to love and be loved."

Jane then wept freely, saying, "Yes, that's right." She was able to commit herself to the treatment from then on. At later times of doubt and confusion for her, and as we both struggled with numerous transference/countertransference vicissitudes and enactments, this moment served as a potent reminder, again for us both, of her purpose and her hopes for the analytic process.

For some analysands, these themes will take years to emerge in any distinct, overt way, while for others they will be almost immediately at the forefront. I maintain, though, that love is a constant and crucially significant presence in analytic work, whether figure or ground, for both analyst and analysand. In a very real sense, analysands are always seeking from the analyst a new relational experience of love, a way of experiencing intimate mutuality that will not result in retraumatization. How does the analyst respond?

This leads to the question of how we define analytic love. Analytic love is hard to define, and often left undefined,[15] perhaps because while it may at times resemble parental love, fraternal love, charitable love, friendly love, erotic love, etc., it is not simply or actually any of those things. It is a thing unto itself.

I offer two defining principles. The first principle is expressed by Loewald in his statement that for things to go well, analysts must have "love and respect for the individual and for individual development" (1960, p. 20). In this statement, I believe Loewald speaks from his highly developed spirituality, expressing the idea that human beings are meant to be loved and respected by their parents from birth, and should in no way be required to earn or merit that love. As Ferenczi, Suttie, Balint, and Fairbairn also articulated, parental love is the birthright of all human beings. Yet for Loewald, it is not just love, but the joining of love with respect, that constitutes the crucial components of the parental role in human development. If parental love is present, but respect for the individual and individual development is not (e.g., as when the child is treated primarily as a narcissistic extension of the parent (Miller, 1981); and of course in cases of abuse, neglect, and exploitation of children by parents), then there will be illness.

As I read him, Loewald implies that faith and belief in human potential is a defining characteristic of analytic love. If the analysand's vitality and authenticity potentials were thwarted in the course of development, he has a second chance to realize those potentials with the analyst. The analyst's love and respect for the potential in a human being serves to encourage analysands whose experiences of deprivation of love, or of love without sufficient respect, have been overwhelmingly discouraging. It is my sense in reading Loewald that the phrase "love and respect" implied for him a sense of awe and reverence for human potential, and that he saw not just the parent/child bond as sacred, but also the analytic bond.

The second defining principle of analytic love is the analyst's commitment to the analysand's safety. I believe that Loewald's reference to parental love and respect as a kind of positive neutrality (1960) is meant to refer to the abstinence involved when a parent makes the effort to refrain, as best as possible, from narcissistically exploiting his child. Similarly, analysts who love and respect the analysand's capacity for development, and who see the analysand as inherently worthy of love and respect, will naturally seek to keep their love free from narcissistic, sexual, and other forms of exploitation of the analysand. This is one of the major ways that the crucial asymmetry (Aron, 1996) of the analytic relationship is upheld.

As psychoanalysts, we dedicate ourselves to the growth and to the safety of the analysand. This dedication is in essence an act of love and an offering of respect. To the extent that we are consistent in this effort, we may be making the first such offering in the experience of many analysands.

How do we get to analytic love? It does not happen simply by our own efforts. No doubt many parents fall instantly in love with their babies the moment they are born, but often a parent's love grows slowly, in tandem both with the infant's emerging sense of self and with the infant's increasingly noticeable recognition of the parent. As Suttie pointed out, children have much to give parents, and not just vice versa. The same must be said for the analytic relationship. By responding to our therapeutic efforts, analysands provide us with a sense of efficacy, pride, and purpose, all of which constitute vitalizing selfobject experience (Bacal & Thomson, 1998). We sustain our analytic purpose with even the most difficult of analysands because we hope that they will get better. We hope that what we provide will bear fruit in the analysand's life, in the form of his healing and growth. Very often, it is the witnessing of the fruits of our labor in the form of the analysand's new-found trust in us, and in their hard-earned healing and growth, that evokes and further stimulates our loving feelings. As an analysand becomes aware of the deepening of our loving feelings toward him, he is not only affirmed, but also encouraged by his own success in evoking those feelings in us. The analysand feels that he has reached and touched us, that he has succeeded in being recognized and valued. Both analyst and analysand feel valued, and recognized, for what they have to give, each inspiring the other to succeed in reaching the goals of treatment. There is mutuality (Aron, 1996) in this interplay that is both vitalizing for the analyst, and therapeutic for the analysand.[16]

When, on the other hand, an analysis is stalemated, it may be that the analyst's need for affirmation is not being met. Racker (1968), influenced by Melanie Klein, sees analysts as motivated to make reparation for making the analysand ill (Racker, 1968, pp. 145–146). The analyst is one whose sense of guilt, stemming from archaic aggression and oral greed and envy, drives him to find an occupation where he can ritually offer concern as a means of making reparation to his internal objects. While this may occur often enough among analysts, I suspect that analysts more universally seek, via their beneficial and curative impact on analysands, a means of confirming that their love is good, as in Fairbairn's formulation.

Bacal and Thomson (1998) address this issue in terms of the selfobject needs of the analyst, some of which are ubiquitous, while others are specific to each analytic dyad. In my own case, when I feel that my love, in the form of my best analytic effort, is being rejected, I can then find myself tempted to focus on how the analysand "provoked" or "elicited" my aversion. This is usually a sign for me that I am narcissistically wounded and preoccupied. In that state, I am at a disadvantage in terms of considering all the possible meanings of the analysand's behavior.

In many cases, stalemates occur when the analysand is not progressing enough to provide the analyst with sufficient evidence of the power and impact of the analyst's love. In this situation, the analysand's withdrawal stimulates the analyst's frustration and counter-withdrawal because his vulnerability to the problematic aspects of his own history of loving and being loved have been stimulated.[17]

I hope that in an analysis I conduct, my patient and I will have been able to experience a full range of feelings for each other (Aron, 1996). Without having in any way avoided taking on sex and aggression, in the end, I would hope that our predominant feelings would include respect, understanding, acceptance, empathy, admiration, caring, the sincere wish for the other's happiness and fulfillment, and love. I hope the experience will have enriched both our lives in many ways, and that we will both be able to internalize the value and meaningfulness of the experience.

Let me return now to Ari.

After the turning point I described earlier, Ari ceased ranting to a great extent, and began to tell me his story. I was able to learn of the way that his father dominated everyone around him, but especially Ari, his only son. A successful and self-made man who was bitterly estranged from seven brothers, Ari's father worked hard, went bankrupt, and built his business back all over again, ultimately dying in his early fifties of a heart attack. Ari's mother worked full-time and devoted herself to trying to assuage her husband. She did not intervene when his father frequently slapped Ari's face, for a wide variety of infractions. Ari was able to remember many of these incidents, with full affect, but one in particular stood out and was especially painful. When his father wanted him to smile for a picture,

Ari would have difficulty because he has a defective tear duct that makes it painful to have the sun in his eyes. Because Ari would squint when he had to pose, his father would smack him, shouting, "Now smile, goddam it!" Almost any picture Ari has of himself as a child was taken shortly after he had been painfully and humiliatingly slapped by his father. Perhaps most shameful of all, and something Ari could not bring himself to speak of in detail, were the few times he saw his father slap his mother.

I was particularly struck by Ari's history of problems with school, and his identity in his family as a wild screw-up, since, in spite of his great difficulty with anxiety and rage, I found him to be exceptionally hard-working, intelligent, and articulate. Ari and his wife were already preparing their son for high school examinations, hoping to enroll him in one of the best schools in New York, which in fact he later attended. As we explored Ari's feelings about this, I was able to ask him, why hadn't he, Ari, been helped to learn in the ways that he was helping his son to learn? This led to many other questions. Was he ever helped to do better in school, or were his experiences of being accused, reproached, and humiliated all he could remember? Were his potentials recognized and nurtured at all? What did his mother think about or do about his father's frequent violence?

Ari began to grieve and weep, openly, in session after session. He wept for his own mistreatment, and for his repetition of this mistreatment with his wife, son, and employees; and for guilt at his sense that he was betraying his parents by acknowledging the abusive and neglectful dimensions of their behavior. I was deeply moved by Ari's tears. I felt honored that he could let himself be this vulnerable with me, and my fond and loving feelings for him deepened. I was quiet during this stage, which lasted for most of a year. My responses were simply sustaining, not probing, not confronting, rarely inquiring other than for simple clarification, interpreting hardly at all.

He eventually moved out of this stage of intense grieving, and soon brought in more material about his conflicts with his wife. Now that he was more in touch with the way his father had used anger against him, I was able to interpret to Ari his identification with his father, how he treated his wife, son, and employees much as his father had treated him. I could confront him in this way because I believe we both knew that we trusted each other. I told him that he was in a war to the death with his wife, and that if one of them didn't try to make peace, they would go on living over each other's dead bodies. I repeated this many times.

Eventually, Ari reported that he was changing his behavior, that he had made love to his wife for the first time in two years, and that he was changing his attitude at work as well, calming down as much as he could, and managing conflict more smoothly. Ari reconnected with his deep love for his wife, which transcended his grievances against her. For the next year and beyond, he focused on calming himself down, gaining more detachment, learning when to keep his mouth shut, when to apologize, how to communicate more effectively.

I thought Ari's efforts were excellent, and I made no effort to conceal the happiness I felt for him. I also pointed out admiringly that even before therapy, although he was often angry, he at least had not hit his wife or his son, and he had come for help when he feared that he might. In addition, Ari had not denied his son the typical childhood gifts that he himself had been denied. I observed that in this way, he had surpassed his father. Instead of feeling perpetual guilt for failing to live up to his father's impossible expectations, I hoped Ari could see that, in many ways, he had made himself a stronger man than his father.

As our work continued, Ari struggled to maintain his determination to control his belligerence and to draw closer to his wife and son. I was particularly moved by his love for and sadness about his father, a man who could not show love, only anger. Ari could now feel his hate toward his father, and still grieve for the love that was lost between them. Most moving was Ari's new-found closeness and affection with his son, who adored his strong, scary father, as Ari had adored his own father. It was powerfully moving to hear the ways that Ari was opening up and sharing himself with his son, and to see his pride in and respect for his son. When I asked him if he had ever told his son how proud he was of him, he teared up and said that although he had never heard a word of encouragement from his father, he was making sure that his son would hear it from him.

I loved Ari for this, certainly in connection with my own resonant feelings about both my father and my son, feelings that were often powerfully called forth while listening to Ari. I loved many of the other tender aspects of himself that he let me see and come to know, and his honesty and courage in engaging the analytic process. For a long time, I'd tried to tolerate Ari's intimidating style of controlling the treatment, tried to set aside my feelings of frustration with his tirades, only to become detached and withdrawn. When I was able to become conscious of the aversiveness I was experiencing toward him as a result of feeling shut out, and when I could subsequently stand up to Ari and persist in my effort to connect with him, he opened his heart. We could then create a new relational experience.

The essence of this new experience, in Ari's case and in general, is that love can be experienced by both analyst and analysand as having greater vitalizing power than hate and fear. The challenge the analyst faces is to find a place from which to help the analysand choose love over hate, again and again, in spite of the many dangers the analysand faces in doing so.

As economic conditions declined in the post-Clinton era, and especially after 9/11, Ari's business began to falter. Ari briefly tried anti-depressant medication, which initially helped him sustain more hope and maintain control over panic and rage. Soon, however, as his business failed to pick up, month after month, Ari made me aware that he had returned to his marijuana habit. He once again came to rely on marijuana as the only means by which he could obtain relief from agonizing fear and shame, no matter how illusory and fleeting that relief may be. He felt defeated, as though life would always end up slapping him in the face, no matter how hard he tried.

Recognizing that Ari was truly closer than ever to losing his business, and sensing that he was giving up on our work, I said something like this at the end of a painful session:

> Ari, I'm aware that you don't feel that anything provides relief for you like marijuana does. But as I've often observed, you pay a terrible price for that relief. You feel more deeply ashamed, and more profoundly alone, in between every high. Now you've turned again to marijuana, because just as in your childhood, you believe that human understanding or solace is totally unavailable and unreliable. I had hoped that our work would have led you to feel otherwise, and I still hope that it might, even though right now it seems like therapy is losing, and marijuana is winning.

As we ended this session, Ari said, with tears, "I don't know. We'll have to see." I felt great sadness and loss when our work ended soon after this session. I am very glad that Ari, several years later, wanted to come back, and try again to find a way to free himself from his pain.

I am aware that how I have presented my work with Ari will be perceived by some as endorsing, in the name of analytic love, provision, direction, reassurance, and exhortation, all shibboleths of "proper" psychoanalysis. In a drive model where interpretation is the exclusively permissible intervention, such forms of responsiveness indeed will have no proper place. In a relational model that acknowledges the centrality of love and the necessity and inevitability of the analyst's emotional participation, however, I believe that these kinds of responses cannot be condemned automatically. I hope too that it is apparent that I do not believe that empathic attunement and allowing oneself to be used as a selfobject are the only modes of analytic work I see as therapeutic. While I believe these analytic modes were appropriate and beneficial in my work with Ari at certain times, equally necessary and beneficial were the many struggles and negotiations we managed around intersubjective recognition, struggles that often mobilized a good deal of aggression and conflict from both sides of the analytic dyad. I contend that any authentic analytic engagement will necessarily include a fluid, oscillating, often simultaneous use of both the analyst's capacity for empathic attunement as well as his skill in negotiating intersubjective difference as a means of reaching mutual recognition. I do not believe that there can be any kind of truly intimate human relationship that does not include both relational experiences.

Instead of presenting Ari, I might have presented more about Jane, an analysand for whom I felt a great deal of love, along with many other feelings, and whose treatment was not quite so complicated. Perhaps I have chosen to present Ari in part because I do not wish to imply that analytic love is a technique that can be used in certain ways to guarantee certain results. Analytic love, like any other meaningful love, is not a demand to be loved in return, or an attempt to control, or a deal you make where you give the analysand love and he gives you health. The best I could do for Ari, I believe, was to believe in him. The experience of someone he respects believing in him, with love and respect, is exactly what he never had. I maintained the hope that this new relational experience for Ari, however fleeting his experience of it may have been initially, was not in vain—and his return at this point, several years after the work described here, is repayment for my faith in him. It was not necessary to contrive these feelings for Ari's benefit and apply them technically. It was simply necessary, as I see it, to persist with dedication in the effort to be his analyst.

Conclusion

Is it necessary for the analyst to love the analysand in order to create new relational experience that is curative? I don't presume to offer a universal, definitive answer. When, how, and if the analyst experiences this love—and if it is experienced, whether or not it is ever made explicit—is co-determined from within each unique analytic dyad. However, the understanding and acceptance of analytic love as a therapeutic agent is also influenced by the values of the analytic community, and determined by the extent to which our theories do, or do not, include and accept love and its vicissitudes as central in development, pathology, and technique. While significant aspects of the work of the theorists discussed in this paper are well established in the clinical repertoire of many contemporary analysts, the complicated and crucial place of love in their work has yet to be more fully articulated and integrated into our theory and practice.

Hoffman, speaking of the ironic and ambiguous aspects of the analyst's influence and authority, concludes that it is nevertheless our responsibility to use the power vested in us "in a way that is as wise, as compassionate, and as empowering of the analysand as possible" (1998, p. 10). In a similar vein, I am saying in this paper that analytic love is indeed complicated and dangerous, and like all loving, carries the potential for devastating disappointment. This knowledge, rather than leading us to ignore, omit, or cancel our love, seems instead a call to persist in loving, as authentically, deeply, respectfully, and responsibly as we can.

Notes

1 This chapter is adapted from an earlier version of a paper by the same title (Shaw, 2003a).
2 Davies' ongoing work in this area (2003), building on the seminal contribution of Searles (1959), focuses on issues connected to post-oedipal sexuality as they are negotiated in the analytic dyad. I do not perceive Davies' emphasis on post-oedipal sexuality as implying any marginalization of the importance of non-sexual aspects of love in development and in analytic work. Similarly, I would hope that my emphasis in this paper on non-sexual aspects of love in the analytic dyad would not be construed as a marginalization of the erotic.
3 I am not alone in making this observation. In Lasky and Silverman, eds (1988), a collection of invited psychoanalytic papers on the theme of love in psychoanalysis, a similar observation is made in the introduction and in four of the 16 papers. Hirsch (1994) makes a similar assertion, as does Mann (2002).

4 Significant exceptions from the classical perspective are found in Coen (1994), Fox (1998), Lear (1990), and Steingart (1995). See also Kristeva (1987).
5 For a thorough exploration of Freud's concerns in this regard, see Carnochan (2001), Collins (1980), Fox (1998), and Kerr (1994).
6 For what may be the most ironic example of the rejection of this concept, see Enid Balint's recent confession that she found her husband's concept of primary love, and especially his use of the word love, essentially useless and irrelevant (Rudnytsky, 2000, p. 14).
7 In a personal communication, Hirsch clarified that his later position (1994) was not a renunciation of his earlier one (Hirsch & Kessel, 1988), but rather an elaboration on his theme, with a different focus.
8 Hirsch and Kessel (1988) are especially illuminating on the influence of existential humanism on the Interpersonal school, noting this influence on the work of Fromm, Searles, Wolstein, and Ehrenberg. I believe this influence was mutual. For example, the popular anthropologist Ashley Montagu was a great admirer of Fromm, Sullivan, Horney, and also Bowlby, and was influenced strongly by their work. Montagu enthusiastically introduced Ian Suttie's 1935 book (referred to in detail later in this paper) to American readers in 1952 (Suttie, 1935/1999); Fromm-Reichman refers to Suttie in 1959. These and other connections (such as Fromm and Fromm-Reichmann's early contact with Buber) would be an interesting area for further study.
9 I am grateful to Donnel Stern (personal communication) for bringing the Edinburgh controversy, Nacht's paper, and Friedman's commentary to my attention.
10 See also Fromm (1950): "Analytic therapy is essentially an attempt to help the patient gain or regain his capacity for love" (p. 87, italics in original).
11 This is also suggested in a reference to Suttie and Sullivan made by Fromm-Reichmann (1959, p. 326).
12 All italics in quotations from Suttie are in the original.
13 Fairbairn does, however, emphasize that the relationship of analyst to patient constitutes a "therapeutic factor of prime importance" (1958, p. 377), and compares the analyst to a reliable parental figure.
14 In addition to the authors reviewed here, I wish to acknowledge the influence on my thinking of contributions made by Maroda (1991, 1999); Orange (1995); Shane, Shane, and Gales (1997); Young-Bruehl and Bethelard (2000); Mitchell (2000a); and Fosshage (1999).
15 Schafer (1991), in attempting to define analytic love, relies on metaphor and the notion of the mystery of the artist's creative power (he quotes Rilke describing Cézanne's work). I read him as saying that to some extent, analytic love is *je ne sai quoi*, something essentially undefinable (pp. 83–84).
16 See also Brothers and Lewinberg (1999); and Searles (1975).
17 See also Ellman (1998, pp. 198–199). My focus on the analyst's experience of and contribution to treatment impasse should not be misunderstood as a recommendation to neglect the significance of the analysand's contributions to any given enactment.

Chapter 8

Analytic Love Revisited

Narcissists 'R' Us![1]

Traumatic narcissism, as I have sought to define it throughout this book, can be understood most simply as the action of subjugation. In the traumatizing narcissist's relational system, the narcissist fortifies himself by diminishing the other. The other is then conquered, controlled, or enslaved at worst—and exploited. Sadly, this happens often enough in relationships that are presented as therapeutic. I have heard story after story, from analysands, supervisees, colleagues, and friends, of how a therapist, from any of the various schools of psychotherapy and psychoanalysis, was able to persuade her patient of her infinite wisdom, and to go on to dictate and control all the significant choices and decisions in a patient's life, sometimes for decades. I have learned of people told to marry or divorce certain people; to cut off all contact with family members, permanently; to assuage and comply with abusers; to dress differently, down to what kind of earrings and bras to wear; to make donations and investments and expect to never see a return . . . The list is quite long and horrible. I have heard these stories told about therapists in remote rural and also in less remote suburban areas. I've heard hair-raising stories of control and exploitation about therapists in world-class cities, therapists who hold high academic or professional positions, or have well-known names through publications and media appearances.

The quality that so many of these controlling, subjugating therapists have in common, besides their charisma, is the ability to persuade themselves and others that all their words and deeds are offered out of selflessness, superior wisdom, and love. Those who fall under the spell of such a teacher, analyst, or guru, will feel elevated, renewed, redeemed—initially. The subjugation comes later. What traumatizing narcissist therapists deeply deny to themselves is that their need of the patient is as great or greater than the patient's need of them. Holding on to the patient means instilling in the patient the fear that all will be lost if she leaves. It's a projection with which, all too often, the patient identifies. What makes traumatizing narcissism so toxic and so confusing to those it traumatizes is that the narcissist delusionally believes his selfish, exploitative actions are the actions of love—and the narcissist is a great persuader.[2]

How does the traumatizing narcissist convince others that they are being loved and not abused? It is extraordinarily easy for analysts, no matter how seasoned, to be unaware of a narcissistic motive underlying any aspect of their work with patients—from silences to interpretive formulations, to how an office looks, how the analyst dresses, anything. A narcissistic motive, in line with my thinking about the traumatizing narcissist, always involves an effort to inflate oneself by deflating another. Insistently pushing an interpretation on an unwilling patient, or denying one's anger at a patient with silence or interpretations drained of affect, are examples of enactments in which the analyst seeks control through deflation of the patient. If these kinds of enactments are not eventually recognized and worked through, with the analyst taking full share of her responsibility, the progress of the analysis will be significantly impeded.

In "On Narcissism," Freud (1914) used the term "paraphrenia" to distinguish paranoia from schizophrenia; it corresponds roughly to what we now call paranoid schizophrenia. Freud thought that this kind of person was not floridly psychotic, and could appear more or less normal—but nevertheless held psychotic beliefs about himself and the world that were not always outwardly apparent. Freud believed narcissism was a paraphrenia, linked to paranoia. He understood that in the paraphrenic, self-regard, or narcissistic libido, is extraordinarily increased; whereas in transference neuroses, as is the case in general with people in love, Freud believed that dependence on the loved one lowers self-regard, because a part of their narcissism has been forfeited, and can only be regained by being loved in return (p. 98). He went on to say that:

> When libido is repressed, the erotic cathexis is felt as a severe depletion of the ego, the satisfaction of love is impossible, and the re-enrichment of the ego can be effected only by a withdrawal of libido from its objects. The return of the object-libido to the ego and its transformation into narcissism represents, as it were, a happy love once more . . .
>
> (pp. 98–99)

Freud here describes in the language of his system how a deflated, rejected seeker of love can snatch victory from the jaws of defeat by narcissistic self-inflation. However, it is Freud's linking of narcissism to psychosis that is the part of his conceptualization that I want to elaborate. First, rather than speak in the mechanistic terms of repressed libido or forfeited narcissism, I would identify developmental exposure to the traumatizing narcissist as the source of a severely depleted sense of self, which makes "the satisfaction of love" impossible. This describes two sorts of people: 1) the sort of person that might have difficulty recognizing the controlling, sadistic aspects of the traumatizing narcissist's love, and instead be dazzled and inflated by the narcissist's grandiosity; or 2) the person who reacts to deflation by transforming himself into the traumatizing narcissist.

I also would not want to say universally that being in love lowers self-regard. Rather, I believe that those who tend to idealize and exalt others with whom they fall in love, or who believe, consciously or not, that being loved by someone deemed impressive and prestigious will cure their self-esteem problems, tend to make choices that eventually confirm their sense of hopelessness about love. Severely, chronically deflated people believe that only others can cause them to feel lovable; yet they all too often seek love from people who are unreliable, withholding, and narcissistic—as though only succeeding in getting love from such people could really prove that they are lovable. Needless to say, they rarely succeed with withholders, and instead remain convinced of their loveless fate; if they should happen to find a saintly partner, they will eventually exhaust the other's compassion, and find reason to find the other disappointing.

By contrast, traumatizing narcissists experience themselves as ideal, and they expect to be loved and to be able to maintain power over anyone who loves them. They have learned to defend against their history of being shamed and subjugated by putting others in the situation they were in—by becoming the shamer and the subjugator. In Freud's language, the traumatizing narcissist has repaired his destroyed self by returning his object-libido to the ego, where it is transformed into narcissism. He has rejected the need for others and has found a "happy love"—in his perfect self. His manic response to developmental traumatic nonrecognition leads him as an adult to paranoid delusions of grandeur and paranoid delusions of persecution. Viewing himself as flawless and blameless, anyone criticizing him is identified as a persecutor. This is the psychosis, the paraphrenia, of traumatizing narcissism.

Throughout the developmental stages of the child who as an adult becomes the traumatizing narcissist, his parents believed that their anger, their unhappiness, their sadism, and any other unpleasant emotions within them, were the result of what their bad, selfish child forced them to feel. *The child who becomes the traumatizing narcissist learns from these parents that whatever does not feel good inside is to be externalized—blamed on the actions of someone who is outside.* Believing in one's own infallible righteousness and superiority, and believing that all the badness is outside, never inside, are delusions that are pathognomonic for traumatizing narcissism.

People who are, again in Freud's terms, experiencing severe depletion of the ego due to deprivation of love, may be powerfully drawn to the traumatizing narcissist. His self-love is enchanting, it is exactly what the neurotic, as opposed to the paraphrenic, does not have and wants to get. The neurotic, according to Freud, is always failing to live up to his ego ideal; whereas the paraphrenic has narcissistically taken himself as his own ego ideal. The traumatizing narcissist offers his love as though he is offering the greatest love ever. For someone who has failed to live up to her own ego ideal, being loved by the traumatizing narcissist solves the problem. He bestows his greatness on her, and she is redeemed.

I refer to Freud's linking of narcissism to psychosis, in particular to what he understood as paraphrenia, to underscore the importance of recognizing the psychotic core of the traumatizing narcissist. It is often well hidden. As Blaise Pascal put it, "Men never do evil so completely and cheerfully as when they do it from a religious conviction" (2011). In whatever context—national, racial, religious, parental, medical, educational, psychoanalytic—wherever there is harm caused by behavior stemming from rigid ideological convictions, ideologues clinging tenaciously to their self-righteousness can be found.

The ideology of the traumatizing narcissist is the stubborn conviction of his own perfection. His dissociated narrative goes something like this:

> I am here for you, in spite of your inferiority to me. I am here to help you because my love is so great. Your love is not good enough, but if you give it to me, I will show you how to root out what is bad and selfish in you. When you succeed in loving me in whatever way I dictate, I will reward you with my approval. But to be sure of being able to use you without having to acknowledge my need of you, any progress you make in pleasing me will always be short-lived, not quite enough. So you will need to continue to strive to make your love for me good enough. You won't succeed—I will see to that—because you will stay with me only as long as I can keep you believing that you need to try harder. If you were to feel really good about yourself, you would not continue to need my approval—and my control of you, and the certainty that you will not leave me, would be threatened.

Analytic Love and Narcissism

The line between altruistic love and narcissism, not necessarily bright and clear in general, simply does not exist for the traumatizing narcissist. In seeking to understand analytic love, that line is important for the analyst to identify and protect. I learned about this early in my career from a patient I will call Mark.

Mark

Mark's father was a very successful and well-known film producer, and a powerful, seductive, charming, and subtly domineering father. Mark was struggling to become a filmmaker in his own right at this time, and to distinguish himself in both senses of the word: from his famous father; and as a filmmaker worthy of critical and public attention. His initial reason for seeking help was that he was married to a woman he loved with whom he wanted to have children, but he was having difficulty with an internet pornography habit that had gotten out of control, and the marriage was now on shaky ground.

As our work progressed, it became clear that Mark had found it difficult to stand up to and differentiate himself from his much admired, self-absorbed, and larger than life father; and that he struggled with painful conflicts about his sense of power, potency, bigness, and manliness. Although Mark admired and looked up to his father, he also often felt that his father was subtly or not so subtly belittling. Being the son of this father meant living up to very high expectations, his father's and his own. Therefore, it was not hard for us to reflect on links from his family history to his internet sexual life, which involved the use of two-way webcams in which he could exhibit himself to professional sex worker partners and verbally control exactly how the cybersex played out. Most of the fantasies involved having these women verbalize some form of phallic worship as he and she watched each other masturbating; less often, but often enough, he also sought pleasure by being verbally humiliated, verbally playing out the fantasy of being physically overpowered and made helpless while watching and being watched by his cyber partners. Could Mark be a powerful, phallic, and potent man and still be his father's son? Or was he in fact merely small, shameful, and abject, as he often felt around his father?

Over the course of several years, our work went well, and toward the ending we had planned, Mark brought up something I had said fairly early on. He referred back to how I had let him know one day that something he was asking of me, to speak in a certain way, and use certain words and not others, was evoking in me an unpleasant, oppressive feeling of being controlled. As I explained this to him that day, I compared him to Jimmy Stewart and myself to Kim Novak in the latter portion of Hitchcock's film *Vertigo*, where Stewart demands of Kim Novak, with frightening, sadistic intensity, that she dress for him and try to act exactly as the mysterious woman he could not save from suicide had done. (The reader may recall that Stewart had been duped, and that the former and latter Kim Novaks were actually one and the same imposter.) I had in mind Mark's use of sex workers, and was trying to suggest that as much as he might disavow the sadomasochistic part of him that came out in those encounters, there was a way that I could feel it in the room between us. I did not, at the time, realize how much Mark had been upset by the way I introduced these themes. Now, more than three years later, he was letting me know. In hearing his complaint, I realized that in my decision to disclose my association to *Vertigo*, I had not inquired of him with curiosity about what it was that I was doing that was making him uncomfortable, and why: I had instead used my inherent authority as his analyst to essentially turn the tables on him and get him to stop doing what was making me uncomfortable. As this realization belatedly dawned on me, I told Mark about it, and told him I was embarrassed and remorseful about my clumsy hurtfulness.

Mark appreciated that, but more importantly, he wanted to know the reason why I had done it in the first place. I thought for a few moments, and told him that at the time, I thought I was trying to help him see something about himself as he was with others, a way in which he could be controlling, that he wasn't aware of. What I realized now, I told him, was that the exchange was an example of me being narcissistic, stabilizing my own self-esteem in that moment by destabilizing his, making my point with a kind of hyperbolic irony while disavowing my retaliatory sadism, rather than with responding with sensitivity to how shameful all this was to him. Mark was stunned, tears came to his eyes, and he said,

> "You mean, you can acknowledge being narcissistic at that moment?"
>
> I said, "Yes, and I'm sure it wasn't only at that moment, unfortunately. And yes, I hope I can acknowledge it, and I want to apologize for it!"
>
> Mark said, "Thank you. You have no idea how relieved I am."

Mark was correct, I had no idea, but he explained that there had never been a time, in all the many conflicts he had had with his father, that he had ever known his father to concede any ground whatsoever. In addition to this, in his work with another therapist before he came to see me, he was also put in the position of having to be the wrong one, because his therapist subtly asserted immaculate infallibility. For Mark, this was a watershed moment in the analysis—a moment when he realized that authority figures, like his father and his analyst, can be admired and looked up to, but that doesn't mean they are always right—even, and probably especially, when they refuse to admit they could possibly be wrong.

I have never forgotten how much my willingness to bring into awareness my narcissistic behavior, and apologize for it, meant to Mark, and the difference it made to him. I have been delighted to receive Mark's baby announcements over the years, and to observe, from afar, Mark's career growing ever more successful. Most importantly, though, I am grateful to Mark. From Mark, and from many other patients, students, supervisees, teachers, and supervisors, I have learned a number of things about the analyst's narcissism, and how, if undetected and unacknowledged, it can turn what might seem like analytic love into a form of traumatizing narcissism.

Where is Love?

My interest in the theme of analytic love (Shaw, 2003a, 2007) is tightly interwoven with my interest in the relational system of the traumatizing narcissist. Over the years I have come to know many patients who grew up feeling unloved, or loved in ways that were stunting and exploitive, and who could not as adults find successful ways of loving and being loved. Whether they had an absent or neglectful parent, or an overbearing, over-involved parent, these patients feel orphaned. For them, Oliver Twist's cry of "where is love?" from the song in the musical *Oliver*, is all too familiar.

The adult children of traumatizing narcissist parents are particularly vulnerable to these feelings of lovelessness, especially as they become aware in therapy, if they have not already, of the theft of their subjectivity, and the depth of their feelings of betrayal. They speak of not knowing how they feel or what they want; of organizing all their ways of relating to others around figuring out what they have to provide for the other; of feeling alone and not taken care of; of feeling unable and unwilling to take any real joy in their accomplishments, no matter how successful they may be. They have painful dreams of loss and aloneness, recurring again and again; they enter relationships that repetitively confirm their fear that they cannot be loved. They have a sense of tremendous potential that they feel they are not realizing, and they blame themselves. These persistent feelings of lovelessness and aloneness are not exclusive to the adult children of the traumatizing narcissist, but they are quite typical for these patients.

The sense of lovelessness and aloneness is not what Freud set out to conquer in his quest to map the mind. It is, though, what Ferenczi was after. Ferenczi saw lovelessness as a developmental relational problem, stemming from deficits in the caregivers' way of loving. The person who suffered from lovelessness was for Ferenczi a traumatized person. He eventually came to see his role as requiring him to provide "something" in his relationship to his patient that could heal the pain of lovelessness. Ferenczi struggled mightily to know what that "something" could be. Greater openness, and care to avoid hypocrisy were part of what he found necessary to provide; but he continued to search for more ways he could bring about healing. In his Clinical Diary (Dupont, 1988), he wrote that patients were right in expecting their analysts to provide:

> a genuine interest, a real desire to help. Or more precisely an all-conquering love . . . which alone makes life seem worth living and which constitutes a counterweight to the traumatic situation . . . Without such a counterpressure, let us say counterlove [*Gegenliebe*], the individual tends to explode, to dissolve itself in the universe, perhaps to die.
>
> (p. 129)

As was true for many important concepts in psychoanalysis, Ferenczi was the pioneer experimenter in analytic love. I interpret the above passage to mean that human beings, seeking at every stage of life, from birth to death, to give and take love, are at risk of significant destabilization (lost-in-space fragmentation; psychic death) in the absence of feeling loved. The risk is potentially catastrophic when those feelings are laid down in the earliest developmental years. For the loveless infant, the part of the self that is most directly connected to love has not been brought sufficiently into being—that part has not been recognized by a loving other.

The traumatizing narcissist parent, cloaked in the righteousness of the complementary moral defense, is not a recognizer of the child's separate subjectivity, and this unrecognition is the root cause of that child's sense of lovelessness. Unrecognition means to the developing child that she herself, as a separate subject, is bad, unlovable. Her lovability exists only to the extent that she makes herself a gratifying object of the narcissist. By the time these people seek psychotherapy, it has usually gotten harder and harder to mask the pain of the "unlovable subject" self with the performance of the "gratifying object" self.

Ferenczi's clinical diary is a testament to his extraordinary determination to discover how the psychoanalyst could be a source or a channel for love that could heal and bring back to life the deadened, loveless part of a person. Had he not died prematurely, we may have had the benefit of knowing how his thoughts about analytic love would evolve. I suspect he might have accepted some of the criticisms made against him, mainly by Freud, that his own need to be loved was a driving force in his willingness to give as much as he did to his patients and that he projected his own experience of feeling traumatically unloved by his mother onto his patients. Ferenczi's *furor sanandi* can easily be seen as a mask for his narcissism, his need to be loved as a hero and savior, disguised as loving concern for the patient; that is how it was seen for decades. However, that is a very black and white way of judging Ferenczi, and psychoanalysts generally. This judgment assumes that there are some psychoanalysts or mental health clinicians of any kind whose self-esteem is completely unlinked to their successes with patients, unlinked to how much patients benefit from their efforts, and to how much they are paid by patients or respected by colleagues. Such an assumption would be preposterous.

The process of trying to find a way for an analyst to heal lovelessness through the provision of love eventually became Ferenczi's chief concern, as we learned from his Clinical Diaries. Analysts such as Loewald, Schafer, Nacht, and many others (see Chapter 7, this book) took up this concern, using the term "analytic love" to describe a way of being lovingly devoted to the health, growth, and healing of their patients. Trying to come up with a rubric of sorts for this thing called analytic love, I suggested in the previous chapter that analytic love consists of two fundamental principles:

1 First, a belief in and reverence for the human potential to grow—in meaningful, creative, and productive ways. Analytic love is reflected in the analyst's faith and hope that these potentials can be found and activated in each person seeking his help.
2 The second principle is the analyst's consistent concern for the analysand's safety. Aside from all the obvious meanings of the word safety that would apply, safety in analytic work requires acute sensitivity on the analyst's part to any tendency toward exploitation of the patient—i.e., use of the patient, subtly or otherwise, for the analyst's inappropriate self-gratification. I now consider analytic love to be crucially reflected in the analyst's willingness to be accountable for the wounding work of psychoanalysis—e.g., the inadvertent restimulation of trauma that is nearly inevitable in any treatment; as well as the mistakes and failures, big and small, of not understanding, thinking one understands when one doesn't, saying too much, saying too little, and so on.

Sensitivity and concern for the necessary pain of analytic work, and the effort to protect the patient from exploitation, are aspects of analytic love that are importantly connected to the themes of traumatizing narcissism and intersubjectivity that I have sought to weave together throughout this book. Intersubjective relatedness is by definition the antithesis of the exploitative, sadomasochistic mode of relating of the traumatizing narcissist. Relational psychoanalysis aims to create an intersubjectively constructed analyst/analysand relationship, which is intended to serve not just as a framework, but as a therapeutic agent in its own right—as a healing contrast and antidote to the trauma of feeling repetitively trapped in complementary relational configurations of domination and submission, with no way out. The intersubjectively created analyst/analysand relationship, with its intrinsic valuation of mutuality, honesty, creativity, and freedom—along with the understanding of the asymmetry (Aron, 1996) of the relationship that safeguards the patient from exploitation—is itself an expression of analytic love.

Keeping faith in a developing child's potential to grow; encouraging the potential to develop meaningful ways of expressing her subjectivity; supporting the expansion of meaning and pleasure in intersubjective relatedness; and steadfastly committing to honoring the developing child's need for safety, especially from exploitation—these are the conditions that we know support healthy growth and development. These conditions are not present in the traumatizing narcissist environment; the agenda is enslavement, not development. For patients who have been trapped in the traumatizing narcissist's relational system, analytic work that carefully minds these concerns provides a framework in which these patients have opportunities to heal and to grow in ways that were not possible given their original developmental experience.

The struggle for the adult child of the traumatizing narcissist to feel entitled to and in possession of his own subjectivity is the same as the struggle to cure lovelessness. It is the struggle to feel real, legitimate; to be able to experience joy, pride, and pleasure for himself, as part of himself. It was working with these patients, many of whom I have referred to throughout this volume, that led me to explore the nature of analytic love—because these patients could not sustain within themselves a feeling of being truly loved. Few, if any, analysts familiar with Ferenczi's experiments with mutual analysis would be willing to go to the lengths he did as he tried to find a way of giving of himself that would heal. However, working with many people I have cared for deeply, for whom happiness continued to be painfully elusive, year after year, has tested my hope and my faith—in psychoanalysis, in my patient's capacity for change, and in myself. It is not so hard, with such patients, to identify with Ferenczi's *furore*, his quest to find "the cure."

What is indispensible, for me, what I hold on to, is the understanding that the psychoanalyst and his therapy can play a crucial role in helping to awaken this potential in the patient—but the analyst is not the owner nor even the purveyor of the healing potential. The therapist's essential value lies in her dedication and skill in helping patients find this potential *within themselves*. If we help them feel even a spark of it, and help them to want to hold on to it and make it grow, then I believe we will be providing what is needed to mobilize themselves and find a pathway out of lovelessness.

I was moved by a session with Meg when I perceived some stirring of hope in a dream she reported. Her previous dreams had been about acute feelings of desolation and loss. This was the first dream she had told me that seemed to present something new.

Meg

Meg is an elegant, thoroughly charming woman in her forties who created and runs her own consulting business that is recognized in her field as highly innovative and successful. A child prodigy, Meg was successful before she'd even finished college, where she had achieved a number of brilliant successes with some high-profile clients.

She contacted me when she began to recognize that she had been raised by her mother in a cult-like branch of a Christian religion. Her realizations had led her to painful confrontations with her mother (her father, long divorced from her mother, was deceased). She had felt it necessary to break off contact with her mother, which she felt was right for her; but she was terribly unhappy.

I learned that Meg had become unusually self-reliant at a very early age, and that she had attempted to mediate her parents' bitter, rageful disputes throughout her childhood and adolescence, when finally her father left her mother, and essentially left Meg as well. As she explained her mother and their relationship to me over the first year or so of our work, we came to understand her very glamorous mother as utterly self-absorbed, and completely obsessed with New Age self-realization, health and spirituality programs, viewing herself as a highly evolved spiritual adept. Her mother's spiritual prescriptions and bromides, offered as though her wisdom was her way of loving, disgusted Meg. Aside from what Meg saw as the intellectual fatuousness of her mother's beliefs, Meg felt that her mother gave her "pearls of wisdom" as a substitute for the love her mother was incapable of giving.

Meg's dreams in our first year of work were emotionally harrowing, vivid depictions of the grief she experienced, and the extraordinary sense of aloneness, lovelessness, and desolation she would feel, again and again, in scenes with her oblivious mother and her father. She didn't see her father's face in these dreams; she would only see his back, through tears, as he was leaving. For most of our work in that first year, Meg was coming to terms with the impact of her necessitated self-reliance. It meant that no matter how much she needed others to be there for her, to help her, to be dependable, there simply was no one. "But your husband?" I would ask, a man I knew she admired for his brilliant intellect and passionately held ideals and values that informed his academic work. I learned that she did not show her pain to him, because she felt her value to him was as a support and help in his work. Meg is used to being an uplifter in her personal and work life, not a downer.

"Are you doing work that you love?" I would ask. "What makes it so impossible to take pride in your success? What would you rather do instead?" My questions often drew one pained, rueful response, in a choked and tearful voice: "I don't know," Meg would say.

Meg gave up on therapy for a while, but then she returned, and in the year between our two periods of work, we both had changed. Meg was still stuck, in ways that were similar to how she had been previously, but I sensed that she was more ready now to push through. I, in turn, had become clearer about something I hadn't been able to formulate previously.

"Meg," I said one morning in our one session that week. I took a deep breath, hoping that what I was going to say would be clear, and that she would really hear me.

"Everything in you, for almost all of your life, has wanted to find expression—in art, in writing, in public speaking, in teaching—in creating. This You, the one that wants to contribute in creative, innovative ways, to give of yourself to help others grow and succeed—this You has never stopped.

At the same time, another You, who feels the bitterness of not knowing what it might be like to feel truly seen and known by mother and father, who gave up on being known and recognized, who knew that everything would always be negated—that You fights the other You every minute of every day. Negating You turns everything Creative You wants and enjoys and succeeds at into nothing. Negating You lets Creative You survive as long as you can keep others happy—but Negating You nips any joy and pride of your own in the bud—so Creative You won't hope, won't care, won't know fulfillment. Couldn't Negating You stop needing to ruin everything for Creative You, already? Hasn't it gone on long enough?"

She was crying silently, as she often does, her tears not falling. She didn't speak for a while, and finally I said, "Do you know what I'm talking about?"

"Yes," was all she said, and we had to end.

The following week, I did not know what to expect—I half expected Meg would be shut down. However, on the contrary, Meg was alive and excited in a way I hadn't seen before. She was excited as she told me that she had realized that she set up every situation and relationship in her life to be a means by which she could use her talents to solve other people's problems and help them have what they wanted. In doing so, she realized, she made herself into exactly the kind of object the other would find most useful; but she, herself, somehow ended up feeling lost, exhausted, drained—and loveless.

"Meg," I asked, "does it have to be only about them? Couldn't it be about you, too? Couldn't the pleasure be mutual?"

"I don't know how to do that, I have no idea how that happens," she answered. She was tearing up again.

"Meg," I said, "I think Negating You just took over and told Creative You to curb your enthusiasm."

"Yup," she said. "It's on!" We laughed.

Although Meg's subsequent sessions were more full of hopelessness and exhaustion, after about a month, she was excited again, and had an important dream.

It had two parts. In the first, she was leaving the apartment she had lived in for years to move in with the man who later became her husband. She was sobbing, because she was going to have to leave behind a lot of her important work-related books, notebooks, and awards. Her boyfriend said, "It's going to be OK. I'm here. I'm with you." Then immediately came the next part of the dream. She was helping a team of executives with a project, and she was full of energy and enthusiasm, and doing a wonderful job. However, she was aware of being watched, perhaps through one of the windows—as though there were someone who suspected something about her.

As we talked about the dream, we understood the first part of the dream to show Creative Meg, sobbing because she could not hold on to the parts of herself that she valued: they were being taken away. This theme had been revisited in previous dreams, with the same intensity of despair. The second part showed Performing Meg—the ideally accommodating perfect object for the benefit of others—with someone watching, perhaps seeing through her performance.

> "But Meg," I said, "your husband was with you in the first part, and he said so clearly, 'I'm with you, it's going to be OK.' You were in pain, but you were not alone—you had a compassionate witness." She listened, tears welling up. "And in the second part, you knew what you were doing—your Perfect Object routine. You were on to yourself. Maybe that was what the feeling of someone watching was about."
>
> "OK," said Meg. "But what about how everything gets taken away, again and again?"
>
> "Meg," I said, "at this point, it's just Creative You leaving yourself, handing yourself over to Negating You."
>
> She seemed taken aback for a moment. I asked, "Is that ok to say?"
>
> "Of course. But how is that going to stop?"
>
> I smiled. Meg is incredibly practical and result oriented. I said, "To be honest, I'm not entirely sure, but I'm sure I'm going to help you figure that out. You've already started turning that around, you know . . . You do know that, yes?"
>
> "I'll take your word for it for now," she replied, smiling.

Meg didn't need help to function per se—she has been an exceptionally productive person all her life. Meg needed to be able to enjoy her work, to take pride in it, and to be able to feel that she can let others help and support her. She is trying to find a way to be the expert creator, leader, and problem-solver she has always been, without feeling so alone, and so drained. Her dream shows the old situations, but with a difference—in the first part, she is not alone: someone who loves her, the man she later married, is there, a witness to her pain. In the second part, Meg does her "make everybody happy" routine—but she is being watched, she doesn't know by whom. I think it is Meg watching—Meg who knows much more about who she is; Meg who is many things, who is multiple; Meg, on to herself, standing in the spaces, watching Meg in the dream compulsively taking care of everyone, knowing that is just one way of being herself. Looking at the dream this way with Meg, emphasizing its leading edge aspects (Tolpin, 2002) (not alone with grief, able to be loved; self-awareness), Meg is not ready to trust that she might be starting to imagine a way out of isolation, loss, and pretense. This is the hope that I will continue to hold for her, having faith that at some point, Meg will truly grieve, and move from melancholia to freedom.

Analytic Love, with Eyes Wide Open

I have chosen to end this volume by speaking of analytic love because, as difficult as it can be to define, one thing is perfectly clear: it does not and cannot spring from a traumatizing, narcissistic relational system. It is probably fair to say that there can be no end to working out what this "analytic love" is all about. I hope that what I have presented in this chapter illuminates the complicated interrelationship between analytic love and narcissism. If an analyst is delusional, she will not know it. She will function, sometimes very highly, with some students, some supervisees, and some patients who will believe in her ability to know what is best for them, who will believe her claim that all that she does and tells them to do is in their best interests, and comes from her love for them. These patients will not see, sometimes for many years, that it is actually their analyst's own self-interest being served, because they will have needed and wanted her approval so much. They will have wanted to place themselves within the glow of her prestige so much, and believed so deeply in her claims to be able to transform them into people like her, a fully-realized master. They will not realize how dependent and how diminished she has made them, so that she could hold on to them, by showing them again and again how far they still have to go.

I can see no systematic way of rooting out the traumatizing narcissist from analytic training institutes. It would be grotesque to see institutes adopting a witch-hunt mentality in an effort to determine who the most offensive narcissists are, so that they could be purged. In that kind of situation, it's likely that an outsider wouldn't be able to discern the difference between the purgers and the purgees. One purpose of writing this book is to create a vocabulary to describe and identify the traumatizing narcissist's relational system, so that we may understand more clearly the impact of narcissism, on our patients and ourselves.

In contrast to the narcissistic system of relating, analytic love is what happens when we do our work with the awareness and acceptance of our own vulnerabilities and fallibility; and with the willingness to acknowledge shame, at least to ourselves, when that is what we are feeling. Analytic love is the balance we find and the tension we maintain between keeping faith with ourselves, and faith in our sincerity and our expertise, while knowing that we are never more than human, always largely unconscious, and as such, always fallible, always vulnerable. Analytic love is a surrender to the process of building a therapeutic relationship—surrender as Ghent (1990) understood the word; surrender of the need to know, of the need to be right, of the need to use our knowledge of the psyche and our position of authority to protect ourselves from being the one who *needs* help, by being instead the one who *dispenses* help. Analytic love encourages us to take risks with our patients, hoping that we are making productive choices but knowing that we may wound in the process. Analytic love is what protects us both, analyst and analysand, from the unfreedom of domination and submission. It is what supports both analyst and analysand in a sustained commitment to the intersubjective construction of the analytic relationship.

Finally, analytic love contains the hope and the faith that where fear of retraumatization and alienation were, compassion, understanding, and mutuality shall be.

Notes

1 This sub-heading is inspired by Muriel Dimen, who previously suggested in a similar vein that Perversion Is Us? (Dimen, 2001).

2 The wonderful performances of Charles Boyer and Ingrid Bergman in the 1944 George Cukor film *Gaslight* depict how persuasive and destructive a charismatic narcissist can be. This is the film that gave the mental health profession the term "gaslighting"—behaving in such a way as to drive someone else crazy, while denying any such intention. However, the Boyer character is thoroughly deliberate about driving the Bergman character crazy, and is therefore a psychopath. The traumatizing narcissist differs in that he operates from a delusional conviction of righteousness.

References

Abraham, K. (1942). A short study of the development of the libido, viewed in the light of mental disorders. In: *Selected Papers of Karl Abraham*. London: The Hogarth Press (first published in 1924), p. 450.

Abraham, N. and Torok, M. (1984). "The lost object—me": Notes on identification within the crypt. *Psychoanalytic Inquiry*, 4:221–242.

Appignanesi, L. and Forrester, J. (1992). *Freud's Women*. New York: Basic Books.

Applebaum, B. and Gebeloff, R. (Feb. 11, 2012). Even critics of safety net increasingly depend on it. *The New York Times*. http://www.nytimes.com/2012/02/12/us/even-critics-of-safety-net-increasingly-depend-on-it.html?scp=2&sq=tea%20party&st=cse (accessed June 1, 2013).

Aron, L. (1996). A *Meeting of Minds: Mutuality in Psychoanalysis*. Hillsdale, NJ: The Analytic Press.

____ (2000). Self-reflexivity and the therapeutic action of psychoanalysis. *Psychoanalytic Psychology*, 17:667–689.

____ (2006). Analytic impasse and the third: Clinical implications of intersubjectivity theory. *International Journal of Psychoanalysis*, 87:349–368.

Aron, L. and Harris, A. (1993). *The Legacy of Sándor Ferenczi*. Hillsdale, NJ: The Analytic Press.

Auerbach, J.S. (1993). The origins of narcissism and narcissistic personality disorder: A theoretical and empirical reformulation. In: J.M. Masling and R.F. Bernstein (Eds.) *Empirical Studies of Psychoanalytic Theories: Vol. 4. Psychoanalytic Perspectives on Psychopathology*. Washington, DC: American Psychological Association, pp. 43–108.

Bacal, H. (1987). British object-relations theorists and self psychology: Some critical reflections. *International Journal of Psychoanalysis*, 68:81–98.

Bacal, H. and Thomson, P. (1998). Optimal responsiveness and the therapist's reaction to the patient's unresponsiveness. In: H. Bacal (Ed.) *Optimal Responsiveness*. Northvale, NJ: Jason Aronson, pp. 249–270.

Bach, S. (1985). *Narcissistic States and the Therapeutic Process*. New York: Jason Aronson, Inc.

____ (1994). *The Language of Perversion and the Language of Love*. Northvale, NJ: Jason Aronson, Inc.

____ (2006). *Getting From Here to There: Analytic Love, Analytic Process*. Hillsdale, NJ: The Analytic Press.

Balint, A. (1933). Love for the mother and mother love. In: M. Balint *Primary Love and Psychoanalytic Technique*. New York: Liveright, pp. 109–127.

Balint, M. (1937). Early developmental states of the ego: Primary object-love. In: M. Balint (Ed.) *Primary Love and Psycho-analytic Technique*. New York: Liveright, pp. 90–108.

____ (1968). *The Basic Fault. Therapeutic Aspects of Regression*. London: Tavistock Publications.

Bateson, G., Jackson, D. D., Haley, J., and Weakland, J. (1956). Toward a theory of schizophrenia. *Behavioral Science*, 1:251–264.

Becker, E. (1973). *Denial of Death*. New York: The Free Press.

Becker, J. (2012). E-mails suggest Paterno role in silence on Sandusky. *The New York Times*, June 30, 2012.

Beebe, B. and Lachmann, F. M. (1998). Co-constructing inner and relational processes. *Psychoanalytic Psychology*, 15:480–516.

Beebe, B., Jaffe, J., and Lachmann, F. (1992). A dyadic systems view of communication. In: N. Skolnick and S. Warshaw (Eds.) *Relational Perspectives in Psychoanalysis*. Hillsdale, NJ: The Analytic Press, pp. 61–81.

Benjamin, J. (1988). *The Bonds of Love: Psychoanalysis, Feminism and the Problem of Domination*. New York: Pantheon.

____ (1995). *Like Subjects, Love Objects: Recognition and Sexual Difference*. New Haven, CT: Yale University Press.

____ (1998). *Shadow of the Other: Intersubjectivity and Gender in Psychoanalysis*. New York: Routledge.

____ (1999). Afterword. In: S. Mitchell and L. Aron (Eds.) *Relational Psychoanalysis*. Hillsdale, NJ: The Analytic Press, pp. 201–210.

____ (2004). Beyond doer and done to: An intersubjective view of thirdness. *Psychoanalytic Quarterly*, 73:5–46.

____ (2009a). A relational psychoanalysis perspective on the necessity of acknowledging failure in order to restore the facilitating and containing features of the intersubjective relationship the shared third. *International Journal of Psychoanalysis*, 90:441–450.

____ (2009b). Response. *International Journal of Psychoanalysis*, 90:457–462.

Berman, E. (2004). *Impossible Training: A Relational View of Psychoanalytic Education*. Hillsdale, NJ: The Analytic Press.

Bernstein, R. (1992). *The New Constellation*. Cambridge, MA: MIT Press.

Black, D. (1975). Totalitarian therapy on the upper west side. *New York Magazine*, December 15, 1975.

Black, S. (1999). *Eugene O'Neill: Beyond Mourning and Tragedy*. New Haven, CT: Yale University Press.

Bohman, J. (2005). Critical thinking. *Stanford Encyclopedia of Philosophy*. http://plato.stanford.edu/entries/critical-theory/ (accessed June 1, 2013).

Bollas, C. (1983). Expressive uses of the countertransference: Notes to the patient from oneself. *Contemporary Psychoanalysis*, 19:1–33.

Bowlby, J. (1969). *Attachment and Loss: Vol. 1: Attachment*. New York: Basic Books.

____ (1973). *Attachment and Loss: Vol. 2: Separation*. New York: Basic Books.

____ (1980). *Attachment and Loss: Vol. 3: Loss*. New York: Basic Books.

Brandchaft, B. (1994). Structures of pathological accommodation and change in analysis. Presented at the Association for Psychoanalytic Self Psychology, New York City, March 1994.

Brandchaft, B., Doctors, S., and Sorter, D. (2010). *Toward an Emancipatory Psychoanalysis: Brandchaft's Intersubjective Vision*. New York: Routledge.

Breger, L. (2000). *Freud: Darkness in the Midst of Vision.* New York: John Wiley & Sons, Inc.
____ (2009). *A Dream of Undying Fame: How Freud Betrayed His Mentor and Invented Psychoanalysis.* New York: Basic Books.
Brenman, E. (2006). *Recovery of the Lost Good Object.* London: Routledge.
Brightman, B. (1984–85). Narcissistic issues in the training experience of the psychotherapist. *International Journal of Psychoanalytic Psychotherapy*, 10:293–317.
Britton, R. (2004). Narcissistic disorders in clinical practice. *Journal of Analytical Psychology*, 49:477–490.
Bromberg, P.M. (1991). On knowing one's patient inside out: The aesthetics of unconscious communication. *Psychoanalytic Dialogues*, 1:399–422.
____ (1993). Shadow and substance: A relational perspective on clinical process. *Psychoanalytic Psychology*, 10:147–168.
____ (1998). *Standing in the Spaces: Essays on Clinical Process, Trauma and Dissociation.* Hillsdale, NJ: The Analytic Press.
____ (2003). One need not be a house to be haunted: On enactment, dissociation, and the dread of "not-me"—A case study. *Psychoanalytic Dialogues*, 13:689–709.
____ (2006). *Awakening the Dreamer: Clinical Journeys.* New York: Routledge.
____ (2011). *The Shadow of the Tsunami: And the Growth of the Relational Mind.* New York: Routledge.
Brothers, D. and Lewinberg, E. (1999). The therapeutic partnership: Developmental view of self-psychological treatment as bilateral healing. In: A. Goldberg (Ed.) *Pluralism in Self Psychology: Progress in Self Psychology.* Vol. 15. Hillsdale, NJ: The Analytic Press, pp. 259–284.
Carnochan, P. (2001). *Looking for Ground.* Hillsdale, NJ: The Analytic Press.
Celenza, A. (2007). *Sexual Boundary Violations: Therapeutic, Supervisory and Academic Contexts.* New York: Jason Aronson, Inc.
Celenza, A. and Gabbard, G.O. (2003). Analysts who commit sexual boundary violations: A lost cause? *Journal of the American Psychoanalytic Association*, 51:617–636.
Cialdini, R. (2008). *Influence: Science and Practice.* New York: Pearson.
Clinton, W. (2004). *My Life.* New York: Knopf Publishing Group.
Coates, S. and Moore, M. (1997). The complexity of early trauma: Representation and transformation. *Psychoanalytic Inquiry*, 17:286–311.
Coen, S.J. (1994). Barriers to love between patient and analyst. *Journal of the American Psychoanalytic Association*, 42:1107–1136.
Collins, S. (1980). Freud, and the "riddle of suggestion." *International Review of Psycho-Analysis*, 7:429–438.
Conason, J. and McGarrahan, E. (1986). Escape from Utopia. *The Village Voice*, April 22, 1986.
Cooper, S. (2004). State of the hope: The new bad object in the therapeutic action of psychoanalysis. *Psychoanalytic Dialogues*, 14(5):527–551.
Davies, J.M. (1998). Between the disclosure and foreclosure of erotic transference-countertransference: Can psychoanalysis find a place for adult sexuality? *Psychoanalytic Dialogues*, 8:747–766
____ (2003). Falling in love with love: Oedipal and postoedipal manifestations of idealization, mourning and erotic masochism. *Psychoanalytic Dialogues*, 13:1–27.
____ (2004). Whose bad objects are we anyway? Repetition and our elusive love affair with evil. *Psychoanalytic Dialogues*, 14:711–732.

Davies, J.M. and Frawley, M.G. (1994). *Treating the Adult Survivor of Childhood Sexual Abuse: A Psychoanalytic Perspective*. New York: Basic Books.

Davis, W. (1994). *Get the Guests: Psychoanalysis, Modern American Drama, and the Audience*. Madison, WI: The University of Wisconsin Press.

DeForest, I. (1954). *The Leaven of Love*. New York: Harper & Brothers.

Dimen, M. (2001). Perversion is us?: Eight notes. *Psychoanalytic Dialogues*, 11:825–860.

DuPont, J. (Ed.) (1988). *The Clinical Diary of Sándor Ferenczi*. Cambridge, MA: Harvard University Press.

Ellman, S. (1998). *Enactment: Toward a New Approach to the Therapeutic Relationship*. Northvale, NJ: Jason Aronson, Inc.

Faimberg, H. (1988). The telescoping of generations: Genealogy of certain identifications. *Contemporary Psychoanalysis*, 24:99–117.

Fairbairn, W.R.D. (1952). *Psychoanalytic Studies of the Personality*. London: Tavistock Publications Ltd.

____ (1958). On the nature and aims of psychoanalytical treatment. *International Journal of Psychoanalysis*, 39:374–385.

Falzeder, E. (1994). My grand patient, my chief tormenter: A hitherto unnoticed case of Freud's and the consequences. *Psychoanalytic Quarterly*, 63:297–331.

Ferenczi, S. (1926). *Further Contributions to the Theory and Technique of Psychoanalysis*. Trans, J. Suttie. London: The Hogarth Press.

____ (1929). The unwanted child and his death-instinct. *International Journal of Psychoanalysis*, 10:125–129.

____ (1933/1980). Confusion of tongues between adults and the child. In: M. Balint (Ed.), E. Mosbacher (Trans.) *Final Contributions to the Problems and Methods of Psycho-Analysis*. London: Karnac Books, pp. 156–167.

Fonagy, P. and Target, M. (1996). Playing with reality: I. Theory of mind and the normal development of psychic reality. *International Journal of Psychoanalysis*, 77:217–233.

____ (1998). Mentalization and the changing aims of child psychoanalysis. *Psychoanalytic Dialogues*, 8:87–114.

Fonagy, P., Steele, M., Moran, G., Steele, H., and Higgitt, A. (1991). Measuring the ghost in the nursery: A summary of the main findings of the Anna Freud Centre—University College London parent–child study. *Bulletin of the Anna Freud Centre*, 14:115–131.

Fosshage, J. (1992). Self psychology: The self and its vicissitudes within a relational matrix. In: N. Skolnick and S. Warshaw (Eds.) *Relational Perspectives in Psychoanalysis*. Hillsdale, NJ: The Analytic Press, pp. 21–42.

____ (1997). Chapter 4 Listening/experiencing perspectives and the quest for a facilitating responsiveness. *Progress in Self Psychology*, 13:33–55.

____ (1999). Forms of relatedness and analytic intimacy. Presented at the 22nd Annual International Conference on the Psychology of the Self, Toronto, October 29, 1999.

Fox, R. (1998). The "unobjectionable" positive countertransference. *Journal of the American Psychoanalytic Association*, 46:1067–1087.

Fraiberg, S.H., Adelson, E., and Shapiro, V. (1975). Ghosts in the nursery: A psychoanalytic approach to the problem of impaired infant–mother relationships. *Journal of the American Academy of Child Psychiatry*, 14:387–422.

Frank, T. (2012). *Pity the Billionaire: The Hard-times Swindle and the Unlikely Comeback of the Right*. New York: Metropolitan Books.

Frawley-O'Dea, M. and Sarnat, J. (2001). *The Supervisory Relationship*. New York: Guilford Press.

Freud, S. (1914). On narcissism: An introduction. In: *The Standard Edition of the Complete Psychological Works of Sigmund Freud, Volume XIV (1914–1916): On the History of the Psycho-Analytic Movement, Papers on Metapsychology and Other Works*. London: Hogarth Press, pp. 67–102.

Friedman, L. (1978). Trends in the psychoanalytic theory of treatment. *Psychoanalytic Quarterly*, 47:524–567.

Fromm, E. (1941). *Escape From Freedom*. New York: Farrar and Rinehart.

____ (1950). *Psychoanalysis and Religion*. New Haven, CT: Yale University Press.

____ (1955). *The Sane Society*. New York: Rinehart & Company.

____ (1956). *The Art of Loving*. New York: Harper Collins.

____ (1959). *Sigmund Freud's Mission: An Analysis of His Personality and Influence*. New York: Harper.

____ (1961). *Marx's Concept of Man*. New York: Frederick Ungar Publishing.

____ (1964). *The Heart of Man: Its Genius for Good and Evil*. New York: Harper and Row.

Fromm-Reichmann, F. (1959). *Psychoanalysis and Psychotherapy*. Chicago: The University of Chicago Press.

Gabbard, G.O. and Lester, E. (1995). *Boundaries and Boundary Violations in Psychoanalysis*. New York: Basic Books.

Gelb, A. and Gelb. B. (2000). *O'Neill: Life With Monte Cristo*. New York: Applause Books.

Ghent, E. (1989). Credo: The dialectics of one-person and two-person psychologies. *Contemporary Psychoanalysis*, 25:169–211.

____ (1990). Masochism, submission, surrender: Masochism as a perversion of surrender. *Contemporary Psychoanalysis*, 26:108–136.

____ (1992). Paradox and process. *Psychoanalytic Dialogues*, 2:135–159.

Gitelson, M. (1962). The curative factors in psycho-analysis. *International Journal of Psychoanalysis*, 43:194–205.

Goldner, V. (2004). When love hurts: Treating abusive relationships. *Psychoanalytic Inquiry*, 24:346–372.

Grand, S. (2000). *The Reproduction of Evil: A Clinical and Cultural Perspective*. Hillsdale, NJ: The Analytic Press.

____ (In press). *God at an Impasse: Devotion, Social Justice and the Psychoanalytic Subject*.

Greenacre, P. (1957). The childhood of the artist: Libidinal phase development and giftedness. *Psychoanalytic Study of the Child*, 12:47–72.

Greenberg, J.R. and Mitchell, S.A. (1983). *Object Relations in Psychoanalytic Theory*. Cambridge, MA: Harvard University Press.

Guntrip, H. (1971). *Psychoanalytic Theory, Therapy and the Self*. New York: Basic Books.

Hamilton, J.W. (1976). Early trauma, dreaming and creativity: Works of Eugene O'Neill. *International Review of Psychoanalysis*, 3:341–364.

____ (1979). Transitional phenomena and the early writings of Eugene O'Neill. *International Review of Psychoanalysis*, 6:49–60.

Herman, J. (1992). *Trauma and Recovery*. New York: Basic Books.

Hewitt, M.A. (2012). Dangerous amnesia: Restoration and renewal of connections between psychoanalysis and Critical Social Theory. *Contemporary Psychoanalysis*, 48(1):72–99.

Hirsch, I. (1983). Analytic intimacy and the restoration of nurturance. *The American Journal of Psychoanalysis*, 43:325–343.

____ (1994). Countertransference love and theoretical models. *Psychoanalytic Dialogues*, 4:171–192.

Hirsch, I. and Kessel, P. (1988). Reflections on mature love and countertransference. *Free Associations*, 12:60–83.
Hoffman, I. Z. (1998). *Ritual and Spontaneity in the Psychoanalytic Process: A Dialectical-Constructivist View*. Hillsdale, NJ: The Analytic Press.
____ (2009). Doublethinking our way to "scientific" legitimacy: The dessication of human experience. *Journal of the American Psychoanalytic Association*, 57:1043–1069.
Hollander, N. (2010). *Uprooted Minds: Surviving the Politics of Terror in the Americas*. New York: Routledge.
Horkheimer, M. (1982). *Critical Theory*. New York: Seabury Press.
Howell, E. (2005). *The Dissociative Mind*. New York: Routledge.
Jacobs, A. (1999). Clinton's a compartmentalizer: Are you? *The New York Observer*, November 1, 1999.
Kalsched, D. E. (1996). *The Inner World of Trauma: Archetypal Defenses of the Personal Spirit*. New York: Routledge.
Kernberg, O. (1975). *Borderline Conditions and Pathological Narcissism*. Northvale, NJ: Jason Aronson, Inc.
Kerr, J. (1994). *A Most Dangerous Method*. New York: Vintage Books.
Klein, M. (1932). *The Psycho-Analysis of Children*. London: The Hogarth Press.
Klein, N. (2007). *The Shock Doctrine*. New York: Metropolitan Press.
Kohut, H. (1959). Introspection, empathy and psychoanalysis. *Journal of the American Psychoanalytic Association*, 7:459–483.
____ (1966). Forms and transformations of narcissism. *Journal of the American Psychoanalytic Association*, 14:243–272.
____ (1968). The psychoanalytic treatment of narcissistic personality disorders: Outline of a systematic approach. *Psychoanalytic Study of the Child*, 23:86–113.
____ (1979). The two analyses of Mr Z. *International Journal of Psychoanalysis*, 60:3–27.
____ (1984). *How Does Analysis Cure?* Chicago: University of Chicago Press.
____ (1990a). Creativeness, charisma, group psychology. In: P. Ornstein (Ed.) *The Search for the Self, Vol. 2*. Madison, CT: International Universities Press, pp. 793–843. (Original work published 1978.)
____ (1990b). On leadership. In: P. Ornstein (Ed.) *The Search for the Self, Vol. 3*. Madison, CT: International Universities Press, pp. 103–128. (Original work published 1969.)
Kristeva, J. (1987). *In the Beginning Was Love*. New York: Columbia University.
Lasky, J. and Silverman, H. (Eds.) (1988). *Love: Psychoanalytic Perspectives*. New York: New York University Press.
Layton, L. (2009). Who's responsible? Our mutual implication in each other's suffering. *Psychoanalytic Dialogues*, 19:105–120.
____ (2010). Irrational exuberance: Neoliberalism and the perversion of truth. *Subjectivity*, 3(3):303–322.
____ (2011). Something to do with a girl named Marla Singer: Capitalism, narcissism and therapeutic discourse in David Fincher's *Fight Club*. *Free Associations*, 62:112–134.
____ (in press). Dialectical constructivism in historical context: Expertise and the subject of late modernity. *Psychoanalytic Dialogues*.
Lear, J. (1990). *Love and Its Place in Nature*. New York: Farrar, Straus & Giroux.
Levine, H. and Reed, G. (Eds.) (2004). Problems of power in psychoanalytic institutions. *Psychoanalytic Inquiry*, 24(1):1–139.
Lifton, R. J. (1961). *Thought Reform and the Psychology of Totalism: A Study of "Brainwashing" in China*. New York City: Norton.

____ (1989). *Thought Reform and the Psychology of Totalism*. Chapel Hill: University of NC Press.

____ (2000a). *Destroying the World to Save It: Aum Shinrikyo, Apocalyptic Violence, and the New Global Terrorism*. New York: Macmillan.

____ (2000b). *The Nazi Doctors: Medical Killing and the Psychology of Genocide*. New York: Basic Books.

____ (2012). Dr Robert J. Lifton's eight criteria for thought reform. http://www.csj.org/studyindex/studymindctr/study_mindctr_lifton.htm (accessed June 1, 2013).

Loewald, H.W. (1960). On the therapeutic action of psycho-analysis. *International Journal of Psychoanalysis*, 41:16–33.

____ (1979). The waning of the Oedipus Complex. *Journal of the American Psychoanalytic Association*, 27:751–775.

Lothane, Z. (1998). The feud between Freud and Ferenczi over love. *American Journal of Psychoanalysis*, 58:21–39.

Lyall, S. (2012). After five books, a measure of peace. *The New York Times*, March 14, 2012.

McWilliams, N. and Lependorf, S. (1990). Narcissistic pathology of everyday life: The denial of remorse and gratitude. *Contemporary Psychoanalysis*, 26:430–451.

Mahler, M., Pine, F., and Bergman, A. (1975). *The Psychological Birth of the Human Infant: Symbiosis and Individuation*. New York: Basic Books.

Mahony, P. (1996). *Freud's Dora*. New Haven, CT: Yale University Press.

Main, M., Kaplan, N., and Cassidy, J. (1985). Security in infancy, childhood, and adulthood: A move to the level of representation. *Monographs of the Society for Research in Child Development*, 50(1–2):66–104.

Mann, D. (2002). *Love and Hate: Psychoanalytic Perspectives*. New York: Brunner-Routledge.

Maroda, K. (1991). *The Power of Countertransference*. Northvale, NJ: Jason Aronson, Inc.

____ (1999). *Seduction, Surrender, and Transformation*. Hillsdale, NJ: The Analytic Press.

Mayer, J. (2010). Covert operations: The billionaire brothers who are waging a war against Obama. *The New Yorker*, August 30, 2010.

Miller, A. (1981). *Prisoners of Childhood: The Drama of the Gifted Child*. New York: Basic Books.

Mitchell, S.A. (1988). *Relational Concepts in Psychoanalysis: An Integration*. Cambridge, MA: Harvard University Press.

____ (1993). *Hope and Dread in Psychoanalysis*. New York: Basic Books.

____ (1997). *Influence and Autonomy in Psychoanalysis*. Hillsdale, NJ: The Analytic Press.

____ (2000a). *Relationality: From Attachment to Intersubjectivity*. Hillsdale, NJ: The Analytic Press.

____ (2000b). You've got to suffer if you want to sing the blues: Psychoanalytic reflections on guilt and self-pity. *Psychoanalytic Dialogues*, 10(5):713–733.

____ (2003a). *Relationality: From Attachment to Intersubjectivity*. New York: Routledge.

____ (2003b). *Can Love Last?: The Fate of Romance over Time*. New York: W.W. Norton and Company.

Mitchell, S. and Black, M. (1995). *Freud and Beyond: A History of Modern Psychoanalytic Thought*. New York: Basic Books.

Nacht, S. (1962). The curative factors in psycho-analysis. *International Journal of Psychoanalysis*, 43:206–211.

O'Neill, E. (1919). *The Moon of the Caribbees and Six Other Plays of the Sea*. New York: Boni & Liveright.

____ (1952). *A Moon for the Misbegotten.* New York: Random House.

____ (2002). *Long Day's Journey into Night.* New Haven, CT: Yale University Press.

Orange, D. (1995). *Emotional Understanding: Studies in Psychoanalytic Epistemology.* New York: Guilford Press.

Ornstein, A. (1974). The dread to repeat and the new beginning: A contribution to the psychoanalysis of the narcissistic personality disorders. *The Annual of Psychoanalysis*, 2:231–248.

Orwell, G. (1949). *1984.* New York: Harcourt, Brace and Co.

Oursler, F. (1949). *The Greatest Story Ever Told.* New York: Doubleday and Co.

Ovid III (1984). *Metamorphoses, Books I–VIII.* (Books 1–8, Volume 3). G. P. Goold (Ed.), Frank Justus Miller (Trans.). Cambridge, MA: Loeb Classical Library.

Pascal, B. (2011). *Pensées.* Radford, VA: Wilder Publications.

Pearce, J. and Newton, S. (1963). *The Conditions of Human Growth.* New York: Citadel Press.

Philipson, I. (2011). The last public psychoanalyst? Why Fromm matters in the 21st Century. Paper presented at Div 39th annual meeting, April 2011.

Plame, V. (2007). *Fair Game: My Life as a Spy, My Betrayal by the White House.* New York: Simon & Schuster.

Putnam, F. W. (1992). Discussion: Are alter personalities fragments or figments? *Psychoanalytic Inquiry*, 12:95–111.

Racker, H. (1968). *Transference and Countertransference.* New York: International Universities Press.

Raubolt, R. (Ed.) (2006). *Power Games: Influence, Persuasion, and Indoctrination in Psychotherapy Training.* New York: Other Press.

Reis, B. (1995). Time as the missing dimension in traumatic memory and dissociative subjectivity. In: J. Alpert (Ed.) *Sexual Abuse Recalled.* Northvale, NJ: Aronson, pp. 215–234.

Rosenfeld, H. (1965). *Psychotic States: A Psychoanalytical Approach.* London: The Hogarth Press.

____ (1971). A clinical approach to the psychoanalytic theory of the life and death instincts: An investigation into the aggressive aspects of narcissism. *International Journal of Psychoanalysis*, 52:169–178.

____ (1987). *Impasse and Interpretation.* London: Tavistock Publications Ltd.

Rudnytsky, P. (2000). *Psychoanalytic Conversations: Interviews with Clinicians, Commentators, and Critics.* Hillsdale, NJ: The Analytic Press.

Russell, P. L. (1993). The essential invisibility of trauma and the need for repetition: Commentary on Shabad's "Resentment, Indignation, Entitlement." *Psychoanalytic Dialogues*, 3:515–522.

St. Aubyn, E. (2012a). *The Patrick Melrose Novels.* New York: Farrar, Straus & Giroux.

____ (2012b). *At Last.* New York: Farrar, Straus & Giroux.

Sartre, J. P. (1946). *No Exit and The Flies.* New York: Knopf.

Schafer, R. (1991). Internalizing Loewald. In: G. Fogel (Ed.) *The Work of Hans Loewald.* Northvale, NJ: Jason Aronson, Inc., pp. 77–89.

Searles, H. (1959). Oedipal love in the countertransference. *International Journal of Psychoanalysis*, 40:180–190.

____ (1975). The patient as therapist to his analyst. In: P. L. Giovacchini (Ed.) *Tactic and Techniques in Psychoanalytic Therapy*, Volume 2. New York: Jason Aronson, Inc., pp. 95–151.

Sedlak, V. (2009) Discussion. *International Journal of Psychoanalysis*, 90:451–455.

Segal, H. (1997). Some implications of Melanie Klein's work: Emergence from narcissism. In: J. Steiner (Ed.) *Psychoanalysis, Literature and War*. London: Routledge, pp. 75–85.
____ (1983). Some clinical implications of Melanie Klein's work: Emergence from narcissism. *International Journal of Psychoanalysis*, 64:269–276.
Shane, M., Shane, E., and Gales, M. (1997). *Intimate Attachments: Toward a New Self Psychology*. New York: Guilford Press.
Shaw, D. (2003a). On the therapeutic action of analytic love. *Contemporary Psychoanalysis*, 39:251–278.
____ (2003b). Traumatic abuse in cults: A psychoanalytic perspective. *Cultic Studies Review*, 2:101–129.
____ (2005). Madness and evil: An insider's view of the Sullivanian Institute. A review essay of the Sullivanian Institute/Fourth Wall Community: The relationship of radical individualism and authoritarianism by Amy B. Siskind. *Contemporary Psychoanalysis*, 41:765–773.
____ (2006). Narcissistic authoritarianism in psychoanalysis. In: R. Raubolt (Ed.) *Power Games: Influence, Persuasion, and Indoctrination in Psychotherapy Training*. New York: Other Press, pp. 65–82.
____ (Ed.) (2007). The analyst's love: Contemporary perspectives [Special issue]. *Psychoanalytic Inquiry*, 27(3).
____ (2010). Enter ghosts: The loss of intersubjectivity in clinical work with adult children of pathological narcissists. *Psychoanalytic Dialogues*, 20:46–59.
Sheaffer, L. (1968). *O'Neill, Vol. 1*. Boston: Little, Brown and Co.
____ (1973). *O'Neill, Vol. 2*. Boston: Little, Brown and Co.
Shengold, L. (1989). *Soul Murder: The Effects of Childhood Abuse and Deprivation*. New York: Fawcett.
Singer, M.T. and Lalich, J. (1995). *Cults in Our Midst*. Somerset, NJ: Jossey-Bass.
Siskind, A. (2003). *The Sullivanian Institute/Fourth Wall Community: The Relationship of Radical Individualism and Authoritarianism*. Westport, CT: Praeger.
St. Aubyn. E. (2011). *At Last*. New York: Farrar, Straus & Giroux.
____ (2012). *The Patrick Melrose Novels*. New York: Farrar, Straus & Giroux.
Stein, R. (2010a). *For Love of the Father: A Psychoanalytic Study of Religious Terrorism*. Stanford, CA: Stanford University Press.
____ (2010b). Notes on mind control: The malevolent uses of emotion as a dark mirror of the therapeutic process. In: A. Harris and S. Botticelli (Eds.) *First Do No Harm: The Paradoxical Encounters of Psychoanalysis, Warmaking, and Resistance*. New York: Routledge, pp. 251–277.
Steiner, J. (1987). The interplay between pathological organizations and the paranoid-schizoid and depressive positions. *International Journal of Psychoanalysis*, 68:69–80.
Steingart, I. (1995). A *Thing Apart*. Northvale, NJ: Jason Aronson, Inc.
Stern, D. (1985). *The Interpersonal World of the Infant*. New York: Basic Books
Stern, D.B. (2004). The eye sees itself: dissociation, enactment, and the achievement of conflict. *Contemporary Psychoanalysis*, 40:197–237.
Stolorow, R. and Atwood, G. (1992). *Contexts of Being*. Hillsdale, NJ: The Analytic Press.
Suchet, M. (In press). *Forgiving the Other: Forgiving the Self*.
Sullivan, H.S. (1953). *The Interpersonal Theory of Psychiatry*. New York: Norton.
Suttie, I. (1935). *The Origins of Love and Hate*. New York: The Julian Press.
____ (1935/1999). *The Origins of Love and Hate*. London: Free Associations Books.

Target, M. and Fonagy, P. (1996). Playing with reality: II. The development of psychic reality from a theoretical perspective. *International Journal of Psychoanalysis*, 77:459–479.

Teicholz, J. (1999). *Kohut, Loewald, and the Postmoderns*. Hillsdale, NJ: The Analytic Press.

Thompson, C. (1943). The therapeutic technique of Sandor Ferenczi: A comment. *International Journal of Psychoanalysis*, 24:64–66.

____ (1964). *Interpersonal Psychoanalysis*. New York: Basic Books.

Tolpin, M. (2002). Doing psychoanalysis of normal development: Forward edge transferences. *Progress in Self Psychology*, 18:167–190.

Volkan, V. (1986). The narcissism of minor differences in the psychological gap between opposing nations. *Psychoanalytic Inquiry*, 6:175–219.

Wallin, D. J. (2007). *Attachment in Psychotherapy*. New York: Guilford Press.

White, W.A. (1937). The origins of love and hate by I.D. Suttie. *Psychoanalytic Review*, 24:458–460.

Wilson, J. (2004). *The Politics of Truth: Inside the Lies that Led to War and Betrayed My Wife's CIA Identity: A Diplomat's Memoir*. New York: Carroll & Graf.

Winnicott, D.W. (1949). Hate in the counter-transference. *International Journal of Psychoanalysis*, 30:69–74.

____ (1958). The capacity to be alone. *International Journal of Psychoanalysis*, 39:416–420.

____ (1960). The theory of the parent-infant relationship. *International Journal of Psychoanalysis*, 41:585–595.

____ (1965). Ego distortion in terms of true and false self. In: *The Maturational Process and the Facilitating Environment: Studies in the Theory of Emotional Development*. New York: International UP Inc., p. 146.

____ (1967). D.W.W. on D.W.W. In: C. Winnicott, R. Shepherd, and M. Davis (Eds.) *Psychoanalytic Explorations*. Cambridge, MA: Harvard University Press, pp. 569–582.

____ (1968). Playing: Its theoretical status in the clinical situation. *International Journal of Psychoanalysis*, 49:591–599.

____ (1969). The use of an object. *International Journal of Psychoanalysis*, 50:711–716.

Wurmser, L. (1981). *The Mask of Shame*. Baltimore, MD: The Johns Hopkins University Press.

Young-Bruehl, E. and Bethelard, F. (2000). *Cherishment*. New York: The Free Press.

Index

Notes are indicated by 'n' plus the note number after the page number.
Clinical case studies (vignettes) are indexed as first names within quotation marks.